"What Meaneth This?"

"What Meaneth This?"

A PENTECOSTAL ANSWER
to
A PENTECOSTAL QUESTION

by

CARL BRUMBACK

GOSPEL PUBLISHING HOUSE
Springfield, Missouri 65802
02-0624

"And they were all amazed, and were in doubt, saying one
to another, 'WHAT MEANETH THIS?' "
Acts 2:12

ISBN   0-88243-624

[PRINTED
IN U·S·A·]

*Dedicated
to my
Beloved
Wife*

CONTENTS

Section I
INTRODUCTION

Section II
WHAT "THIS" IS NOT

Section III
WHAT "THIS" IS

A. THE INITIAL, PHYSICAL EVIDENCE OF THE BAPTISM WITH THE HOLY GHOST

B. THE GIFT OF TONGUES

C. TONGUES—A SIGN

Section IV

CONCLUSION

PREFACE

It was my privilege, while pastoring in Tampa, Florida, during 1942-1944, to be associated with two pastors in a daily radio broadcast. Since there were a number of national and local broadcasts which were reaching that area with the evangelistic message, we dedicated our program to the preaching of the deeper truths of the Word. We did not neglect to proclaim the gospel to the unsaved, but we did attempt to meet the vital need for ministry to the Christians in our radio audience. And what a real joy it was to lead many hungry hearts, step by step, into a fuller and richer experience with God!

In the course of our studies in the Scriptures we arrived at the subject of speaking with tongues—or, as it is technically known, the *glossolalia*. It fell my lot to gather material and to speak on this distinctive doctrine of the Pentecostal Movement of which we three pastors were and are members. I found that I had a rather difficult task on my hands, for though there was some excellent material on tongues from the Pentecostal viewpoint, it was mostly in incidental form—tracts, pamphlets, and sometimes a chapter in a book. It never had been compiled into a single volume whose scope was specifically and comprehensively the subject of tongues.

Despite the difficulties involved, I was enabled of the Lord to assemble enough material for a series of twelve messages. At the conclusion of the series there was an insistent demand that they be placed in printed form. Fully aware now as never before of the need of a thorough and exhaustive work on tongues from a Pentecostal viewpoint, and aware also that my radio messages were but a brief sketch of such a work, I agreed to attempt to meet the need. For the past two years I have devoted my time almost wholly to the research necessary for a comprehensive study of the subject. Kind friends have given me access to their libraries, and in the providence of God it has been possible for me to spend several months in the Library of Congress in Washington D. C., where I found a surprisingly large selection of volumes on tongues.

What has been the result of this intensive and specialized study? It may not be wise to voice one's conclusion in the preface of his book, but I believe a word of personal testimony will not be altogether out of place here. For years I had been taught that speaking in tongues was Scriptural truth, and in addition I had experienced rich edification from the almost daily exercise of tongues in my own life. Nevertheless, I had never so thoroughly searched the Scriptures that I was satisfied that I was "ready always to give an answer to every man" who might ask a reason for my belief in tongues. During the past two years I have had ample opportunity to examine carefully the teaching in the Word of God, to analyze the arguments of many of the leaders of religious thought both for and against the Pentecostal viewpoint, and to pray earnestly that the Spirit of Truth would lead me into all truth. The result? I am absolutely and unalterably convinced that there is a firm foundation laid for my Pentecostal faith in His excellent Word. Like Timothy, I have found that the things which I had learned from the lips of others, I could be "assured of" by a full and honest study and appropriation of the Holy Scriptures.

So it is that I offer to the public what at this time is the only comprehensive work on tongues in the Pentecostal movement. It is my sincere hope that this volume may be useful in the strengthening of conviction within our own ranks; that it may provide the information so long desired by many of our non-Pentecostal friends; that it may remove some of the obstacles from the minds of those who have vigorously opposed this part of the Pentecostal message; and that it may stimulate in every reader a searching of the Scriptures and a seeking of God in prayer for "every good and perfect gift" which He desires to give to His saints of the Twentieth Century.

The apostle Paul said, "None of us liveth to himself, and no man dieth unto himself." And I feel sure that every author will agree with me when I humbly add, "No man writeth unto himself!" It would be impossible for me to express the deep gratitude which I owe to the authors and speakers whom I have so frequently consulted in the writing of this volume. It would also be impossible to express the feeling of obligation which I have to the friends whose helpful suggestions and kind criticisms have been so invaluable to me. But I can pray that the blessing of the Lord will rest abundantly upon them and upon this book in which we have been "laborers together with Him."

CARL BRUMBACK

Washington, D. C.
November 14, 1946

SECTION I

INTRODUCTION

"Be this known unto you, and hearken to my words."
Acts 2:14

CHAPTER 1

"What Meaneth This?"

JERUSALEM was happy. The great Feast of Pentecost with its memories of Sinai and its thanksgiving for the wheat harvest was at hand. "Devout men, out of every nation under heaven" were wending their way once again toward their beloved Zion. They were coming to worship at her temple and to pay her homage. The ancient city was content in the knowledge that her children still longed to celebrate the feasts of the Lord within her walls. She rejoiced that she could fling wide her gates in another glad welcome to her sons from afar.

The pilgrims were singing as they came, and their sweet songs brought great joy to Jerusalem. Her children were rising up from the north and the south, the east and the west, and calling her blessed! "Hear, O Israel!"

"I was glad when they said unto me, Let us go into the house of the Lord. Our feet shall stand within thy gates, O Jerusalem. Jerusalem is builded as a city that is compact together. Whither the tribes go up, the tribes of the Lord, unto the testimony of Israel, to give thanks unto the name of the Lord. For there are set thrones of judgment, the thrones of the house of David. Pray for the peace of Jerusalem:

they shall prosper that love thee. Peace be within thy walls, and prosperity within thy palaces. For my brethren and companions' sake I will now say, Peace be within thee. Because of the house of the Lord our God I will seek thy good."[1]

But Jerusalem was not at peace. The ominous events of the recent Passover had cast a shadow over her preparations for the day which was "holy unto the Lord," a day "to eat, and to drink, and to send portions, and to make great mirth." The crucifixion of Jesus of Nazareth, accompanied as it was by the gross darkness, the awful earthquake, and the rending of the sacred veil in the temple, had disturbed the peace of Jerusalem. And even after His death the Nazarene continued to trouble the city, for it was being commonly reported that He had risen from the dead and appeared unto many of His followers. In direct conflict with this report was the story told by the soldiers on watch at the tomb who contended that while they slept "His disciples came by night and stole Him away." These conflicting rumors were being circulated among the thousands of strangers arriving in the city for Pentecost. The name of Jesus was on the lips of everyone; and, as in the days of His ministry, so now "there was a division among the people concerning Him."

The speculation and strife were further increased when it was discovered that over one hundred of His most intimate disciples had been in the city for a number of days. It was said that the rulers were keeping them under strict surveillance, but so far the disciples had limited their activities to attending the hours of prayer at the temple and gathering for

---

[1]Psalm 122.

private worship in a large upper room. It might be that they were awaiting the great day of the Feast to make public proclamation of their belief in the resurrection of the Prophet. Many of the people who had witnessed the miracles and signs and wonders which God had done by Jesus in their midst, and others attracted by their tales of His power, were eager to hear the resurrection story from the lips of His disciples. Thus it was, as Pentecost drew nigh, that the interest of the multitude was focused upon the lowly followers of the Nazarene.

And what of the little band of "about an hundred and twenty"? The doubts and fears which had filled their hearts at the last Passover had been forever dispelled at the sight of their risen Lord. For to them Jesus had "showed Himself alive after His passion by many infallible proofs, being seen of them forty days." They had stood transfixed on Mount Olivet "while He blessed them, and was parted from them, and carried up into heaven. Then returned they unto Jerusalem, . . . and when they were come in, they went unto an upper room"—and "all continued with one accord in prayer and supplication."

How slow of heart they had been to believe all that the prophets had spoken! Now they knew that "Christ ought to have suffered these things, and to enter into His glory." Now they knew that His kingdom was not of this world. Now they knew that He had ascended unto the Father and would soon let "the house of Israel know assuredly, that God hath made that same Jesus both Lord and Christ." Is it any wonder that they were "continually . . . praising and blessing God," as they waited for the promise of the Father? Nor could it be long before the Heavenly Gift would be sent from the Father by their exalted Lord, for had He not promised but a few days ago, "Ye shall be baptized with the Holy Ghost not many days hence"?

"And when the day of Pentecost was fully come, they were all with one accord in one place." One hundred and twenty hearts beat as one as they sat together that morning, waiting for the "power" that would enable them to be witnesses unto the Lord Jesus Christ "both in Jerusalem, and in all Judea, and in Samaria, and unto the uttermost part of the earth."

"And suddenly," the Word declares, "there came a SOUND. . . ." It was a deep, strange sound that seemed to come from above—"from heaven." Voices raised in prayer were instantly hushed, and a profound stillness filled the room. A still, small voice whispered to each disciple, "The hour is come!" The sound, which perhaps at first seemed far away, now appeared to be coming closer. It was like the roaring of a whirlwind, the howling of a tempest— "as of a rushing, mighty wind!" Nearer and nearer it came. Louder and louder its volume. At last, with an all-pervading, majestic roar it burst into the room, "and it filled all the house where they were sitting."

What overpowering feelings must have gripped the disciples as they realized that God Himself, the Holy Ghost, was there in the room with them! No doubt the soul of each one echoed the cry of Jacob at Bethel, "Surely the Lord is in this place!" Unlike Jacob, however, they were not frightened. Nor were they as Moses, who at Sinai cried, "I exceedingly fear and quake!" They remembered the words of their Lord, "I will not leave you comfortless. I

will come to you. . . . I will pray the Father and
He shall give you another Comforter." This "sound
as of a rushing mighty wind," they knew, only
accompanied their new Friend, the *Paracletos,* in
His descent from heaven.

It was not long, however, before that which
their ears heard became secondary to that which
their eyes saw. There appeared to their startled gaze
a lambent flame of fire, suspended above their heads.
As they watched, the mass of fire was cleft asunder,
broken up into separate parts, and distributed
throughout the room. And lo, every flaming fragment assumed the shape of a cloven tongue, and "sat
upon each of them"![1]

The disciples were only beginning to consider
this second miraculous manifestation of the Holy
Spirit *with* them when, suddenly, they felt a
strange power moving with*in* them. Some spiritual
force was breaking up the fountains of the great
deep in their souls, and at the same time the windows
of heaven were being opened upon them. The words
of Jesus were brought to their remembrance, "Ye
know Him; for He dwelleth *with* you and shall
be *in* you." And that Holy One, who came into
these disciples, was not content to occupy only the
inner sanctum of their souls. As in Solomon's day
the glory of the Lord filled the temple, so now the
Holy Spirit filled these true temples. "They were all
filled with the Holy Ghost."

The Gift had come! The disciples, in the midst
of mighty manifestations of power, and overwhelmed

---

[1] Of course, we do not claim infallibility for any description which is not actually found in the Scriptural record.
Our purpose is merely to recapture as far as possible the
atmosphere surrounding the tremendous events of that day.

by holy emotions, nevertheless knew that the most
important fact of all was that the Spirit of Truth
had come. As at Mt. Sinai it was not the thunder nor
the lightnings nor the fire nor the trumpet which
was paramount, but the giving of the Law; so at
Pentecost it was not the sound nor the tongues of
fire nor the subsequent speaking with other tongues
which was paramount, but the giving of the Holy
Spirit. The manifestations in each case were but
subservient and symbolical. The signs at Pentecost,
though clearly supernatural, were only the accompaniments of the gift of the Spirit. They were but the
physical and visible revelations of spiritual and
invisible realities. The tremendous truth was that
"He" had come!

He, the blessed Holy Spirit, had disdained to
descend on the temple of Herod, the center of worship
for Christ-crucifying Israel. Instead, He would honor
this unpretentious upper room with His presence. He,
the gracious Spirit of God, had refused to fill with
Himself the ritualistic rabbis, or the pompous priests,
or the sanctimonious scribes. He would incarnate
Himself in humble Galileans. What marvelous, infinite, matchless grace! How confounding to the
proud! How reassuring to the lowly! Yea, how true
the words of the prophet, "For thus saith the high
and lofty One that inhabiteth eternity, whose name
is Holy: I dwell in the high and holy place, with
him also that is of a contrite and humble spirit"!

Is it any wonder that the disciples felt that they
must give vent to the mighty deluge of glory which
was flooding their souls? That they must give voice
to the captive praises which were pleading to be set
free? But what words of theirs could express the
inexpressible ecstasy, or describe the indescribable

delight, or speak the unspeakable joy of being filled with the Holy Ghost? The New Testament priests, like the priests of old, "could not stand to minister by reason of the cloud: for the glory of the Lord had filled the house of God." They were helpless to perform the service of the Lord, as the Third Person of the Trinity filled His temple.

Then it was that the Spirit Himself helped their infirmity. Taking control of their mental faculties and vocal organs, He began to give expression to the rapturous praises which the disciples felt in their hearts but could not express with their lips—"And they . . . began to speak with other tongues, as the Spirit gave them utterance." The words that fell from their lips were unknown to them, but not unknown was the fact that the pent-up praises within them were finding a release that satisfied their souls. The Spirit of the Lord had set the captive praises free to sweep forth from the inner depths and to ascend up on high to the throne of God. Angelic hosts bending a listening ear, must have bowed their heads, and folded their wings, and cried one to another, "Surely the Lord inhabiteth the praises of His people!"

Meanwhile, these demonstrations of divine power were attracting a great crowd of curious spectators. Thousands of excited Jews were turning aside to solve the mystery of the sound of a tempest on that calm morning. As they gathered together, they were met by still another mystery—the cloven tongues of fire upon the heads of the Galileans. But the strange sound and the glowing tongues were to be surpassed by an even greater mystery—the speaking with other tongues. With a shock of amazement the onlookers discovered that these Galileans, who had been identified as followers of Jesus of Nazareth, were not speaking in their simple Galilean tongue but in "other tongues"! And those "other tongues" were recognized by some of the bystanders as their very own! In fact, almost every man in the crowd, by listening carefully, was able to single out of the languages spoken by the enraptured worshipers his own tongue or dialect.

The attention of the multitudes was immediately centered upon the *glossolalia* manifested by the Galileans. And small wonder, for "the voice they uttered was awful in its range, in its tones, in its modulation, in its startling, penetrating, almost appalling power; the words they spoke were exalted, intense, passionate, full of mystic significance; the language they used was not their ordinary and familiar tongue, but was Hebrew, or Greek, or Latin, or Aramaic, or Persian, or Arabic, as some overpowering and unconscious influence might direct . . . and among these strange sounds . . . there were some which none could interpret, which rang in the air like the voice of barbarous languages, and which . . . conveyed no definite significance beyond the fact that they were reverberations of one and the same ecstasy."[1]

In the vast audience were many who felt that they were witnessing an extraordinary visitation of God. They recognized the sound of the rushing, mighty wind and the tongues of fire as Scriptural signs of the presence of the Lord. Had He not manifested His power to Elijah at Horeb in the "strong wind" and the "fire"? And had not the prophet been carried up to heaven in a whirlwind, and parted from Elisha by "a chariot of fire" and "horses of

---

[1]Neander.

[20]

fire"? But what was the explantion of this distinctly new manifestation, this speaking with tongues?
To them, as to a more modern critic, it seemed
that "the sudden communication of a facility of
speaking foreign languages is neither logically possible nor psychologically and morally conceivable."
And yet—

"Every man heard them speak in his own language. And they were all amazed and marvelled, saying one to another, Behold, are not all these which
speak Galileans? And how hear we every man in our
own tongue, wherein we were born? Parthians, and
Medes, and Elamites, and the dwellers in Mesopo-
tamia, and in Judaea, and Cappadocia, in Pontus,
and Asia, Phrygia, and Pamphylia, in Egypt, and
the parts of Libya about Cyrene, and strangers of
Rome, Jews and proselytes, Cretes, and Arabians, we
do hear them speak in our tongues the wonderful
works of God. And they were all amazed and were
in doubt, saying one to another, What meaneth
this?"[2]

"What meaneth this?"—the cry of the "devout
men, out of every nation under heaven," when confronted with this initial appearance of the *glossolalia.*
"What meaneth this?"—the cry of all thinking men
who through the succeeding ages have contemplated
this phenomenon of Pentecost. "What meaneth
this?"—the cry of Bible students who through the
centuries have read with wonder God's record of
that extraordinary day. "What meaneth this?"—
the cry which has lost none of its challenge though

---

[1]H. A. W. Meyer, *Commentary on Acts*, p. 48.

[2]Acts 2:6-12.

almost two thousand years have passed since first it was uttered.

What is your answer to this Pentecostal question? Do you know what meaneth this speaking with tongues by the charter members of the Christian Church? Do you understand how the simple folk from the hill country of Galilee could speak with tongues of ancient and cultured nations? Do you have an answer that fully satisfies both the heart and mind? Or must you echo the cry of your Pentecostal predecessors, who on that day were "amazed and in doubt, saying one to another, *What meaneth this?*"

CHAPTER 2

Who Answered at Pentecost?

AMONG the spectators that day there were, in all probability, a number of priests, rabbis, and scribes, who had also turned aside to investigate the sound of the wind and the report of the strange tongues. It is hard to believe that they did not attempt to answer the excited queries of the common people around them. Indeed, it was incumbent upon these authorities in matters religious to display their superior knowledge. They dared not remain silent for their reputation as spiritual leaders was at stake. So undoubtedly the priests advanced their opinions, the rabbis loudly voiced their theories, and the scribes expressed their speculations about the *glossolalia*. But somehow the opinions, the theories, and the speculations of these exalted individuals did not satisfy the inquirers any more than the pitiful explanation of the foolish mockers who cried, "These men are full of new wine."

Once again there was a need for someone to speak "as one having authority and not as the scribes." And God, who through His gift of the Holy Ghost had caused the multitude to ask, "What meaneth this?" also had someone there who could answer the question. The Word states, "But Peter,

[23]

standing up with the eleven, lifted up his voice, and said unto them, Ye men of Judea, and all ye that dwell at Jerusalem, be this known unto you, and hearken to my words." Yes, it was the rugged fisherman apostle whom God had chosen to give His answer to the question, "What meaneth this?"

Why was Peter God's choice as spokesman on this day of Pentecost, rather than one of the priests, rabbis, or scribes? Was it because his position as the foremost apostle of the early church and the future author of several New Testament epistles made him more certain of a respectful hearing from the crowd? The Christians of that day and all the succeeding ages have thus revered Peter, but not so this contemporary throng of Jews. To them he was but a poor, despised follower of the crucified Nazarene. The rabbinical scholars scorned him as an ignorant, unlettered Galilean. Why, then, did God choose such a man to expound the true meaning of this speaking in tongues?

For two substantial reasons: first, *Peter's knowledge of and reverence for the Scriptures;* second, *his personal experience of being filled with the Holy Spirit and speaking with tongues.* Three years at the feet of the Master Expositor of the Law, the prophets, and the psalms had made Peter a lover of the Word. He had learned to cast aside as worthless the traditions of men and to take hold of "the more sure word of prophecy" which "holy men of old spake as they were moved by the Holy Ghost." His message, so filled with quotations from the Old Testament prophecies, proves that he was a careful and diligent student of the Scriptures. It was no accident, nor was it altogether due to the immediate inspiration of the Spirit, that Peter was ready to

give an answer from the Word to them that asked
him.

The infilling of the Spirit had brought with it an
illumination of hitherto veiled truths. This was
according to the promise of the Lord Jesus, "When
He, the Spirit of Truth, is come, He will guide you
into all truth." He had enlightened the minds of the
apostle and his fellow disciples, enabling them to
recognize fulfillments of prophecies. When Peter
began to speak with other tongues, the words of the
prophet Joel flashed across his mind: "And it shall
come to pass afterward that I will pour out my
Spirit upon all flesh; and your sons and your daughters shall prophesy." No doubt the words of the Lord
Jesus also were brought to his remembrance: "These
signs shall follow them that believe; in My name
. . . they shall speak with new tongues." Peter
knew that these prophecies were true, and that they
actually had come to pass in his own life. And though
he could not fully comprehend all the mysteries of
the *glossolalia*, he did know the truth and had the life
of that truth. Is it any wonder that he was ready to
give an answer to the question, "What meaneth
this?" Is it any wonder that his voice rang with
authority as he, filled with the Word of God and
the Spirit of God, applied that Word with such
logic, such conviction and such power?

It may be that some will say that Peter in his
sermon that day did not give a straightforward, full
answer to the question about tongues. Admittedly, he
did not give a long discourse on tongues at Pentecost.
The main purpose of his message was to present
Jesus as Savior, Lord, and Messiah, and this he
accomplished so successfully that three thousand
Jews thus acknowledged Jesus. Peter did not have

time to satisfy fully the curiosity aroused by the sign; he was too busy preaching unto them Jesus to whom the sign pointed. Therefore, of necessity, his answer regarding tongues was only introductory and suggestive.[1]

The full answer to "What meaneth this?" must needs await the pens of Mark, Luke and Paul. For through these inspired men God preserved for all time a promise of the Lord Jesus concerning tongues; a record of its manifestation at Jerusalem, Caesarea, and Ephesus; and a detailed discussion of its exercise in private and public worship.

However, even with the wealth of material in the Word of God in regard to tongues, the Church as a whole since apostolic days has been in ignorance about this spiritual gift. This ignorance, which has been theoretical as well as experimental, has been due largely to the lack of clear, Scriptural teaching upon the subject. Sundry and divers interpretations of the tongues passages have been given through the ages, but very few have added much to the definite knowledge of the Church about tongues. In fact, as one reads the works of the most noted commentators and expositors, he finds that their discussions of tongues are characterized by much hesitancy and indefiniteness. The authors themselves seem to be groping their way through a fog, and consequently, are unable to lead their readers to any definite conclusions. Statements like the following

---

[1]Nevertheless, Peter did as follows: (1) He refuted the ridicule of the mockers (v. 15). (2) He identified tongues with the outpouring the the Spirit (v. 16). (3) He revealed that speaking with tongues was a form of prophesying (vs. 17, 18). (4) He showed that it was a sign confirming the exaltation of Jesus (v. 33).

occur repeatedly in their dealing with the subject, "Much difficulty in understanding this passage"; "the meaning here is obscure."

Why all this obscurity and uncertainty about tongues on the part of writers who have been distinguished by their clarity and conviction in other doctrines? Why have these highly esteemed men been unable to answer "What meaneth this?" We believe that their failure is due to reasons similar to those which rendered the priests, rabbis, and scribes incapable of the right answer at Pentecost: they have not made a thorough study of tongues in the Scriptures, nor have they had an experience like that of Peter and his fellow disciples, viz., speaking "with other tongues as the Spirit gave them utterance."

For many years the *glossolalia* was not a "live" topic for discussion among Biblical scholars. Its appearances through Church history had been confined to certain spiritual awakenings in which the gift had not become so frequent and widespread as to cause much public comment. The fragmentary and faulty speculations on the subject by little interested scholars seemed to content the church of bygone years. Their treatment of tongues was as good as anything that had been advanced up to that time, and the church did not feel that there was an urgent necessity of becoming fully informed on it when there were so many grave issues at stake in those days. Since the early part of the Twentieth Century, however, this rather lackadaisical attitude towards tongues has disappeared. The subject of tongues now ranks as one of the leading questions in the religious world. What has brought about this change? A world-wide revival of this miracle

[27]

of vocal utterance. Established denominations have regarded with ever-increasing horror the phenomenal growth of the so-called "Tongues Movement." And what has especially troubled the leaders is that many of the lay members have constantly asked them, "What meaneth this speaking in tongues? What about this Pentecostal Movement?"

Driven by the questioning of their followers, but with little desire for the task, many ministers, religious educators, authors, and denominational leaders have been forced to make an investigation of Scriptural tongues and of the Pentecostal movement. It soon became evident to the majority of them that some of their preconceived ideas about tongues would have to be discarded. They could not possibly accept the Pentecostal teaching, but they realized that many of the traditions of the fathers did not constitute strong opposition to the doctrines advocated by the Pentecostalists. And without a personal experience of speaking in tongues, they found that the Scriptural manifestations and teachings about tongues were rather difficult to interpret to their people. Some other means than reasoning from the Scriptures must be adopted if the laity's doubts were to be dissolved and the influence of Pentecostalism halted. Then someone made the discovery that it was easier to defend the flock from false doctrine by turning the spotlight of investigation on the "Tongues People" themselves. Not that the investigators were fearful of their ability to prove that the Scriptures were on their side, but if the effects of error could be shown in the lives of its advocates, the cause of truth could be saved much more easily through this means.

This type of investigation has resulted in a uniform pattern which most non-Pentecostal authors seem to have followed in writing about tongues: (1) a brief and altogether inadequate explanation of the Scriptural passages on tongues; (2) a making void of the evident meaning of the Word by the citing of examples of fanaticism; (3) a one-sided study of the Irvingites, and other "tongues groups" prior to the Twentieth Century: (4) a discussion of the latest discoveries in psychology and pathology and their application to speaking with tongues; (5) descriptions of isolated contacts with present-day "Tongues People"; (6) attacks on personalities within the Pentecostal Movement who may have been guilty of immorality or some other form of un-Scriptural conduct.

We trust that you believe us when we say that we have no desire to question the spiritual integrity or intellectual honesty of these authors. We have received much personal profit from the writings of many of these men along other lines, and even in their writings on tongues we have found some discussions which are highly commendable. But we are convinced that any work which follows the above pattern cannot justly be said to answer, "What meaneth this?" The failure of these men to give a clear and definite interpretation of the Scriptures regarding tongues, and the absence in their spiritual experience of anything remotely similar to tongues, reveal their inability to speak with authority on the subject.

It is our sincere belief that the Pentecostal Movement of this Twentieth Century is the only body of believers since the early church, who can fully answer, "What meaneth this?" To some, this statement, coming as it does from a Pentecostal author, will undoubtedly seem the last word in religious conceit. We trust that all will not so interpret it. The favor of God is not merited any more by Pentecostal believers than by non-Pentecostal believers. It has been through the grace of God alone that we have discovered the truth regarding tongues, and crossed the threshold into this marvelous Pentecostal experience. We dare not set ourselves upon a spiritual pedestal and say to all others, "We are holier than thou." If there be those among us who do assume such an attitude, they need to be abased before the God of all grace, and learn anew "that no flesh should glory in His presence."

We Pentecostalists owe to the Church as a whole the great body of doctrines which we have embraced as our fundamental beliefs. We gladly acknowledge our obligation to the great men of the past whose lives and teachings serve as guideposts to God. We confess ourselves debtors to all preceding revival movements, for we have received much inspiration and instruction from them. Yea verily, it is only "with all saints" that we are able to comprehend the Lord Jesus Christ in His truth and His life.

Nevertheless, we are cognizant of the fact that there has been a steady progression in the revelation of New Testament truths since the Dark Ages. Each new discovery of truth has been made by men who have had the courage to set aside the traditional teachings of their predecessors, and to go all the way back to the Scriptures themselves. There they have uncovered truths which long had been hidden in the dust of obscurity, and which have appeared to their contemporaries as new doctrines, but which in reality were an integral part of the "apostles' doctrine." With regard to tongues, we in Pentecost have followed this principle of penetrating past the confused and uncertain teachings of the fathers to the Word of God itself. In the providence of God, we have unearthed from the treasure house of His Word the facts about the supernatural signs and gifts which characterized the life and worship of those early Christians. And while we do not forget our unworthiness, yet because of our study of the Scriptures and our own experience, we can say humbly but positively, we know what meaneth this speaking in tongues.

It is only natural, but surely regrettable, that such a claim should stir up a storm of controversy in the religious world. There is cause for rejoicing, however, in the fact that it has also stirred up a spirit of investigation. Thousands upon thousands have searched the Scriptures to see whether the claim of the Pentecostalists could be supported by "thus saith the Lord." They have also subjected the life and worship of the Pentecostal people to the closest scrutiny. To the glory of God, may it be stated that many honest, hungry-hearted men and women have been convinced that the doctrines and experiences of the Pentecostal people are "according to the Scriptures." What was truly said of the investigators on the day of Pentecost can be as truly said of their successors in the Twentieth Century:

"Such awakening, such spirit of inquiry and investigation, such clear proof of a readiness to challenge appearances rather than succumb too readily and run the chance of delusion, made for every man that was there a strong, convinced witness in time to come, and in the home and country of each. From being gaping hearers, they became instructed and impressive preachers. And the unsettledness of their mind gave place to deep unmoved conviction."[1]

---

[1] *Pulpit Commentary,* Vol. 41, p. 76.

If you are a non-Pentecostal reader, you have undoubtedly read considerable material in opposition to the Pentecostal view of tongues. We heartily commend you for giving careful study to that side of the argument. At the same time, we are happy that you also desire to acquaint yourself with a comprehensive survey of the tongues question as taught by the Pentecostal movement.[1] We are happy that you are granting to us the privilege extended by Agrippa to Paul, "Thou art permitted to speak for thyself."

GEORGE BARTON CUTTEN, President Emeritus of Colgate University and a non-Pentecostal author, says of the apostle Paul, "*Glossolalic* himself in a very high degree, this circumstance does not remove from him the liberty of critical appreciation in regard to this gift, but on the other hand confers on his criticism a value and peculiar interest."[2] Is it asking too much if we, who are *glossolalic* today, covet the same attitude from you toward us as we endeavor to give a Pentecostal answer to a Pentecostal question?

---

[1] It is not the prerogative of any one author to interpret infallibly the doctrinal beliefs of the entire Pentecostal Movement concerning tongues. Nevertheless, we feel that in most instances this volume will set forth only that which is generally believed by the Movement; and in those instances where we may advance a personal conviction not generally accepted by the Movement, we shall be careful to designate it as such.

[2] *Speaking With Tongues*, p. 23.

SECTION II

WHAT "THIS" IS NOT

"These are not drunken, as ye suppose, seeing it is but the third hour of the day." Acts 2:15.

From the above quotation we can see that Peter's answer to "What meaneth this?" was first negative in character. Before he could proceed with an orderly presentation of positive truth he was forced to answer the mockers who said, "These men are full of new wine."

Through the centuries of Church history various theories about tongues have been introduced by religious leaders. And during the past forty years, in which the *glossolalia* has been revived on a universal scale, these theories have been supplemented by arguments directed against the present-day Pentecostal Movement. In giving our answer to "What meaneth this?" we find it convenient to follow Peter's wise example; i.e., to state first what "this" is not, and then to give our reasons for rejecting these theories and arguments.

(The words, "THIS" IS NOT, should be prefixed by the reader to the title of each chapter in this section.)

CHAPTER 3

Linguistic Ability

ON the day of Pentecost languages were spoken by the disciples which, though unknown to them, were understood by different groups in the multitude. This remarkable phenomenon has given rise to a number of theories regarding the exact nature and purpose of that speaking with other tongues. In this chapter we shall deal with six of the most familiar of these theories.

1. TO ACCELERATE THE SPREAD OF THE GOSPEL

This is perhaps the oldest and most widely known of the six. Briefly stated it is this: The speaking with tongues in the early church was a supernatural communication of the gospel in languages unknown to the speaker but known to the hearer. Without the gift of tongues the disciples would have been faced with the arduous task of mastering many languages before they could witness to the uttermost part of the earth. Therefore, God gave to them the ability to preach the gospel in languages that they had never learned, and in that manner the good news was spread quickly over the whole world.

[35]

It is absolutely true that at Pentecost foreign languages were spoken by the one hundred and twenty, and understood by the bystanders. It is equally true that this phenomenon has been repeated in many and varied circumstances since that day. Stanley Howard Frodsham, in his book *"With Signs Following,"* has given multiplied instances of this particular phase of the *glossolalia*. Scores of testimonies are recorded there which illustrate the fact that speaking with tongues has been used of God to acquaint foreigners with the gospel in a supernatural and spectacular manner, and if we had the time and space, we could give a number of other examples which have come to our attention. Nevertheless, we vigorously object to the teaching that this was the primary purpose of tongues in the early church. It was the exceptional and not the usual manifestation of tongues in those days, and likewise in its subsequent manifestations.

Let us look at the one case in the Word where it is definitely stated that the tongues were understood by the listeners. This occurred at Pentecost. The record does not imply that any outsiders were present when the disciples began to speak in those hitherto unlearned languages. It seems that some time elapsed before the curious crowd came together and recognized the tongues as their own. Why, then, were the disciples speaking in tongues ere the multitude, for whom the tongues were intended, arrived? Were they practicing for their approaching audience? Certainly not! They were ecstatically praising God, declaring His glory in much the same manner as the Psalmist. They were not speaking with tongues because the crowd gathered, but the crowd gathered because they were speaking with tongues! And not a single word is said about their *preaching* in tongues, even after the audience had assembled before them. The awestruck spectators simply overheard the Galileans worshipfully declaring the wonderful works of God. They had been allowed to witness a wonderful worship service in which the worshipers poured out supernatural praises to the Lord.

The only preaching on that occasion was done by Peter, who "lifted up his voice, and said unto them, Ye men of Judea, and all ye that dwell at Jerusalem, be this known unto you, and hearken to my words." How could all these men of different nationalities and tongues have anything made known unto them, or hearken to Peter's words, unless they knew what he was saying? Surely, Peter did not speak some fifteen or more tongues simultaneously. Yet *all* heard and *all* understood, and out of that vast congregation, composed of so many diverse groups, three thousand accepted the invitation and were saved. The only possible explanation is that Peter spoke in a single language which was familiar to all, either the popular language of Palestine, Aramaic, or the universally understood Greek. Thus we can see that even at Pentecost the *glossolalia* was not needed for a clear comprehension of the gospel. Hearing their native tongues spoken by the Galileans astonished the multitude, but it was Peter's message, in a language known by all, which conveyed the gospel to them.

Nor is there the slightest implication that the apostles ever employed tongues as a means of preaching the gospel to foreigners. Such a supernatural method of communicating the gospel was not necessary, for they could speak Aramaic, or Greek, or Latin, the three languages of the inscription on the Cross, and be understood anywhere and everywhere.

since these three tongues were the media of intercourse throughout the whole Roman Empire. Paul makes it very clear in 1 Corinthians 14 that when he was teaching or preaching, he did not employ the gift of tongues.

And speaking of 1 Corinthians 14, we should surely expect to find some basis for the belief that this gift was exercised to accelerate the spread of the gospel, for practically the whole chapter is devoted to a discussion of tongues. But the proponents of this theory must search in vain for its confirmation there. On the contrary, the general rule for the speaker in tongues is that "no man understandeth him." Paul exhorts him who speaks in a tongue to pray that he may interpret what he utters, for otherwise those who hear will not understand and will not be edified. The very fact that the gift of tongues was in constant operation in the Corinthian assembly, where all spoke the same language, should be proof enough that this theory rests upon a false conception of the purpose of tongues. It is altogether inapplicable to the whole of 1 Corinthians 14 where a private as well as a public use of the gift is discussed by the apostle. The most ardent advocates would hesitate to say that the Corinthian believer who spoke to himself in a tongue (1 Cor. 14:28) did so that he might supernaturally acquaint himself with the gospel.

But it is folly to spend more time upon this absurd and illogical theory which has absolutely no support in the Scriptures. There is perhaps only one thing which can be said in its favor; viz., it does recognize the supernatural nature of tongues.

2. ARCHAIC, POETIC GLOSSES

The comment of D. A. HAYES in his book *"The Gift of Tongues"* (p. 25), will be sufficient for our consideration of this view of tongues:

"Erneste, Bleek, and Baur have labored with great learning to show that 'other tongues' may be interpreted to mean strange words, or archaic, poetic *glosses*. These *glosses* were not in use in ordinary language, but in this moment of extraordinary experience they seemed to flow naturally to the lips, and being taken from many different dialects and languages they were in reality other and new tongues to those who found themselves using them. The objection to this suggestion is that it gives a technical and grammatical meaning to the word 'tongues'—a meaning which is not to be found anywhere else in the Old or the New Testament, and which Luke would not be at all likely to use in this connection, and which the Parthians and Medes and Elamites surely could not have used in any case. If all these foreigners not only heard the disciples speaking in their own native tongues, but also discovered that they were using archaic and obsolete expressions in those tongues, we have a miracle unnecessarily heightened. To tell the wonderful works of God in foreign languages would surely be enough, without telling them in an antiquated and strange and stilted phraseology. One would think that the preaching would have been more effective in the common speech."

3. EJACULATIONS OF THE SUB-CONSCIOUS MIND

Mr. Hayes, in company with many other men who have written on the subject, advances this explanation of speaking with tongues: "The foreign

[39]

languages spoken at Pentecost are explicable to us as due to abnormally quickened memories, reproducing to these Jews and proselytes phrases and sentences heard from them, and all unconsciously stored in minds that had no use of them in normal conditions."[1] In other words, the ejaculations in other tongues had been impressed upon the subconscious minds of the Galileans while mingling with the foreign Jews and proselytes on other occasions; then at Pentecost, when the disciples were in a state of ecstasy, these strange words, which had been deposited in the memories of the disciples, came tumbling forth to be recognized by the men to whose native tongue they belonged.

The latest discoveries in psychological research lend credence to this view, and it would seem that Mr. Hayes is well aware of this fact, for he writes: "Chrysostom said of this whole section of the first epistle (1 Corinthians 14) that it was exceedingly obscure; Chrysostom had never seen any instance of this charism, and he felt himself very much in the dark concerning it. We know more about psychology than Chrysostom did, and we have seen the gift of tongues in our own community. We think, therefore, that these chapters are not so obscure to us as they were to him."[2] According to this statement, it appears that the tongues which so astonished the spectators at Pentecost can be largely explained by means of psychology in this enlightened age.

It is undoubtedly true that tremendous strides have been taken in the field of psychology since Chrysostom's day. Today, we have psychiatrists,

---

[1] *The Gift of Tongues*, p. 56.
[2] Ibid, p. 14.

neurologists, psychopathologists, psychotherapists, psychoanalysts——all experts in their specialized branches, who are performing a legitimate and helpful service to the world. Yet, despite all the technical advances which have been made by these specialists in human behaviorism, the Bible is still the highest authority on the subject. Psychology, according to the dictionary, is "the science of the human mind or soul and its operations." Any student of the Word of God must admit that the Word presents not only the clearest revelation of God, but also the clearest revelation of man. This wonderful Book, which James so aptly describes as a mirror reflecting the image of the whole man, was inspired by the Spirit of God, and this glorious fact accounts for its incomparable knowledge of man.

Thus, when we attempt to interpret Scriptural instances of human behaviorism, we do well to interpret them according to the Scriptures, rather than according to Twentieth Century psychical knowledge. Any view of Scriptural phenomena, whose conclusions have been gained as a result of a modern, psychological approach, and not as a result of a reverent study of the phenomena in the light of other like phenomena in the Scriptures, will almost certainly be false.

A doubt immediately arises in our mind as to the correctness of any theory concerning Scriptural truth, when, as in the case of Mr. Hayes, we see such a dependence upon psychology or any other science of the natural man. Whether merely witnessing the speaking in tongues in his own community qualified Mr. Hayes as an authority on the subject, or not, we shall leave with you to decide, but we emphatically repudiate the assertion that knowing more about psychology enabled him to give a clearer explanation of the miraculous tongues in the early church. Has not God plainly told us that "the natural man receiveth not the things of the Spirit of God: for they are foolishness unto him: neither can he know them for they are spiritually discerned"? The egotism of man is never so evident as when he tries to search out with the natural mind the mysteries of God; when he attempts natural explanations of supernatural manifestations. Poor, blinded creatures! Ever groping after truth in the darkness of our own reasonings, when God has decreed that only in His light do we see light. Ever the victim of our foolish pride which attributes omniscience to our finite minds!

Man, unless enlightened by the Holy Spirit, always makes one of two mistakes in dealing with the Bible: he either leaves God out of the picture entirely, or else limits the Holy One of Israel. The miraculous element in the Word is especially subjected to this policy. It is either treated with utmost scorn as folklore, or shorn of its supernatural character until scarcely recognizable as such. Take, for instance, this theory in regard to the speaking with other tongues on the day of Pentecost. How similar it is to countless other theories which had their origin in the minds of unbelieving men, whose only thought is the ultimate removal of every miracle from the Bible.

This view pretends to acknowledge the omniscience and omnipotence of the Spirit of God, but makes certain that His enabling of the disciples to speak with other tongues is explicable by purely rationalistic means. And, as if it were not enough to reduce the *glossolalia* to ejaculations of the subconscious mind, the proponents of this theory, in their efforts to furnish conclusive proof, come perilously close to blasphemy. We have observed with horror their attempts to prove that what they call similar phenomena in history—psychic ejaculations by persons in a delirious fever, in a state of insanity, or in a spiritistic trance—are essentially the same as the tongues spoken at Pentecost. Regardless of the consequences of such an identification, these men feel that they must reject any possibility of the Holy Spirit operating in any manner which is not comprehended by the mind of man. And it seems that if men are determined in their opposition to the miraculous, Satan can furnish them with enough pseudo-proof to confirm them in that opposition.

As for us, in our approach to the speaking with tongues, as well as every other clearly defined miracle in the Word, we proceed on the eternal fact that "God is." This is our simple but reasonable explanation of all the miracles which present such insurmountable difficulties to the materialistic mind. Why must we manufacture endless conjectures about a realm whose mysteries can be discerned only by faith in Almighty God? Let the wise and prudent of this world condemn us as "escapists" if they will; but let us continue to escape from all false and foolish notions and to see our God as men of faith have always seen Him, the God with whom "all things are possible!" What does it matter if Meyer declares: "The sudden communication of a facility of speaking foreign languages is neither logically possible nor psychologically and morally conceivable"? "*All* things are possible with God!"

Read again Acts 2:4. Who is He that enabled the disciples to speak with other tongues? The Holy Spirit! The Third Person of the Trinity! The God of all flesh! Is there anything too hard for Him? Why should it be thought necessary for Him to borrow phrases from the pilgrims who came to the feasts? Why should He be confined to quickening the memories of the one hundred and twenty in order to bring forth praises to the Father? He as God could say, "I *create* the fruit of the lips!" Ah! beloved, the words in which the disciples declared the wonderful works of God "as the Spirit gave them utterance" were not borrowed from the pilgrims; they had their origin in the mind of the Spirit who "searcheth all things, yea, the deep things of God."

If it were true that the speaking with other tongues at Pentecost was a result of "abnormally quickened memories," it might follow that a similar reason can be offered for other types of supernatural utterance in the Bible. Consider, for example the case of Babel (Gen. 11:6-9). We read that "the whole earth was of one language and of one speech." We also read that the "Lord did there confound the language of all the earth . . . that they might not understand one another's speech." Just how this took place we are not told; but undoubtedly, the builders of the tower began to speak in languages and dialects which they had never heard, indeed, which had never existed before. What is the psychologist's explanation of that act of God?

And perhaps a still more amazing miracle of utterance is that of the articulate ass. (Numbers 22:28-30). Surely the rationalist is in for a difficult time if he attempts to convince us that these words sprang from the subconscious mind of the ass! If the Lord could open the mouth of that dumb beast and cause it to speak in the language of its master, Balaam, cannot that same Lord work a lesser miracle in a

[44]

man who already exercises human speech? And cannot He who originated the words in the mouth of the beast, also originate the words in the mouths of the disciples, even though the words be derived from other tongues?

Nor can it be proved that the speaking with tongues was only a collection of disjointed phrases and sentences which were utterly separated in meaning one from another. While its ejaculatory nature is definitely shown, yet from Paul's description of the gift of tongues in 1 Corinthians 14 it would seem to be a fluent and co-ordinated discourse. To state briefly our reasons for this conclusion, we call your attention to Paul's discussion there of the gift of prophecy. In verse 30 we see that the prophet spoke forth a revelation of truth; i.e., though he was in an ecstasy, still the thought content of his message was connected and entire so that he could speak "unto men unto edification, and exhortation, and comfort" (v. 3). Verse 5 tells us that tongues, coupled with its companion gift, the interpretation of tongues, is equal to prophecy; i.e., the same three-fold purpose is realized. This being so, it would be necessary for both the interpretation of the tongue and the tongue itself to be equal to prophecy in the coherency and cohesiveness of thought content.

One further thought. If the psychiatric theory be correct (viz., that the phrases and sentences in other tongues were borrowed subconsciously from the foreign Jews and proselytes), then we should expect the words to be devoid of mention of the life, death, and resurrection of the Lord Jesus, for the pilgrims knew only the Old Testament revelation. Does it not seem strange that the speaking with tongues, so particularly reserved for the New Testament dispensation, should be confined to Old Testament truth? Then too, its continued exercise among Christian believers (1 Cor. 14) would seem to belie the supposition that its thought content and the words themselves were borrowed from the pilgrims.

What amazes us about this confused and inconsistent view of tongues is that fundamentalists like Mr. Hayes are eagerly grasping it as the answer to "What meaneth this?" We have become accustomed to the attempts of the modernists to explain away the supernatural in the Bible, but we must confess that we are dismayed to behold some fundamentalists following in their train. How dogmatically have the fundamentalists opposed the destructive critics of the miraculous element in the Word! How tenaciously have they contended for the faith against the forces of doubt and unbelief! This makes it all the more remarkable when they join hands with the modernist and sing the praises of this psychological interpretation of the *glossolalia*. Beloved, what communion hath light with darkness? What part hath he that believeth with an infidel? How can we deny the modernist the right to explain the virgin birth, the resurrection, Paul's conversion, etc., on natural grounds, and yet applaud them as they explain the miracle of tongues on the same grounds? May God reveal to our fundamentalist friends the compromise and un-Scripturalness of such a position.

4. ONE PURE AND MIGHTY HUMAN LANGUAGE

ABRAHAM KUYPER in his volume, *"The Work of the Holy Spirit"* (p. 133, 138), tells us that the language spoken by the disciples was "the one pure and mighty human language . . . which one day

[46]

all will speak, and all the brethren and sisters from all nations and tongues will speak." To the hearers "it seemed as though they heard them speaking in their own tongues. To the Parthian it sounded like Parthian, to the Arabian like Arabic, etc." He spends several pages showing that the *glossolalia* was an extraordinary "phenomenon of sounds." And he also states that "at Jerusalem, only they understood it who were specially wrought upon by the Holy Spirit. The others understood it not."

The Word does not say that what the disciples began to speak, as the Spirit gave them utterance, was "one pure and mighty human language," but "other tongues"—the tongues enumerated there. And it not only *seemed* to be in the tongues of the listeners; it not only *sounded* like the Parthian and the Arabic; it *was* the Parthian and the Arabic! That is what God's Word says as plainly and definitely as it is possible to say anything, and we prefer to believe God! Nor does the record furnish any basis for the belief that the disciples' ecstatic speech was only an extraordinary phenomenon of sounds. That speech was in definite languages. Luke may not have known the precise description for the heavenly wind and the cloven tongues of fire, but he was positive that the one hundred and twenty spoke in the tongues of the pilgrims. Paul, in 1 Corinthians 14:18, does not thank God for emitting more *sounds* than all the Corinthians; he praises God for the abundant exercise of the gift of *"tongues"!* Certainly Paul would not instruct the believers to pray that they might interpret an unintelligible succession of sounds —a gibberish. And finally, the record does not inform us that the audience understood the various tongues through being "specially wrought upon by the Holy

Ghost." They had only the natural ability, common to man, to recognize their own language; they did not have the gift of interpretation of tongues.

5. A MIRACLE OF HEARING RATHER THAN OF SPEAKING

Some expositors take the position that the disciples spoke in their own Galilean tongue, and the audience heard and understood them as if they were speaking in all the different tongues listed in the account. The Galilean words, after leaving the lips of the one hundred and twenty, were changed into corresponding words in the many tongues. It was a miracle of hearing rather than of speaking.

We suppose that there is but one book in the world that is read in such a manner as to produce a theory like this one. Why the evident meaning of the Word of God should be so wrested is beyond our comprehension. Luke distinctly says: "They began to *speak* with other tongues" (v.4); "the multitude came together and was confounded, because that every man heard them *speak* in his own language" (v.6); "we do hear them *speak* in our own tongues" (v.11).

DEAN ALFORD says of this supposition: "There can be no question in any unprejudiced mind that the fact which this narrative sets before us is, that the disciples began to *speak* in *various languages;* viz., the languages of the nations below enumerated, and perhaps others. All attempts to evade this are connected with some forcing of the text, or some far-fetched and indefensible explanation. . . . The words, 'in our own tongue (lit., dialect), wherein we were born,' are very decisive as to the nature of the miracle. The hearers could not thus have spoken, had they been spiritually uplifted into the comprehension of some ecstatic language spoken by the disciples. They were not spiritually acted on at all, but spoke the matter of fact: they were surprised at each recognizing, so far from his country, and in the mouths of Galileans, his own native tongue."

THE PULPIT COMMENTARY (vol. 41, p. 48) adds this significant note: "Not to mention that this is far more difficult to imagine, and transfers the miracle from those who had the Holy Spirit to those who had it not, it is against the plain language of the text."

WM. ARTHUR (Tongues As of Fire, P. 76): "Had it been as here supposed, the symbol of the miracle would not have been cloven tongues, but *manifold ears.* The double declaration of the narrative corresponds with the symbol. As regards the speakers, it says *they* 'spake with other tongues'; as regards the hearers, that they heard every man in his own tongue.

"When Paul finds fault with the use of the gift of tongues in Corinth, he does not blame the hearers for lacking an ear that would interpret their own tongues into foreign ones, but blames the speakers for speaking with the tongue words not easy to be understood 'by the unlearned,' not being interpreted. This proves that a foreign language was used as an instrument of speech.

"If the supposition of the miracle of hearing, instead of in speech, has been resorted to with a view to simplify the miracle, it defeats its own object; for to sustain that supposition, the miraculous influence must have been exerted on a number of persons as much greater than in the other case, as hearers were more numerous than the speakers. At the same time, the nature of the miraculous operation would be in every respect equally extraordinary."

6. KNOWLEDGE OF FOREIGN LANGUAGES

According to some expositors, the *glossolalia* was a God-given ability to learn languages quickly. It was a talent, as in art or music, but given supernaturally by the Spirit for the purpose of preaching the gospel to foreigners. One noted commentator thought that it was the ability to learn and speak ancient Hebrew, but what a time he had trying to expound 1 Corinthians 14! The theory and the Scriptures just didn't seem to fit together.

We object that the disciples at Pentecost were not required to learn any of the "other tongues," but spoke them forth immediately at the impulse and guidance of the Holy Spirit. Paul plainly shows that "if I pray in an unknown tongue, my spirit prayeth, but my understanding is unfruitful." How could this be if he had learned the tongue? And the preceding verse (13) says, "Wherefore let him that speaketh in an unknown tongue pray that he may interpret. Conybeare and Howson conclude that "this verse distinctly proves that the gift of tongues was not a knowledge of foreign language as is often supposed."

Speaking in tongues cannot be divested of its supernatural character any more than the other eight gifts in 1 Cor. 12:8-10. To reduce it to mere linguistic ability, even though divinely quickened, is to lower it to a plane that is not given it in the Scriptures. In a sense, any unbeliever, if he be a master of languages, and thus able to speak and interpret those languages, could be said to possess the gifts of tongues and interpretation of tongues.

Paul dispels much ignorant speculation about the speaking with tongues by declaring that it is one of the nine *spiritual* gifts, given only to the members of the Body of Christ, the Church. It is not a natural talent, but, as Horton so splendidly comments, "The linguistic skill of man is no more employed in speaking with tongues than the surgical skill of man was employed when at Peter's word, 'Rise up and walk,' the lame man instantly arose and leaped and walked! It is, in short, a miracle."[1]

---

[1] *Gifts of the Spirit*, p. 136.

CHAPTER 4

Christian Eloquence

IT hardly seems necessary to discuss any more attempts to reduce tongues to the sphere of the natural, but we must deal with them if we are to tell thoroughly what "this" is not.

1. THE SANCTIFIED TONGUE OF A NEW CONVERT

Mark 16:17 gives us the words of the Lord Jesus regarding tongues: "And these signs shall follow them that believe; in my name shall they cast out devils; they shall speak with new tongues." T. J. McCrossan has gone to some length to prove that the "new tongues" refer to the sanctified speech of a new convert. He explains that "the word for 'tongue' here is 'glossa' and its first meaning is 'an organ of the body.' The word for 'new' here is 'kainos,' and means 'new, fresh, anew or renewed.'" By examining the use of the word 'kainos' in other passages (Mk. 2:21; 2 Cor. 5:17; 2 Pet. 3:13; Rev. 21:1; Lam. 3:23) he is led to believe that "Mark 16:17 is a prediction that when a sinner really accepts Christ by faith, and becomes a new creature, one sure and certain visible sign will follow

[53]

—he will speak with a new or renewed tongue."[1] He concludes his argument with a description of an engineer, who was "perhaps the worst curser in the whole city" before his conversion, but after that blessed experience the cursing gave place to songs and praises and testimonies of Christ.

We agree with Mr. McCrossan that the word "believe" in Mark 16:16, 17 refers primarily to saving faith, the heart belief unto righteousness (Rom. 10:10), but we cannot agree that the word, especially in verse 17, is limited to the faith exercised at conversion.

It seems to us that he makes the phrase "them that believe" mean only new converts. While it is true that faith is born at the time of conversion, it is not true that faith lives and dies there. "The just shall *live* by faith;" i.e., faith is an essential principle of the whole Christian life (Heb. 11:6). The words, "them that believe," refer not only to new converts, but also to all Christian believers. Verse 20 is a definite indication of this fact: "And they went forth, and preached everywhere, the Lord working with them, and confirming the word with signs following." As long as the apostles and other disciples continued believing in the Lordship of Jesus over every realm, "these signs" continued to follow them.

A word now about the nature of these signs. They are definitely on a supernatural plane, and why tongues should be singled out from among the others to be stripped of its supernatural character, we do not know. Spiritualization may be an ex-

---

[1] *Speaking With Other Tongues, Sign or Gift—Which?* pp. 20, 21.

cellent means of obtaining some fine truths for the flock, but we must be careful lest in our spiritualizing we remove the literal meaning of the inspired writer. "New tongues" undoubtedly refers to the tongues miraculously spoken by the disciples at Pentecost and in subsequent instances in the New Testament. It does not appear likely that Mr. McCrossan would desire to treat the drinking of any deadly thing as other than drinking a literal poisonous substance; or the casting out of devils as other than the examples found in the ministry of the Lord and His disciples; or the laying on of hands for the recovery of the sick as other than that practiced in the Word; or the taking up of serpents as other than that incident in which Paul was delivered (Acts 28:3-6).

Since Mr. McCrossan admits the supernatural character of tongues in other parts of the volume from which we have quoted, we cannot understand why he endeavors to treat "new tongues" in such a manner. It may be that he is trying to substantiate a theory, or it may be that he, like some other Bible teachers, has allowed his knowledge of Greek to obscure his ability to think clearly and consistently. We do not wish to be uncharitable, but after encountering so many elaborate theories which claim as their foundation Greek roots and tenses, but which are "guilty of arbitrary and artificial exegesis for which there is no foundation in the text or in logic,"[1] we are convinced that the best way of interpreting the Scriptures, especially the historical events. is to take them at face value.

PHILLIPS BROOKS has well remarked: "There is a

---

[1] Mackie, *The Gift of Tongues*, p. 22.

knowledge which is not light but darkness, just as there is a luster on the surface of the ocean which keeps you from seeing down into the ocean's depths. There is a superficial knowledge of the things to which men give their study—of nature, of history, of literature, of man—which, while it is wonderfully accurate in the facts which it receives, does not help to reveal, but glosses over and shuts away from our intelligence the depths and essential glories of the things to which these facts relate. To such, a sort of knowledge is not light but darkness."[1]

Let it be clearly understood that we deeply appreciate Greek scholarship. We give unqualified admiration to the brave souls who have burned the midnight oil so that they might master that difficult but wonderful language. Our own inability to read the Greek New Testament does not cause us to disparage those fortunate fellows who can, for we "esteem them highly for their works' sake." Nevertheless, we are not ignorant of the conditions, cited by Brooks, to which all Greek scholars are liable. It is a fact that some do prize the Greek so highly that they feel it is next to impossible to understand the Scriptures or to speak authoritatively on them without a knowledge of the Greek. In effect, this attitude renders Scriptural truth as inaccessible to the non-Greek (or non-Hebrew) student of today, as it was to the non-Greek and non-Latin student of the days prior to the translation of the Bible in the languages of the people.

The Authorized (or King James) Version is generally acknowledged to be unrivaled in the beauty

---

[1] *Sermons Preached in English Churches*, p. 95, E. P. Dutton & Co., New York, N. Y.

of its language, but the greatest virtue of this beloved version is often overlooked—its doctrinal accuracy. The modern versions (RV, ASV, RSV) may be more correct translations insofar as minor details are concerned, but the best conservative scholarship has adjudged each of them guilty of mistranslations on points of basic scriptural truth. ARTHUR WAY, the noted Greek scholar, has pointed out in the preface of his *Letters of St. Paul* that the Authorized Version was written in an age of doctrinal controversy when exactness of translation was mandatory. The translators were so scrupulous in their desire to use the precise words that their translation, at times, seems a bit stilted, but, according to Way, this extreme literalness produced a Bible which, *in matters of faith*, stands as the supreme authority. We believe that, if we are to gain as much light as possible on the Word, we should refer constantly to the many other translations, but when outstanding Hebrew and Greek scholars confirm again and again the authoritative position of the Authorized Version, we feel justified in our belief that it is the most trustworthy of all versions and the closest to the original of anything we have today.

2. SPIRITUAL ELOQUENCE IN THE NATIVE TONGUE

"VAN HENGEL thinks that the 'other tongues' and the 'new tongues' with which the disciples spoke were their own tongue, given other and new power by the baptism of the Holy Spirit. They had been tongues without fire, and now they were tongues of fire. Their new inspiration had made them new tongues. They were new men and new women, and they spoke with new language and with other tongues than they had known before this wonderful spiritual exaltation. They spoke in Aramaic and they used their own tongue, but their unwonted fluency and fervor, and possibly their adoption of new and strange phraseology, made their own tongue seem like other and new tongues to them."[1]

A brief word will be sufficient for this view whose salient points have been answered in previous arguments. Van Hengel apparently had forgotten the record in Acts 2 when he conceived this opinion. That record, we repeat, states that the "other" tongues were definite languages other than their own Galilean tongue. Peter's sermon in Acts. 2:14-36 was preached with "unwonted fluency and fervor" because of his baptism with the Holy Spirit, but he did not speak with another tongue as he did in Acts 2:4. Paul, in 1 Cor. 14:19, declares emphatically that he did not employ the *glossolalia* when teaching in public.

3. NEW EXPOSITIONS OF THE SCRIPTURES

"HERDER thought that the Pentecostal tongues were simply new interpretations of the ancient prophets, new expositions of the Scriptures. The old preachers of righteousness seemed to be speaking again through the lips of these men and the Pentecostal inspiration gave to the old writings new life. The apostles preached with new and strange power, and the ancient oracles were transformed in their speech. To this we object that the text demands that the tongues be interpreted to mean languages and not expositions."[2] To which we add our "amen."

---

[1]Hayes, *The Gift of Tongues*, p. 23.
[2]Ibid, p. 26.

CHAPTER 5

The Exclusive Possession of the Apostolic Age

IT is an undeniable fact that speaking in tongues was present in the early church; an abundance of Scriptures proves this beyond the shadow of a doubt. The big question, then, is not, Did it occupy a place in the early church? but, Should it occupy a place in the church of today? Such a question obviously deserves a primary position in our consideration of the subject. If speaking in tongues belongs wholly to the apostolic era, and hence is not a present-day possibility, it possesses only a historical significance for us, and we could well devote our time and study to a more vital and practical theme.

1. THE STATEMENT OF THE THEORY

Christendom for many centuries has believed that tongues should be regarded as the exclusive possession of the apostolic age. Endorsement of this view by some of the most eminent scholars of the Church has caused it to be accepted with little reservation by both clergy and laity. And certainly, it would be conceded that the proponents of this theory have compiled a number of fairly plausible arguments to support their relegating of tongues to the remote and irrecoverable past.

They tell us that the supernatural signs and gifts were given to attest the deity of the Lord Jesus, and to authenticate the disciples and their message. The church faced a hostile world. Jew and Gentile were united in their fierce opposition to the gospel of the crucified Nazarene, who had been "declared to be the Son of God with power, according to the Spirit of Holiness, by the resurrection from the dead." How necessary it was then that God should supernaturally confirm the message by stretching forth His hand to heal; and that signs and wonders might be done by the name of His holy child Jesus. The unbelieving and unsympathetic world required visible proofs of the resurrection of Jesus Christ. It is doubtful whether the gospel, minus the miraculous signs, ever could have gained a firm foothold in that "evil and adulterous generation"; assuredly, it would not have created half the stir it did in the world of that day.

But these miraculous powers granted to the first preachers of the gospel should be regarded as only a temporary measure. When their purpose had been fulfilled (viz., the establishing of Christianity as the divine revelation), they began to disappear from the scene. To expect a continuance of them after they had accomplished that whereto God had sent them, reveals a lack of understanding of the plan of God for this age.

Above all, the completion of the canon of the Scriptures removed all necessity for such extraordinary measures From that time on, the church possessed the full and perfect revelation of God and His salvation for man. To desire a further revelation by any other means, or to desire a confirmation of the Word by miraculous signs, is to discredit the Word of God. God, who spoke in time past by miracles, speaks now by His Word. With regard to the signs and wonders of the First Century, we live today in the silence of God. This, it is claimed, is a historical fact universally accepted by the Church, for no major ecclesiastical body has considered that speaking with tongues, or any of the other phenomena of the apostolic age, was to be continued throughout the entire dispensation.

The theory is before us. We trust that its main points have been clearly and fairly stated. One thing that is immediately apparent to every student of the Word about this teaching, and that is admitted even by its advocates, is the total absence of *any definite declaration* by the Lord of His intention to cause tongues and other powers to cease shortly after the establishing of the Church. We have looked in vain for one positive statement in the Scriptures to this effect. It may be that we are lacking in perspicacity, or are guilty of obstinacy, but until we see some clear-cut statement in the Word of God we must recognize this view as a supposition of man. To build a whole theory on the sand of a few doubtful implications is not the best means of insuring its Scriptural correctness or its ability to withstand the attacks of its opponents, especially if the opposition is supported by explicit passages of Scriptures.

2. THE AUTHENTICITY AND TEACHING OF MARK 16:15-20

Such support we believe we can can claim from Mark 16:15-20. No one can doubt that this passage extends the scope of tongues and the other signs far past the boundaries prescribed by the above theory. It contains a definite promise by the Lord Himself, which deals a death blow to the assumption that He willed the termination of tongues and other confirmatory signs at any time during this dispensation. Those who would "shut up these great blessings within the ideal realm called the 'apostolic age,' "[1] must successfully answer this passage, or be reduced to silence.

The favorite method of dealing with these verses is to question their authenticity, to subject them to a barrage of doubts as to their right to be included in the sacred canon. Undoubtedly, this method provides an escape from any doctrine or experience which is not easily comprehended by the natural man. Modernists have long employed this means to remove passages which are distasteful to them, but fundamentalists, in this instance, do not seem to scruple about following suit. The casting of suspicion upon the genuineness of a portion of Scripture is quite a potent weapon, because, even though no actual proof of its lack of genuineness can be advanced, the portion is so clouded with doubt that it loses its power as evidence. Realizing then the importance of establishing the authenticity of Mark 16:15-20, we offer the following arguments (from the Pulpit Commentary) in its favor:

"OBSERVATIONS ON THE GENUINENESS AND AUTHENTICITY OF THE LAST TWELVE VERSES OF MARK'S GOSPEL

"These verses have been admitted by the Revisers of 1881 into the text, but with a space between verse

---

[1] A. J. Gordon.

8 and verse 9, to show that they have received them with some degree of caution and reserve, and not without having carefully weighed the evidence on both sides. The most important features in the evidence are the following:

"1. THE EVIDENCE OF MANUSCRIPTS

"OF THE UNCIAL MANUSCRIPTS. The two eldest, namely, the Sinaitic and the Vatican, omit the whole passage, but under different conditions. The Sinaitic omits the passage absolutely. The Vatican omits it, but with a space left blank between the eighth verse of Mark 16 and the beginning of Luke, just sufficient for its insertion; as though the writer of the manuscript, hesitating whether to omit or to insert the verses, thought it safest to leave a space for them.

"But there is another and much later Uncial Manuscript (1), of about the eighth century. Of this manuscript it may be said that, although some four centuries later, it bears a strong family resemblance to the Sinaitic and the Vatican. This manuscript does not omit the passage, but it interpolates between it and the eighth verse an apochryphal addition, and then goes on with verse 9. This addition is given at p. 538, second edition, of Dr. Scrivener's admirable work on the Criticism of the New Testament.

"It should be added here that there is a strong resemblance between the Sinaitic and Vatican manuscripts; so that practically the evidential value of these three manuscripts amounts to little more than one authority.

"*With these three exceptions, all the Uncial Manuscripts maintain the twelve verses in their integrity.*

"(2) The Cursive Manuscripts. *The evidence of the Cursives is unanimous in favor of the disputed verses.* It is true that some mark the passage as one of which the genuineness has been disputed. But against this there has to be set the fact that the verses are retained in all but two old manuscripts, and those two in all probability not independent. It has been clearly shown by Dean Burgon that the verses were read in the public services of the Church in the fourth century, and probably much earlier, as shown by the ancient Evangelisteria.

"2. Evidence of Ancient Versions

"*The most ancient versions,* both of the Eastern and of the Western Churches, *without a single exception, recognize this passage.* Of the Eastern versions the evidence is very remarkable. The Peshito Syriac, which dates from the second century, bears witness to its genuineness; so does the Philoxenian; while in the Curetonian Syriac, also very ancient, far earlier than the Sinaitic copy of that version, the Gospel of Mark is wanting, with the exception of one fragment only, and that fragment contains the last four of these disputed verses. The Coptic versions also recognize the passage.

"The same may be said of the versions of the Western Church. The earlier version of the Vulgate, called the Old Italic, has it. Jerome, who used the best manuscript of the old Italic when he prepared his Vulgate, felt himself obliged to admit this disputed passage, although he did not scruple to allege the objections to its reception which were the same as those urged by Eusebius. The Gothic Version of Ulphilas (fourth century) has the passage from verse 8 to verse 12.

"3. EVIDENCE OF THE EARLY FATHERS

"There are some expressions in the 'Shepherd of Hermas,' written in all probability not later than the middle of the second century, which are evidently taken from Mark 16:16.

"The evidence of Irenaeus (A.D. 177) is yet more striking. In one of his books ('Adv. Haer.' iii. 10) he quotes the beginning and the end of Mark's Gospel in the same passage, in the latter part of which he says, 'But in the end of his Gospel, Mark saith, 'And the Lord Jesus, after He had spoken unto them, was received into heaven, and sitteth at the right hand of God,' confirming what was said by the prophet, 'The Lord saith unto my Lord, Sit thou on My right hand, until I make Thine enemies Thy footstool.'

"This evidence of Irenaeus is conclusive as to the fact that in his time there was no doubt as to the genuineness and authenticity of the passage, in Asia Minor, in Gaul, or in Italy.

"There yet remains the question of internal evidence.

"Now, to begin with, if it is assumed that Mark's Gospel ended at the close of verse 8, the abruptness of the conclusion is very striking in the English, and still more so in the Greek. It seems scarcely possible to suppose that it could have ended here. . . .

"On the other hand, having regard to the mode in which Mark opens his gospel, we might suppose that he would condense at the close as he condenses at the beginning. The first year of our Lord's ministry is disposed of very briefly; we might, therefore, expect a rapid and compendious conclusion. Two or three important evidences of our Lord's resurrection are concisely stated; then, without any break, but where the reader must supply an interval, he is transported into Galilee. How natural, therefore, that he should refer in some way to our Lord's presence in Galilee after His resurrection; which he does in the most effective manner by quoting the words which Matthew (27:16 etc.) tells us were spoken by Him in Galilee. Then another stride from Galilee to Bethany, to the last earthly scene of all—the Ascension. The whole is eminently characteristic of Mark. His Gospel ends as we might expect it to end, from the character of its beginning. *On the whole, the evidence as to the genuineness and authenticity of this passage seems irresistible.*"[1]

To this lengthy quotation we would add a few brief observations of our own: These twelve verses are not un-Scriptural; they agree with the other Gospel accounts of the resurrection events; and verses 19 and 20 present a perfect preview of the Book of Acts. And surely Mark, writing as it is believed to the Romans, would not end his Gospel with the word, "afraid." v. 8. What a feeble way to end the story of the Lord of life and death! But enough evidence has already been presented to convince the non-bigoted man that the passage belongs in the canon of Scripture. If some of you are still not convinced, we would suggest that you read again the entire chapter as it is in the Authorized Version. Study these verses with an honest, prayerful heart, laying aside, as much as possible, your preconceived opinions. It will not be long before a consciousness of God's presence will permeate your soul, and you will know that these words were inspired of the Spirit of God as an integral part of the Holy Scriptures.

---

[1]From the *Introduction to the Gospel According to Mark*, in the *Pulpit Commentary*.

Before we comment on the actual teaching of verses 15-20, it may be helpful for us to quote them in full: "And he said unto them, Go ye into all the world, and preach the gospel to every creature. He that believeth and is baptized shall be saved; but he that believeth not shall be damned. And these signs shall follow them that believe! in my name shall they cast out devils; they shall speak with new tongues; they shall take up serpents; and if they drink any deadly thing, it shall not hurt them; they shall lay hands on the sick, and they shall recover. So then after the Lord had spoken unto them, he was received up into heaven, and sat on the right hand of God. And they went forth, and preached everywhere, the Lord working with them, and confirming the word with signs following. Amen."

Please notice first that the all-inclusive command, the Great Commission, comes to us today with as much force as it did to the disciples to whom it was originally spoken. Then follows a twofold promise to the believer:[1] first, a promise of salvation; second, a promise of miraculous signs.

A. J. GORDON writes: "It is important to observe that this rich cluster of miraculous promises all hangs by a *single stem, faith*. And this is not some exclusive or esoteric faith. The same believing to which is attached the promise of salvation, has joined to it also

---

[1] From the use of the singular "he" in verse 16, it would seem that Mark is emphasizing the very personal nature of saving faith; while his use of the plural "them" and "they" in verses 17, 18, 20 would indicate the corporate nature of faith for miracles. But though two or more are usually found participating in the latter type of faith, it is also true that Mark records another promise of the Lord Jesus (9:23), "If *thou* canst believe, all things are possible to *him* that believeth."

the promise of miraculous working. Nor is there any ground for limiting this promise to apostolic times and apostolic men, as has been so violently attempted. The links of the covenant are very securely forged, *'He that believeth* and is baptized shall be saved,' in any and every age of the Christian dispensation. So with one consent the church has interpreted the words, 'And these signs shall follow *them that believe,'* in every generation and period of the church's history— so the language compels us to conclude.

"And let us not unbraid this twofold cord of promise, holding fast to the first strand because we know how to use it, and flinging the other back to the apostles because we know not how to use it. Whatever practical difficulties we may have in regard to the fulfillment of this word, these ought not to lead us to limit it where the Lord has not limited it. For if reason or tradition throws out half of this illustrious promise into eclipse, the danger is that the other half may become involved. Indeed we shall not soon forget the cogency with which we heard a skillful skeptic use this text against one who held the common opinion concerning it. Urged to 'believe on the Lord Jesus Christ' that he might be saved, he answered: 'How can I be sure that this part of the promise will be kept with me, when, as you admit, the other part is not kept with the church of today?' And certainly, standing on the traditional ground, one must be dumb before such reasoning. The only safe position is to assert emphatically the perpetuity of the promise, and with the same emphasis to admit the general weakness and failure of the church's faith in appropriating it. . . .

"Both the one and the other ('he that believeth and is baptized shall be saved' and 'these signs shall follow them that believe') apply to ourselves down to the present day and indeed for all future time. Everyone applies the first part of the saying to ourselves, teaching everywhere that faith and baptism are necessary in all ages to salvation, and that unbelief in all ages excludes from it. But what right has any to separate the words that Jesus immediately added from His former words! Where is it said that these former words have reference to all men and all Christians, but that the promised signs which should follow those who believe referred solely to the Christians of the first age? What God hath joined together, let not man put asunder."[1]

What a great gulf ofttimes lies between the promise and the possessing of that promise! We all know that it is possible for eternal salvation, so freely promised to the sinner, to be rejected. It is likewise possible for miraculous signs to be offered to us who believe, only to be neglected. The Lord Jesus Himself has solemnly assured us that "these signs shall follow them that believe." May our faith be quickened to appropriate what He has promised.

3. TONGUES GIVEN TO CHURCH

Another definite statement in the Word, which further substantiates our belief that speaking with tongues should continue through this dispensation, is found in 1 Corinthians 12:28: "And God hath set some in the church, first apostles, secondarily prophets, thirdly teachers, after that miracles, then gifts of healings, helps, governments, diversities of tongues." The apostle obviously does not have reference just to the local church at Corinth, but to

---

[1] *Ministry of Healing,* p. 22, 23, 24, 26.

the complete Church, "which is His body, the fullness of Him that filleth all in all." Every truly born-
again believer, from Pentecost until the coming of
the Lord Jesus, is a full-fledged member of that
Church. We Twentieth Century believers are as
much a part of that Church as were the First
Century believers, and it is our privilege, as joint
heirs with them of the promises of God, to claim
"diversities of tongues."

Some may object that our use of this verse in our
argument is unwarranted since the word "apostles"
occurs therein. They remind us that God did give
the apostles to the whole Church, in that their
doctrine is the foundation of Christian faith for all
time, and yet, the actual ministry of the apostles
was confined to the First Century. This being so,
the same can also apply to tongues, miracles, and
gifts of healings, for they, too, were set in the Church
as a temporary measure.

But even if we grant that there are no longer
apostles in the Church,[1] does this necessitate the belief that the other ministries and miraculous gifts
mentioned in this verse have also passed away? Not
at all. We know of no Bible scholar who contends
that teachers, helps, and governments (also pastors
and evangelists; see Eph. 4:11) are not with us
today. It is true that these lesser ministries were

---

[1]It is our personal conviction that the term "apostle," in
its strictest Scriptural sense, can be applied only to those
extraordinary ambassadors of the First Century who were
infallibly inspired to provide the Church with her doctrines
and practices. Perhaps a loose usage of the term might permit its application to great leaders since that time, but certainly it is not to be applied promiscuously to everyone who
is "sent," simply because the definition of apostle is "sent
one."

ofttimes included in an apostolic ministry, but they were by no means confined to the apostles. And by the same token, the miraculous powers—prophecy, gifts of healing, diversities of tongues, etc.—can be regarded as gifts which were designed by God to continue throughout this age, for they, too, were not confined to the apostles. Thus, even though these unique men have passed from the scene, the other ministries and powers remain as permanent and perpetual gifts to the Church.

4. WHEN TONGUES SHALL CEASE

We have made the assertion that there is not a single, positive statement in the Word to support the theory that tongues were to disappear from the Church. Undoubtedly, this assertion has caused a number of readers to demand, "What about 1 Corinthians 13:8: 'Love never faileth: but whether there be prophecies, they shall fail; *whether there be tongues, they shall cease;* whether there be knowledge, it shall vanish away'? Is this not positive enough for you Pentecostalists?"

Frankly, we cannot understand how any real student of the Scriptures can justify the use of this verse in this matter. A theory must be lacking fearfully in Scriptural support, when it is necessary to strengthen it by such perverted treatment of a text. To make 1 Cor. 13:8 fit the theory, it is necessary not only to wrest the verse from its context, but to disregard the thought of the verse as a whole.

"Verse 8, we see, displays a contrast between the imperishable nature of love and the impermanence of spiritual gifts. Prophecy, tongues, knowledge— these shall fail, cease, vanish away. Our friends the critics of Pentecost repeatedly emphasize the

[71]

ephemeral character of the first two. Let me emphasize also the impermanence of the third: knowledge. There is a sort of implication abroad that we are cherishing in prophecy and tongues things that are worthless because impermanent, while our critics are pursuing in 'knowledge' something that is invaluable because enduring. 'Whether there be knowledge it shall vanish away' is the clear statement of the Word."[1] [2]

When shall tongues cease? According to the apostle Paul, this will occur "when that which is perfect is come." v. 10. Some would have us to believe, though they must have difficulty in believing it themselves, that the "perfect" to which Paul refers was the completion of the sacred canon. We agree fully that the Scriptures are the perfect revelation, but we cannot agree that they are the "perfect" of which Paul writes. The reference is to the perfect age which will be ushered in by the coming of the Lord Jesus Christ. So it is interpreted even by our critics, except when they are attempting to establish a case for the disappearance of tongues. The language is too plain to be interpreted in any other light. Look at those words, "face to face" (v. 12); they are personal words, which can mean only one thing—seeing our glorified Saviour "as He is." Surely the poet caught the true meaning of the Word:

"Face to face shall I behold Him,
    Far beyond the starry sky;

---

[1] Harold Horton, in *Gifts of the Spirit*.

[2] Dr. Ironside, in his *Addresses on the First Epistle to the Corinthians*, points out that *"cease"* is a stronger word than *"fail;"* but it can scarcely be said to be a stronger word than *"vanish."*

> Face to face in all His glory,
> I shall see Him by and by!"

Rather than teaching the termination of tongues, 1 Cor. 13:8 and its context teach the continuance of tongues until the Church is caught up to meet the Lord in the air. "The same thought is expressed in 1 Cor. 1:7, where Paul commends the Corinthians for 'coming behind in no gift, waiting for the coming of the Lord Jesus Christ.' In this spirit, then, the whole Church ought to await the Bridegroom.'"[1]

Our treatment of this passage would not be complete without one more quotation from *Gifts of the Spirit*, by Harold Horton:

"Gifts by their very nature are impermanent because they are fragments of a coming whole; but they are none the less essential for the period over which they are designed to be operative. The very virtue of a spiritual gift is in its impermanence, as the virtue of an acorn is in its impermanence. To make permanent the acorn would be to extinguish oak forests forever. To make permanent the gifts would be to ensure merely fragmentary knowledge and power forever. To sacrifice an acorn is to get a forest hanging thick with them. To look to the 'end' of spiritual gifts is to look to the great whole of which they are but the fragmentary representatives and samples.

"Impermanence is not a fault. It is merely a necessary characteristic of some very delightful things. The gifts of the Spirit are ephemeral like the faculties of the body. But no man neglects his eyesight because of its impermanence. Rather the reverse. Eyesight,

---

[1] T. B. Barratt, *In the Time of the Latter Rain*, p. 158.

like spiritual gifts, belongs to the temporal part-knowledge stage of our eternal development. But who gouges out his eyes or cuts off his ears because he accepts the superior importance of spirit or mind or soul? When that which is perfect is come we shall not need spiritual gifts—or ears. We need both at present. Gifts or no gifts here, we shall be endowed with marvelous wisdom and power hereafter. But shall we neglect the opportunity God gives us in the gifts to help with miracles in the edification of ourselves and the building up of His Church and the deliverance of the needy *now?* Was the Lord Jesus really mocking us when He promised that miracles should be wrought in His name? Mark 16:16. The gifts are the only chance of a miracle *now.* Heaven is a continuous and superlative series of miracles.

"Gifts do not terminate in the simple sense conveyed by the commentators. Gifts only cease in the sense that they are swallowed up in the whole of which they are a part. It is not a bad thing but a good thing to possess *now* a part of that divine ability we shall have forever. It is a thing to covet earnestly."

5. INFERENCES FROM THE LAST PAULINE EPISTLES

SIR ROBERT ANDERSON tells us: "And it is a matter, not of opinion, but of fact, that whereas Pentecostal gifts and evidential miracles hold a prominent place in the teaching narrative of the Acts, and in the teaching of Epistles written during the period historically covered by the Acts, the later Epistles are silent with respect to them. The natural inference is that they had ceased."

He says further, "Why then was it that he could

not heal Epaphroditus when he lay 'sick nigh unto death' by his side at Rome? How was it, at a still later date, he had to leave Trophimus lying sick at Miletum? And a miracle at the Court of Nero might have shaken the world. Never indeed was an evidential miracle more needed, if received beliefs and theories about miracles be true. But miracle there was none.

"If with an open mind we peruse the Acts of the Apostles, and then turn to 2 Timothy, we shall find proofs of a tremendous change. When the magistrates at Philippi thrust the apostle into the dungeon, a great earthquake shook the foundation of the prison; heaven came down to his deliverance, and his persecutors were brought as suppliants to his feet. But now the days of earthquakes and 'mighty signs and wonders' were past; and as a 'pattern to them that should afterward believe,' the lonely and despised prisoner in Rome was to learn the deeper mysteries of the life of faith beneath a silent heaven."[1]

In answering Sir Robert's inferences about the "mighty signs and wonders," we shall help to establish the fact of the continuance of the *glossolalia*, for it, too, is a "sign and wonder." Our answer, of necessity, must be brief, but we trust that it will show every reader that even such apparently weighty arguments as these do not constitute real opposition to our view.

To begin with, the assumption that the Epistles of Paul's last imprisonment are devoid of references to miraculous powers, is false. In 1 Timothy 4:14 Paul counsels his son in the gospel, "Neglect not the gift that is in thee which was given thee by prophecy,

---

[1] *Spirit Manifestations and "The Gift of Tongues."* p. 23, 24.

with the laying on of the hands of the presbytery." And again in 2 Timothy 1:6, "Wherefore I put thee in remembrance that thou stir up the gift of God, which is in thee by the putting on of my hands." The "gift" of which Paul speaks in the latter verse was undoubtedly one of the extraordinary gifts of the Spirit which was imparted, as in the experience of the Samaritans (Acts 8:17) and the Ephesians (19:6), with the laying on of the apostles' hands. And with this almost all commentators agree. It may well be that the gift which he received at his ordination by the presbytery was also of a miraculous nature. The "gift" in 2 Timothy 1:6 should be sufficient proof, however, that the last Epistles do contain some reference to the continuing exercise of the supernatural workings of the Holy Spirit; for how could Timothy "stir up the gift" if it had already ceased?

But even if there were a total absence of mention of the miraculous in these last letters of the apostle, would that be absolute proof of the cessation of the miraculous? Not any more than the lack of direct mention of the Lord's supper in the later Epistles proves that it was no longer observed in the churches. Then, too, 2 Thessalonians, one of Paul's earliest Epistles, does not refer to the exercise of the signs and wonders, but no one infers from this that they were not in existence then.

The truth of the matter is simply this: An ordinance or doctrine does not have to be restated in every Epistle to be accepted as truth. Each Epistle was written with a distinct purpose, and sometimes lacks, and at other times contains, some teaching which is found or not found in other Epistles. Separately, they teach similar but not necessarily identical truths, and when placed together in the sacred canon, they present the complete and perfect revelation of God to man. To isolate an Epistle, or group of Epistles, and to say that their failure to mention a truth taught elsewhere in the Word cancels that truth, is one sure way to produce false interpretations of the Scriptures.

And what of Paul's "failure" to heal Epaphroditus and Trophimus? Frankly, we cannot explain this, and it would be as much folly for us to formulate an opinion and state it as an absolute fact, as it is for Sir Robert to do so. We do not know all the circumstances connected with these two cases, and therefore cannot speak with authority regarding them. The disciples thought that blindness from birth could be attributed unquestionably to sin either in the parents or in the child (John 9:1, 2). But the Master said, "Neither hath this man sinned, nor his parents: but that the works of God should be made manifest in him." And why did Jesus allow Lazarus to die? It was "for the glory of God, that the Son of God might be glorified thereby." And what of the lame man "whom they laid daily at the gate of the temple"? Surely the Master must have passed often by this terribly crippled man, and yet He left him in Jerusalem sick. Why did He not heal him, as He had countless others? We assume that it was because the lame man's hour had not yet arrived; because his faith had not yet matured; because the glory of God was to be more manifest in his being healed through Peter and John.

And can we not surmise that for some kindred reason God merely delayed the healing of Epaphroditus and Trophimus? The record does not state that Paul could not heal these men because his miraculous powers had deserted him. On the contrary, it may be that the words regarding the recovery of Epaphroditus, "but God had mercy upon him," indicate a miracle wrought through the importunate prayers of Paul. (Elijah prayed but once for the fire, but it was necessary for him to pray many times for the rain.) And it may be that Trophimus, whom Paul left sick, was healed at a later date. Who can tell? Three things we do know, however: (1) healing of the sick was a definite promise given to the believer of the whole Church age; (2) it was never revoked, not even qualified by a definite statement in the New Testament; and (3) these two exceptional cases, which are susceptible to various interpretations, cannot be advanced as proof that God was disclosing His desire to remove the miraculous gifts from the Church.

Finally, what significance should be attached to the fact that Paul wrought no miracle before Nero, but rather was forced to remain a lonely and despised prisoner in Rome? Those who believe that this reveals a cessation of the miraculous seem to have forgotten that this was not the first time the apostle had suffered imprisonment. For two long years he was kept bound by Felix, and no earthquake brought deliverance to him as at Philippi. He appeared before Felix, Festus, and Agrippa, but miracle there was none. And yet, no one dares to assert that the days of mighty signs and wonders were past, for the voyage to Rome is replete with them.

What, then, does Paul's experience at Rome teach? That when the purposes of God can be served best through miracles, He performs them; and when the purposes of God can be served best without miracles, He omits them. A miracle by the Lord

Jesus before Herod might have spared Him the sufferings of Calvary, "but He answered him nothing." Luke 23:9. James could have been set free, like Peter, but Herod was permitted to kill "James the brother of John with the sword." Stephen, like Paul at Lystra, could have been quickened and restored to the church, but "devout men carried Stephen to his burial." In other words, we cannot build doctrine on all the sovereign dealings of God in the lives of His servants. What was His will in one instance in their lives, was not His will in another instance; and what was His will for one servant was not His will for another. The purposes of God in Paul's deliverance at Philippi and in his continued imprisonment at Rome were not the same. It is to the differences in purpose that we must attribute the earthquake at Philippi and the absence of an earthquake at Rome, not to the supposed termination of signs and wonders. He who permitted John Bunyan to languish in the Bedford jail to pen *Pilgrim's Progress*, willed that His servant Paul should remain in bonds so that he might write the "Prison Epistles." And why should God deliver him, when according to the apostle's own confession, "the time of my departure is at hand"? Paul's work was done, but not so the work of the God of Paul, for He continued to work on, "confirming the Word with signs following."

6. PURPOSE OF THE SIGNS IN APOSTOLIC DAYS

It seems to us that the reason why there has been such an elaborate effort to prove that God desired the withdrawal of tongues, interpretation of tongues, prophecies, healings, etc., is that the true

nature and purpose of these powers have been mis-
understood. Chapters 10 through 23 of this volume
will present the Pentecostal view of the nature and
purpose of tongues, but a general explanation here
should help to bring a clearer understanding of these
signs and wonders as a whole.

These miraculous powers were not given to take
the place of the New Testament, which was still to
be written. They were for confirmation, not substitution, of the Word. And it should be clearly
understood that these signs were never considered
to have the same authority as the word spoken by
the apostles. We do not read that the early believers
continued steadfastly in the truths made known
through tongues and interpretation, prophecy, etc.,
but that "they continued steadfastly in the *apostles'*
doctrine." The teaching of the apostles constituted
the highest authority in the First Century church.
All other revelations were judged according to the
apostles' doctrine, upon which rests the entire New
Testament as we have it now. What was the spoken
Word then, has since been incorporated into the
written Word, so that now the Church has the
perfect, final and infallible revelation of God.

But does it follow that with the completion of
the sacred canon the signs should cease? Why should
they not continue to confirm the written Word even
as they confirmed the spoken Word? Mark 16:20.
We are immediately informed by DR. HARRY A.
IRONSIDE that "now with God's complete revelation
in our hands, we do not require signs to manifest it
as the word of the Lord. When preached in power, it
authenticates itself."[1] As if the apostles did not

---

[1] *Addresses on the First Epistle to the Corinthians.*

preach the Word in power! As if the mere transcribing of the truth of God's Word could lessen or increase its authenticity or power! As if each portion of the Word were not permeated by the same spirit and life as the other portions with which it was afterwards canonized! Nay, for the very same reason that the signs followed the message in the First Century (viz., the providing of a miraculous background for the message and the investing of the disciples with divine authority), they should follow the same message today.

The March 3, 1934 issue of the *Sunday School Times* carried an article from the book, *Miraculous Healing*, by HENRY W. FROST, D.D., Home Director Emeritus for North America, China Inland Mission. In this article Dr. Frost asks, *"Are signs still needed? In answering this question, two great facts are to be kept in mind. First, in the greater part of the world and among the largest number of people the Bible has never been circulated, and the missionary may make no appeal to it. Second, among Christianized peoples the apostasy of Modernism has greatly undermined confidence in the authenticity of the Scriptures, so that the preachers' appeal to it is largely non-effective The first of these facts brings us face to face with the condition which prevailed in Christ's day as a result of non-enlightenment; and the second forces us to confront a similar condition as a result of unbelief."*

The gospel in this Twentieth Century is still faced by a hostile and skeptical world. What fierce antagonism our missionaries encounter when they attempt to invade the strongholds of Judaism, Mohammedanism, Hinduism, Buddhism, and Confucianism! How strong is the opposition of the demon-inspired devotees of pagan religions the world over! What hatred and malice confront the courageous soldiers of the Cross, when they enter the lands under the control of Roman Catholicism! And is not unbelief widespread even in the so-called Christian nations of today? Do not spiritism and clairvoyance exercise an ever-increasing evil influence over the spirits of men? Is not anti-Christian activity multiplying on every hand? Then, why should it be decreed that the need of confirmatory signs no longer exists, since the Church today is surrounded by conditions startlingly similar to those of the First Century?

Dr. Frost continues: "It is therefore true that there are large parts of the world where healing-miracles, in proof of the living and all-powerful Christ, may well be looked for, and it may confidently be anticipated, as the present apostasy increases, that Christ will manifest His deity and lordship in increasing measure through miracle-signs, including healings. The missionary abroad, therefore, may have it in mind, in case of the sickness of others, that God may choose to make him a miracle worker; and the worker at home may understand that He may choose to make some sick saint, as He made the apostles, a spectacle, or—as it reads literally—a theater unto the world, and to the angels, and to men. 1 Cor. 4:9. And what true child of God will not be willing to be used by Him in these ways, as in any and every other?"

And DR. JAMES M. GRAY, in his *Christian Workers' Commentary*, commenting on Mark 16, writes (page 319): "As a matter of fact, however, such signs do still follow the teaching of the gospel on foreign mission fields, and doubtless will be practically universal again as the end of the age draws near and the coming of the King."

One further thought about the purpose of the signs. They were not given only for confirmation of the Word, but to meet a definite physical, mental or spiritual need. While it is true that some miracles were given as manifestations of divine power alone, and did not fulfill a particular need in an individual or group, still the vast majority of miracles combined both of these elements. The mighty works of the Lord Jesus flowed out of a heart moved with compassion for the hungry multitude, the loathsome leper, the deaf, the dumb, the blind, the lame. And this compassion was one of the prime factors in His continued miracles through the early church. In this respect, Jesus Christ is "the same yesterday, and today, and forever" (Hebrews 13:8). His love for the sick and the suffering has not grown cold. Wherever a need exists in body, soul, mind, or spirit, He stands ready to meet that need. For this cause He gave gifts unto men and confirmed the Word with signs following. What beneficial purposes the nine gifts of the Spirit (1 Cor. 12:8-10) and the signs of Mark 16:17, 18 would serve in this old world, where "the whole creation groaneth and travaileth in pain together until now." And we are persuaded to believe that these purposes represent the supreme element in these gifts and signs given to a needy Church and a needy world by the God of love.

7. THE REAL REASON FOR THE RETROGRESSION OF MIRACLES

Why did the signs and wonders begin to disappear from the Church after the First Century? Why have miracles been so rare in the history of the Church?

Not because the Lord decreed their withdrawal, as so many assert, for His unrevoked, unqualified promise is that "these signs shall follow them that believe." We must change the direction of our search from the God who made the promise to the ones to whom the promise was and is made. Why has not the Church constantly cast out devils, spoken with new tongues, taken up serpents without harm (accidentally, of course—Acts 28:3-6), been preserved from the effects of deadly poison (inadvertently taken, or administered by an enemy), laid hands on the sick for their recovery? Because of unbelief!

BENGEL declares, "The reason why many miracles are not now wrought is not so much because faith is established, as that unbelief reigns."

CHRISTLIEB says, "It is the want of faith in our age which is the greatest hindrance to the stronger and more marked appearance of that miraculous power which is working here and there in quiet concealment. Unbelief is the final and most important reason for the retrogression of miracles."

JOHN WESLEY lays the blame squarely on the Church, telling us that the sign-gifts decreased "because the love of many, almost all Christians so-called, waxed cold. That was the real cause why the extraordinary gifts of the Holy Ghost were no longer to be found in the Christian Church."

D. M. PANTON writes: "Sapped in faith, in holiness, in aloofness from the world, the church relaxed its grasp of the gifts, which, as manifestations of the Spirit, invited persecution; relied less on the Spirit, as it leaned more on the State; abandoned the powers of faith as it fell back to justification by works; until the divine and marvelous glory of the first splendid powers of faith was replaced by scarlet robes and crosses and censers of gold, and over the portal of God's spiritual temple was inscribed *Ichabod*."[1]

We might cite also an observation by EDWARD IRVING, who, despite his being misled in attributing too much importance to the gifts of the Spirit, grasped as few other men during the centuries of Church history the teaching of the Scriptures with respect to the supernatural:

"The true reason why the gift of tongues hath ceased to be in the Church is the exaltation of the natural methods of teaching above, or into copartnery with, the teaching of the Holy Ghost; the meanness of our idea, and the weakness of our faith, concerning the oneness of Christ glorified with His Church on earth; the unworthiness of our doctrine concerning the person and office of the Holy Ghost, to knit up the believer into complete oneness with Christ, every thread and filament of our mortal humanity with His humanity, immortal and glorious; to bring down into the Church a complete Christ, and keep Him there, ever filling her bosom, and working in her members; the shortcoming of our knowledge, in respect to the gifts themselves; our having ceased to lament their absence, and to pray for their return; our want of fasting, and humiliation, and crying unto the Lord; our contentment to be without them; our base and false theories to account for their absence, without taking guilt to ourselves. Any one of these causes were sufficient, all of them are far more than sufficient, to account for their long absence from the bosom of the Church. These are the true reasons; the commonly given reason, that they were designed

---

[1] *Irvingism, Tongues, and Gifts of the Holy Ghost*, p. 44.

only for a short time, is utterly false and most pernicious."[1]

Even DR. IRONSIDE expresses a similar thought: "Some insist that these gifts have absolutely disappeared, but I do not know of any scripture that tells us that. I do not know of any scripture that says that the age of miracles is past, and I would not dare to say that the sign gifts all ended with Paul's imprisonment. I know from early church history that this is not true.

"In the beginning the apostle writes to these very Corinthians, 'I have espoused you as a chaste virgin to Christ.' It was a separated company, the affianced bride of the Lamb, and as this Church went forth it was the delight of the blessed risen Lord to lavish upon her gift after gift. These Corinthians 'came behind in no gift,' we are told, but it seems to me we can see in the Book of Acts that as time went on and the Church began to drift a little, and as dissension and other things came in that grieved the Lord, there was more reserve on His part in bestowing gifts. That, I believe, explains the lack of many of these gifts today. The church has gotten so far away and there is so much strife, division, worldliness, and carnality that He no longer delights to lavish His gifts upon her as He did in the beginning."[2]

Fellow Christian, the promise is unto us: "And these signs shall follow them that believe; in My name they shall . . . speak with new tongues." Let us not comfort ourselves with the excuse that tongues (or any of the other signs or gifts) were

---

[1]*Complete Works of Edward Irving*, Vol. V. p. 560.
[2]*Addresses on the First Epistle to the Corinthians.*

meant to cease; let us not condone our acceptance of this mistaken hypothesis simply because all major ecclesiastical bodies have embraced it (for one thousand years of Church history, 500-1500 A. D., the doctrine of justification by faith was not espoused by any major ecclesiastical body): but let us "cry out, and say with tears, 'Lord, I believe; help Thou mine unbelief.' "

CHAPTER 6

Absent From Church History

SO often it is asserted that the *glossolalia* was almost wholly removed from the Church by the end of the First Century, the latest date of its existence being given as the Third Century, after which the gift completely disappeared. This assertion, however, rests entirely upon an ignorance of the facts of Church history. According to the *Encyclopedia Britannica*, the *glossolalia* "recurs in Christian revivals of every age."[1]

In this chapter we wish to sketch briefly this recurrence from its first manifestation at Pentecost down through the centuries to the present time. It is not within the scope of this volume to give an exhaustive survey of tongues in Church history, nor to consider all the doctrines and practices of the various religious groups in which this phenomenon occurred. Perhaps it will be sufficient to say that many more well-authenticated instances could be cited, and that we do not identify ourselves with all that has been done and taught by those who in time past witnessed to the presence of this miracle of utterance in their midst.

---

[1]Vol. 22, p. 283, 1944 edition.

FIRST CENTURY

LUKE: "And they were all filled with the Holy Ghost and began to speak with other tongues as the Spirit gave them utterance (Acts 2:4).

PAUL: "I thank my God, I speak with tongues more than ye all" (1 Cor. 14:18).

SECOND AND THIRD CENTURIES

DR. PHILIP SCHAFF, the well-known Church historian, in his *History of the Apostolic Church,* Book 1, Sec. 55, writes:

"The speaking with tongues, however, was not confined to the day of Pentecost. Together with the other extraordinary spiritual gifts which distinguished this age above the succeeding periods of more quiet and natural development, this gift also though to be sure in a modified form, perpetuated itself in the apostolic church. We find traces of it still in the second and third centuries."

IRENAEUS (115 to 202 A.D.) was a pupil of Polycarp, who was a disciple of the apostle John. He wrote in his book *Against Heresies,* Book V, vi: "In like manner do we also hear many brethren in the Church who possess prophetic gifts, and who through the Spirit speak all kinds of languages, and bring to light for the general benefit the hidden things of men and declare the mysteries of God, whom also the apostles term spiritual."

TERTULLIAN (160-220 A.D.) invited Marcion to produce anything among his followers such as was common among the orthodox Christians: "Let him exhibit prophets such as have spoken, not by human sense but with the Spirit of God, such as have predicted things to come, and have made manifest the secrets of the heart; let him produce a psalm, a vision, a prayer, only let it be by the Spirit in an ecstasy, that is, in a rapture, whenever an interpretation of tongues has occurred to him." He also gives a full description of a certain sister who often spoke with tongues. (See Smith's *Dictionary of the Bible*, Vol. 4, p. 3310).

FOURTH CENTURY

PACHOMIUS (292-348 A.D.)—According to A. Butler in his book *Lives of the Saints*, published in 1756, Pachomius after seasons of special prayer was able to speak the Greek and Latin languages, which he had never learned, under the power of the Spirit.

AUGUSTINE (354-430) wrote: "We still do what the apostles did when they laid hands on the Samaritans and called down the Holy Spirit on them by the laying on of hands. It is expected that converts should speak with new tongues."

FIFTH CENTURY TO REFORMATION

ALEXANDER MACKIE in his book *The Gift of Tongues* (p. 27) says: "From patristic times until the power of the Reformation had made itself distinctly felt, the gift of tongues is an almost forgotten phenomenon. The attention which the Reformation drew to the Scriptures is the reason for the reappearance of the gift. Men do not usually have the gift of tongues unless they know there is a gift of tongues. The revival of the Bible made also necessary in some minds a revival of states of mind and actions such as were those of the men who lived in Bible times and who were esteemed holy. During the long silence of those weary centuries there was evidence, however, of those psychological and physiological tendencies and actions which we find go hand in hand with the appearance of the gift in the history of the Corinthian church, or in the history of all the more modern sects which we shall discuss. Simply because the ages preceding the Reformation were deficient in a Scriptural vocabulary we fail to find these phenomena described and classified as related to the gift of tongues."

But even in the Dark Ages God gave some gracious revivals. From the Twelfth to the Fifteenth Century there were revivals in southern Europe in which many spoke in other tongues. Foremost among these revivalists were the Waldenses and Albigenses.

The *Encyclopedia Britannica* states that the *glossolalia* was present "among the mendicant friars of the Thirteenth Century."

In the *History of the Christian Church,* by Philip Schaff, we read of VINCENT FERRER who died in 1419. "Spondamus and many others say this saint was honored with the gift of tongues."

REFORMATION TO TWENTIETH CENTURY

In a German work, Souer's *History of the Christian Church,* vol. 3, p. 406, the following is found: "DR. MARTIN LUTHER was a prophet, evangelist, speaker in tongues and interpreter, in one person, endowed with all the gifts of the Holy Spirit."[1]

FRANCIS XAVIER, who died in 1552, is reported to have had a remarkable exercise of the gift of tongues, according to Schaff and *The Catholic Encyclopedia.*

The *Encyclopedia Britannica* (Vol. 22, p. 283) tells of tongues "among the Jensenists and early Quakers, the converts of Wesley and Whitefield, the

---

[1]We have not been able to determine the author's conception of the nature of tongues, and therefore we would hesitate to enter this quotation as conclusive evidence. The same can be said of the references to Augustine and Dwight L. Moody.

persecuted Protestants of the Cevennes, and the Irvingites."

DR. MIDDLETON once wrote: "After the apostolic time, there is not, in all history, one instance either well attested, or even so much as mentioned, of any particular person who had ever exercised that gift (tongues), or pretended to exercise it in any age or country whatever." JOHN WESLEY wrote in protest against this statement (see *Wesley's Works*, Vol. V, p. 744): "Sir, your memory fails you again. . . . It has been heard of more than once, no further off than the valleys of Dauphiny."

THOMAS WALSH, in his diary of March 8, 1750, wrote: "This morning the Lord gave me language that I knew not of, raising my soul to Him in a wonderful manner."

In *The Message and Mission of Quakerism* (Page 17), by W. C. Braithwaite, quoting from Burrough's *Preface to Great Mystery*, we read: "While waiting upon the Lord in silence, as often we did for many hours together, we received often the pouring down of the Spirit upon us, and our hearts were glad and our tongues loosed and our mouths opened, and we spake with new tongues as the Lord gave us utterance, and as His Spirit led us, which was poured down upon us, on sons and daughters, and the glory of the Father was revealed. And then began we to sing praises to the Lord God Almighty and to the Lamb forever."

Regarding DWIGHT L. MOODY, here are a few quotations from page 402, *Trials and Triumphs of Faith* (1875 edition), by the Rev. R. Boyd, D.D. (Baptist), who was a very intimate friend of the famous evangelist:

" 'When I (a Y.M.C.A. member) got to the

rooms of the Young Men's Christian Association (Victoria Hall, London), I found the meeting 'on fire.' The young men were speaking with tongues, prophesying. What on earth did it mean? Only that Moody had been addressing them that afternoon! What manner of man is this? thought I, but still I did not give him my hand. . . . Many of the clergy were so opposed to the movement that they turned their backs upon our poor, innocent Young Men's Christian Association for the part we took in the work; but afterward when the flood-gates of divine grace were opened, Sunderland (near London) was taken by storm. I cannot describe Moody's great meeting: I can only say that the people of Sunderland warmly supported the movement, in spite of their local spiritual advisers.' "

Some years ago DR. F. B. MEYER visited Esthonia, one of the Baltic provinces of Russia, where he found some simple peasant congregations of Baptists. He wrote to the *London Christian* of the wonderful work of the Holy Ghost that he saw among them. He stated: "It is very remarkable, at a time when the Lutheran Church of this land has lost its evangelistic fervor, and is inclined to substitute forms and rites for the living power of Christ, that God raised up a devoted nobleman, Baron Uxhall, to preach the gospel in all its simplicity, and is renewing among the peasantry those marvelous manifestations which attended the first preaching of the gospel when God bore witness to the message of salvation with signs and wonders and gifts of the Holy Ghost. To have come across a movement like this is intensely interesting. The gift of tongues is heard quite often in the meetings, especially in the villages, but also in the towns. Here at Reval, the pastor of the Baptist Church tells me that they often break out in his meetings. They are most often uttered by young women, less frequently by men. When they are interpreted they are found to mean, 'Jesus is coming soon; Jesus is near. Be ready; be not idle.' When they are heard, unbelievers who may be in the audience are greatly awed. A gentleman who was present on one occasion was deeply impressed by the fact that those who spoke were quite ordinary people until they were uplifted as it were by a trance and then they spoke with so much fluency and refinement."

TWENTIETH CENTURY

Time and space will not allow our recording of the multiplied thousands of testimonies which could be given by those who have spoken with tongues in this century. For the reader who desires an extensive survey of the modern exhibitions of this phenomenon, we would suggest that he obtain a copy of the book *With Signs Following*, by Stanley Howard Frodsham.[1] This monumental work has twenty-four chapters, twenty-two of which are devoted to a detailed discussion of the miraculous signs which have followed the preaching of the Word in this world-wide Pentecostal revival. We are confident that all will find much valuable information, and will receive much spiritual blessing, from a careful reading of this book.

We shall leave until the next chapter the controversy concerning the similarity between the present-day exercise of tongues and that of the early Christians. But to conclude this brief historical sketch, we

---

[1] Gospel Publishing House, Springfield, Mo.

would say that it cannot be successfully denied that there is definite proof of the presence of tongues in the Church throughout the centuries. We grant that this miracle of utterance has not been as commonplace as it was in the apostolic era, but neither has it been entirely absent from Church history.

CHAPTER 7

The Babblings of Fanaticism

IS the speaking with tongues of today the same as that of the early disciples, or is it but a cheap imitation of that miracle of utterance? Is it true that the *glossolalia* has been restored to the Church, or is this nothing more than a fanatical gibberish? Is this thing "from heaven, or of men"?

These questions are of utmost importance to thousands of Twentieth Century Christians. They want to know whether or not to believe the claim of Pentecostalists that once again believers are speaking with other tongues as the Spirit gives them utterance. One reason for the ever-increasing questionings is that more and more knowledge of the so-called "Tongues People" is being gained every day, and it is being discovered that most of the widely circulated charges against these people are exaggerated, and in many instances are absolutely false. Even church leaders are beginning to modify their former assertions, for they too are becoming better acquainted with the Movement as a whole. We welcome this change of attitude on the part of our fellow believers in the Lord Jesus Christ, whom we all love and adore. Nevertheless, we realize that there are many

[97]

who are of the same opinion still, who continue to attack us in none too flattering terms. They insist that it is a mistake to recognize the "Tongues People" as anything more than a group of ignorant heretics, whose false teachings and fanatical demonstrations do more harm than good for the cause of Christ. And so it is necessary, if we are to provide further information for our friends and to answer our opponents, to present a brief discussion of those who speak with tongues today.

One point we would mention before we enter this discussion. The appellation, "Tongues People," which is so often used in connection with this body of believers is somewhat misleading. It conveys the impression that speaking with tongues is the sum and substance of all our teaching and practice. Such is not the case, as we shall show presently. The term Pentecostal, it would seem to us, is a much more correct designation of this great Twentieth Century Revival Movement. While it is true that the word Pentecostal has been the subject of much unnecessary reproach (unfortunately, everyone from snake-handlers to fire-eaters seems to prefer that name!), still we feel that the term has a special application to the people whom one prominent fundamentalist commended as "responsible for stirring up more interest in the Person and Work of the Holy Spirit than any other contemporary religious movement."

1. DOCTRINAL BELIEFS

The Pentecostal Movement is thoroughly fundamental. Ample proof of this fact can be seen in the recognition extended to various Pentecostal organizations by the NATIONAL ASSOCIATION OF EVANGELICALS and similar fundamentalist groups. The great doctrines of the Church—the infallibility of the

Scriptures, depravity of man, deity of the Lord Jesus Christ, His virgin birth, vicarious death, literal resurrection, ascension, and second coming, the reality of heaven and hell, etc.—which have caused tremendous controversy and division in some of the older denominations, are accepted without question by Pentecostal people as a whole.

In addition to these vital tenets of faith, commonly held by our fundamentalist brethren, we embrace some beliefs peculiar to us as Pentecostalists. We have written at length in Chapter 5 of our conviction that the supernatural signs and gifts of the apostolic church can be possessed by believers today. Speaking with tongues is easily the most spectacular of these signs and gifts in operation in the Pentecostal Movement, and the one which distinguishes its adherents from all other Christians. The specific purpose of this whole volume is to set forth our Pentecostal belief with respect to tongues, and in this way our most distinctive doctrine[1] will be submitted to all for the closest scrutiny.

Believe us when we say that we are honest in our desire for truth. If our beliefs will not stand the searchlight of investigation, then the sooner we know it the better for us. If "this" which we teach and experience is not "that" which was taught and experienced by the early disciples, then we do not want "this." But if "this" of today is the same as "that" of yesterday, as we believe it is, then we shall continue to proclaim to all, both far and near, "This is that!" (Acts 2:16).

---

[1]It is not our main doctrine, as some critics suggest. Our main doctrine is Jesus Christ and Him crucified, resurrected, glorified and coming again!

2. SOCIAL AND INTELLECTUAL STATUS

Some time ago we sat in a Pentecostal convention which was being given a welcome to the city by a denominational leader who represented the local ministerial alliance. In the course of his remarks he complimented us on our ability to reach a "certain class" which other religious groups are failing to reach. It was a "left-handed compliment," but it did not make us particularly unhappy, for, though it did not exactly minister to our pride, there was an element of truth in the statement. Many of the larger denominations in their efforts to reach the so-called "higher classes" have almost forgotten the "common people" who "heard Him gladly." Bishop Moore, of the Methodist Church, has exhorted his brethren (and we trust not in vain) to "go back to the low, the least, the lost, and the last!" So far, we Pentecostal preachers need no exhortation to "go back," for we are content with "our calling"—and God forbid that we should ever be ashamed of any of them whom He is not ashamed to call His "brethren!"

It is blessedly true that within our ranks there are some who are "wise men after the flesh," some "mighty," and some "noble." For these we lift grateful hearts to the "one God and Father of all, who is above all, through all, and in you all." Hayes (speaking of tongues) has said, "They will flourish most among the poorer and the illiterate classes, but they will by no means be confined to these. Past experience proves that educated and high-bred people are likewise influenced by them."[1] On the whole, the Pentecostal Movement of today is composed of

---

[1] *The Gift of Tongues,* p. 93.

the same class of people as those found in the church of the First Century.

3. MORAL STANDARD

CONYBEARE AND HOWSON have stated: "We must not be led from any apparent analogy to confound the exercise of the gift of tongues in the primitive church with modern exhibitions of fanaticism, which bear a superficial resemblance to it. If, however, the inarticulate utterances of ecstatic joy are followed (as they were in some of Wesley's converts) by a life of devoted holiness, we should hesitate to say that they might not bear some analogy to those of the Corinthian Christians." In other words, if the similarity of the tongues of today and the tongues of New Testament times is to be established, there must be a comparison made not only of the tongues themselves, but also of the moral conduct of the persons thus exercised in the present and in the past.

How does the average Pentecostal Christian compare with the New Testament Christian? The same Christ who wrought a life of devoted holiness in the early disciples is doing the same blessed work today. It is not necessary for us to say that His work among us is often hindered by our imperfections, for everyone knows that human nature in the Twentieth Century is the same as human nature in the First Century. Nevertheless, the consuming desire of every true Pentecostal believer is to worship and serve the Lord in the beauty of holiness.

DR. A. B. SIMPSON, the late Founder and President of the Christian and Missionary Alliance, made this comment about the Pentecostal Movement in one of his annual reports:

"We believe there can be no doubt that in many

cases remarkable outpourings of the Holy Spirit have
been accompanied with genuine instances of the gift
of tongues and many extraordinary manifestations.
This has occurred both in our own land and in some
of our foreign missions. Many of these experiences
appear not only to be genuine, but accompanied by a
spirit of deep humility and soberness, and free from
extravagance and error. And it is admitted that
in many of the branches and States where this
movement has been strongly developed and wisely
directed, there has been a marked deepening of the
spiritual life of our members, and an encouraging
increase in their missionary zeal and liberality. It
would therefore be a serious matter for any candid
Christian to pass a wholesale criticism or condemnation upon such movements, or presume to limit the
Holy One of Israel."[1]

Over a quarter of a century has elapsed since Dr.
Simpson made this statement, and every passing year
has borne out the correctness of his view. While
others were looking only upon the extravagances and
errors of the Movement, this man of God saw what
others either could not or would not see; viz., the
presence of God. He refused to judge the whole Mov-
ment by the individuals who erred from the truth in
doctrine or conduct. To him it was "a serious
matter for any candid Christian to pass a wholesale
criticism or condemnation upon such movements."
Would to God that other critics would take a
lesson from him in this respect! How many have
blindly rejected this revival simply because they have
known of some individuals who may have been

---

[1]Quoted by T. B. Barratt, *In the Days of the Latter Rain*,
p. 157.

guilty of immorality or some other form of un-Scriptural conduct. Pentecost, like every other revival movement in the Church, has had within its ranks those who have brought shame and reproach to the entire body; but they are the exception and not the rule. We are confident that Pentecost would be spared from many vicious unfair attacks in the future, if our critics would agree that only he who belongs to a perfect organization should cast the first stone.

"The supernatural signs, the gifts of the Spirit, the bodily demonstrations are all a part of this Pentecostal Movement," said the late T. B. Barratt, of Olso, Norway; "but the great moral influence of this revival, the mighty spiritual impetus, is of far greater importance." Surely abundant proof of this statement is found in the thousands of clean, wholesome young people in Pentecost. With what amazement ministers of other ranks regard the spiritual enthusiasm of Pentecostal young people! And the leaders of the "YOUTH FOR CHRIST" Movement all over this country can testify to the clear-cut, Christian experiences of Pentecostal youth. What a testimony to the world are these splendid young men and women! Surrounded on every hand by the temptations of an evil and adulterous generation, they are examples of "the expulsive power of a new affection"; they are witnesses to the saving, keeping and satisfying power of the Lord Jesus Christ.

If all spoke well of this great revival today, we should have reason to doubt its genuineness. We do not expect the world that crucified our Lord and Master to grant us its favor. Neither can we hope for the good will of them that have "a form of godliness but deny the power thereof." But we do desire earnestly the right hand of fellowship of all who love the Lord Jesus in sincerity. It may be that there are some beliefs and practices in Pentecost which are unacceptable to a number of non-Pentecostal Christians, but surely it is possible for us all to exercise love toward one another in spite of our differences of opinion. How much more edifying it will be if, while we refuse to cast aside our own distinctive doctrines, we as fellow members of the Body of Christ shall also refuse to cast the shadow of suspicion upon the moral character of those who disagree with us.

4. EMOTIONALISM

It wearies us to read and hear the constantly recurring statement that the people who speak in tongues are emotionally unbalanced. The critics are continually identifying them with abnormal personalities whose neurotic tendencies stamp them as former inmates or candidates for the psychopathic wards in the state institutions. Every revival movement has its share of cranks, fanatics, neurotics and feeble-minded individuals; and Pentecost is no exception. That they receive more notoriety from outsiders than people in other religious organizations is undoubtedly due to the fact that the congregation is given a more prominent part in the services. We do not minimize the difficulty in dealing with certain individuals, but generally speaking, they are kept in control by the gentle but firm hand of the minister.

We do protest the charge, however, that *all* Pentecostal people are abnormal. Perhaps it would help to clarify our discussion if we give a definition of the word "normal": "In accordance with an established law or principle; conforming to a type or standard; regular, natural." Now if the critics are comparing Pentecostal people with other people in their emotional life outside of the realm of the religious, the critics are absolutely wrong, for there is no difference at all; Pentecostal people conform to the pattern which is natural to their nationality and clime. And if the critics imply that in the religious realm Pentecostalists are unstable emotionally, we answer that it all depends with whom the comparison is made. If it is made with the Christians of the First Century, we claim accord with them. If it is with some professors of religion today, we thank God that Pentecostal believers are abnormal!

Man recognizes the desirability of manifest emotion in every realm except the religious. It is accepted as a vital part of human existence and is appealed to by all who deal with men, and it seems that the children of this world are wiser than the children of light in their recognition and use of the emotional element. They would not dare to remove it from the stage, or screen, or radio, because they know that the public would shun unemotional entertainment, even as it shuns the dry, unimaginative services of the average church today. Certainly, an appeal is made to the mind, but the wise worldling knows that this must be supplemented by an emotional appeal. How many political contests would be won by candidates who ruled out applause and cheering by their supporters? How many athletic contests would be as well attended if all singing, shouting, cheering and handclapping were eliminated? How many wars would be won by a nation that forbade any display of emotion? And yet, if such manifestations of emotion occur in the church, an immediate cry is raised that they are shocking exhibitions of irreverence and fanaticism!

It may be that modern theology and formalism

would suppress all outward expressions of emotion, but the Scriptures do not. Search the Scriptures as you will; you cannot find in them a sanction of the stoical, purely intellectual worship which is advocated by church leaders today. You will find, rather, the command to love the Lord our God *with our whole being,* and you will also find many God-approved instances of the inclusion of the emotional in worship and service. God created man not only as a physical, intellectual, and spiritual being but also as an emotional creature. Emotion is a perfectly proper element in man, and he is normal only when that element is given expression, no matter what the sphere of activity. It is our firm conviction that the deliberate attempt to take from church worship all expression of the emotions is in disagreement with the Scriptural examples; it frustrates the plan of God, and forbids the entrance of God into that part of our nature.

This does not mean, of course, that Pentecostal people desire only the emotional. While it is true that they want a freedom to manifest their feelings which is denied them in some places, at the same time they are eager for a full knowledge of the Word of God. Nowhere have we found a people with a deeper love and understanding of the Scriptures than Pentecostal people. It should not be inferred from this statement that there is no possibility of ignorance and error on their part regarding the Scriptures. All that we mean to say is that the average Pentecostal congregation is at least the equal of any average non-Pentecostal congregation in regard to its appreciation of the Word. We cannot believe that emotional expressions, which do not interfere with, but rather increase, the desire to grow in grace and the knowledge of our Lord and Saviour Jesus Christ, should be considered indecent and out of order.

5. PHYSICAL DEMONSTRATIONS

How the critics love to describe the happenings in Pentecostal services! How they rejoice to refer to the shaking, the shouting, the dancing, the prostrations, and then to turn very soberly to the inquirer, and say, "We would ask if this is anything like the quiet, sober account of the Scriptures?"[1] The inquirer, if a true student of the Scriptures, could well ask in return, "To what 'quiet, sober account' do you refer? To the account of Pentecost, when such extraordinary and rather noisy manifestations caused the mockers to say, 'These men are full of new wine'? To the account of the healing of the lame man who 'leaping up stood, and walked, and entered with them into the temple, walking, and leaping, and praising God'? To the account in Acts 4 where the disciples 'lifted up their voice with one accord'? To the prostration of Saul by the power of God? To the rejoicing and praising God with a loud voice by the multitude at the triumphal entry, which the Lord Jesus approved, saying, 'I tell you that, if these should hold their peace, the stones would immediately cry out'?"

Many good Christian people today are much like the devout men who watched the disciples at Pentecost. They are acquainted only with the formal worship of their own circle, where for years there has been a total absence of any kind of physical

---

[1]What makes the critics so certain that they know the exact nature of the bodily demonstrations, speaking with tongues, etc. in the early church? They have no greater authority than the Scriptures, and we all have access to them.

demonstration. Consequently, when these people attend a Pentecostal meeting, they become amazed and terrified at the things which they see and hear, attributing them to fanaticism and extreme emotionalism. But if these dear folk would only take time to examine the Word of God, they would discover that these Pentecostal demonstrations have abundant Scriptural precedent. And if they searched the records of the great revival movements of Church history, they would find similar manifestations. The contemporary critics of the revivals in New Testament days and in Church history were sure that those revivals were not of God because of the physical demonstrations. From our vantage point, we can see something more than the bodily manifestations; we can see the revivals as a whole—their effect on history, the hundreds of thousands swept into the kingdom—and we can only conclude that the critics were wrong; the work was of God. And may God open the eyes of the critics of this Pentecostal revival, who condemn it *en toto* because of the physical manifestations, to see the great moral and spiritual benefits as well.

A sane and sensible attitude toward bodily demonstrations has been expressed by JOHN WESLEY in his *Journal*, Sunday, November 25, 1759:

"The danger was to regard extraordinary circumstances too much, such as outcries, convulsions, visions, trances, as if they were essential to the inward work, so that it could not go on without them. Perhaps the danger is to regard them too little; to condemn them altogether; to imagine they had nothing of God in them, and were a hindrance to His work. Whereas the truth is: (1) God suddenly and strongly convinced many that they were lost sinners, the natural consequences whereof were sudden outcries and strong bodily convulsions; (2) to strengthen and encourage them that believe, and to make His work more apparent, He favored several of them with divine dreams, others with trances and visions; (3) in some of these instances, after a time, nature mixed with grace; (4) Satan likewise mimicked this work of God in order to discredit the whole work; and yet it is not wise to give up this part any more than to give up the whole. At first it was, doubtless, wholly from God. It is partly so at this day; and He will enable us to discern how far, in every case, the work is pure, and where it mixes or degenerates. . . . The shadow is no disparagement of the substance, nor the counterfeit of the real diamond."

Thus, from the pen of the eminent Founder of Methodism we can deduce these two facts: (1) bodily demonstrations must not be magnified beyond their rightful sphere; (2) nor must they be rejected because of irregularities. Our prayer for Pentecostal leaders is that God will enable them to keep the Movement in the safe, Scriptural channel; neither plunging it into the dread rocks of fanaticism, nor allowing it to be cast upon the dreary beaches of formalism.

6. THE TONGUES

To give you an idea of the opinion of many regarding the nature of the tongues exercised by Pentecostal people today, we quote from the tract, *Speaking with Tongues,* by J. FRANKLIN FISHER:

"At this point we wish to ask in all candor, 'Are the demonstrations of the Pentecostal Movement in our times of the same nature as in apostolic times?

Are those strange sounds and utterances coming from seekers in Pentecostal churches to be thought of as repetitions of Pentecost?' Common sense and honesty answer 'No.' The Scriptures answer 'No.' To palm off as Pentecostal the mutterings and gutturals of present-day tongues manifestations is as repugnant to the intelligence as it is to the Word of God."

Now that we have this none too flattering description of the Pentecostal tongues of today before us (and it is but representative of descriptions by other opponents), we might ask of these men, "What do you believe the *glossolalia* sounded like in apostolic times? How do you know that the tongues of today and the tongues of those days are utterly dissimilar?" In chapters 3 and 4 we discussed a number of their theories regarding the phenomenon, but gave no description of the manner in which they thought the tongues were exercised. As a matter of fact, very few writers have attempted to describe in detail what the utterance actually sounded like to the hearers. The non-Pentecostalists who have tried to explain the nature of New Testament tongues can be divided generally into two groups: (1) those who disparage tongues both past and present; and (2) those who overestimate the utterance of apostolic days to the discredit of the utterance of today.

The first group does not regard the phenomenon too highly even as it was manifested on the day of Pentecost. HAYES says, "There may have been an occasional word or phrase that was understood, but for the most part it was a strange and bewildering jargon, more like the gibbering of a maniac or the maundering of a *drunken* man than anything else these auditors had known in their experience. An orderly discourse in a foreign tongue, understood by

[110]

many who were present, would never have given any occasion for such criticism."

We protest this un-Scriptural description of the utterances of the disciples at the impulse of the Holy Spirit. What they spoke was not "a strange or bewildering jargon, . . . the gibbering of a maniac or the maundering of a drunken man," but *"other tongues"*— definite languages. MATTHEW HENRY'S comment should cast some light on the criticism of the mockers: ". . . the scorn which some made of it who were natives of Judea and Jerusalem, probably the Scribes and Pharisees, and chief priests, who always resisted the Holy Ghost; they said, 'These men are full of new wine, or sweet wine; they have drunk too much at this festival-time.' v. 13. Not that they were so absurd as to think that wine in the head would enable men to speak languages which they had never learned; but these, being *native* Jews, knew not, as the others did, that what was spoken was really the languages of other nations, and therefore took it to be gibberish and nonsense, such as drunkards, those 'fools in Israel,' sometimes talk."

And such is the reaction of many today when they hear an utterance in tongues. Simply because they do not understand the tongue, they label it as unintelligible prattle, gibberish, and babblings of fanaticism. And yet, these same critics must admit that there are hundreds of languages and dialects spoken on this earth, with which they are totally unfamiliar, and which also sound like meaningless jargon. Especially is this true of the tongues spoken by the more primitive peoples in the remote corners of the globe. But does their unfamiliarity with these tongues cause the critics to label them as gibberish and not tongues? Of course not! Then who are they to pass wholesale condemnation on all the utterances of Pentecost today? Have they applied to these utterances the laws of philology—observing the syllables, the distinct words and phrases, differences in pronunciation, etc.? Why are not these "strange sounds and utterances coming from seekers in Pentecostal churches to be thought of as repetitions of Pentecost"? Surely it is not a difficult thing for the Spirit of God, who knoweth all tongues, to cause Christian believers to speak in one of the lesser known tongues.[1] [2]

And what authority does the second group of writers have for demanding that the tongues should always be recognized by a listener? We have shown in Chapter 3 (see also Chapter 10) that only at Pentecost is there any record that the tongues were understood. And it is very plain that the tongues at Corinth were unknown not only to the speaker but

---

[1]We do not mean to imply from this defense of present-day tongues that the utterances of all are in genuine languages. It is inevitable that all physical manifestations will be counterfeited, and speaking with tongues is no exception. What some speak is, in reality, only a gibberish, and nothing more. It is the result of an attempt to imitate the genuine, without possessing the enabling power of the Holy Spirit. Anyone who has heard the real cannot fail to recognize the false. Such gibberish is not as prevalent, however, as some critics imagine. The true speaking with other tongues, as the Spirit gives utterance, far exceeds the false and fanatical imitation. It is impossible in a movement so large to eliminate entirely all human efforts to simulate the workings of the Spirit of God, but we do label it as gibberish, and try our very best to correct the situation.

[2] Dr. Agide Pirazzini, possibly one of the greatest philologists in America, having taught Hebrew, Greek, and Oriental languages at the Biblical Seminary in New York for thirty years, has identified the utterances of some Pentecostal believers as Aramaic, the language which Jesus spoke.

[112]

also, as a general thing, to the hearer. It was a rare occasion, even in the exercise of tongues in the early church, for anyone to recognize the tongues. All that is required for the *glossolalia* to be stamped as genuine is that an utterance be given by the believer in a language unknown to him.

Still many tell us today that they would be far less incredulous toward the Pentecostal Movement if only they could identify the ecstatic utterances of Pentecostal believers as belonging to a definite language. Something about their statement is reminiscent of doubts expressed by Thomas, "Except I shall see, . . . I will not believe." Both Pentecostal and non-Pentecostal believers, who are absolutely trustworthy, have gone on record that they have definitely identified some of the tongues supernaturally spoken by believers today, but the critics will not accept their testimony. It may be that it will please God to grant unto these doubters a personal experience like that of the multitude at Pentecost. If so, we pray earnestly that they may have the honesty and the courage to acknowledge that God indeed is moving today as in ages past.

ROBERT C. MCQUILKIN, President of Columbia Bible College, writer of the notes on the Sunday School lessons for the *Sunday School Times,* has written a pamphlet entitled, *What is Pentecost's Message Today?* first published in the *Sunday School Times.* On page 27 of this pamphlet he writes:

"Does such speaking in tongues take place today? To deny that it may take place, we must first refuse to receive or believe the word of quite a number of honored Christians who testify in most definite ways to having heard foreign languages spoken by those not acquainted with them.

"If we reject such testimony and deny that such manifestations of the Spirit are possible today, what shall we do with the prophecy of Joel, quoted by Peter in the second chapter of Acts? Peter said that the outpouring of the Spirit at Pentecost was in fulfillment of that prophecy of Joel: 'And it shall come to pass in the last days, saith God, I will pour out of My Spirit upon all flesh.' Now it is evident that this prophecy was not completely fulfilled at Pentecost, nor has it been fulfilled in any day since. There still remain these wonders in heaven above and on the earth beneath that shall precede the great and terrible 'day of the Lord'; we still await that day when the sun shall be turned into darkness and the moon into blood (Acts 2:17-21). But if the prophecy still awaits a further and more complete fulfillment, shall we say that the Spirit of God may not again be poured out in mighty power and in supernatural demonstrations? There seems to be trustworthy evidence that these supernatural manifestations have occurred from time to time through the ages, in individual cases. There is nothing in Scripture to make such workings of God impossible; rather we might expect that they should occur. And is it not reasonable to expect that in connection with the culminating judgments of this age and the ushering in of a new age there should be a mighty outpouring of the Spirit of God? It is this expectation of a special 'latter rain' outpouring that has led many earnest Christians into the Pentecostal Movement.

"Let us not limit God in His working, and let us not fail to be ready for new and great outpourings of the Holy Spirit in the closing days of this age. For the days are upon us when nothing will avail to break through the overwhelming power of the enemy except supernatural power beyond what most Christians have known anything about."

If speaking in tongues were taken out of this Pentecostal Movement, perhaps nine-tenths of the opposition would disappear; Pentecost might possibly become the most popular religious movement in the Protestant world. How often have we been counseled to leave that part out of our doctrine and worship.

But we cannot give up tongues! What these well-meaning counselors fail to realize is that there is an intimate connection between tongues and all the other blessings which God has bestowed upon us. We know that it has brought reproach and persecution to us; we know that fanatical elements in our ranks have added unnecessarily to that reproach and persecution; but speaking in tongues must remain a part of our doctrine and worship. As we continue to set forth our Pentecostal view of this subject, it will become increasingly clear why we are willing to suffer the scorn and ostracism of some religious groups today rather than to give up tongues. To us, speaking with tongues, and what it signifies, is worth all the reproach that accompanies it. The "cost" in Pentecost has been counted, and the glory far outweighs all opposition by man.

CHAPTER 8

By the Power of Beelzebub

THERE are but two ultimate sources of supernatural power—divine and satanic. It is true that much strange phenomena can be attributed to highly developed human powers, but the fact remains that there are some extraordinary happenings which are clearly supernatural. These are the result of the direct intervention of either God or Satan; no other explanation can be reasonably offered.

So concluded the Pharisees and Scribes when confronted with the miracles of Jesus of Nazareth. The casting out of the blind and dumb demon (Matthew 12:22-32; Mark 3:22-30; Luke 11:14-23) was inexplicable on natural grounds. It was evident to all that such a marvelous act emanated from a supernatural source. The amazed multitude cried out, "Is not this the son of David?" But the Pharisees and scribes could not attribute the miracle-working power of Jesus to God, for that would demand their acknowledgment also of His teachings and claims. How could they make such an acknowledgment of One who had not submitted to their authority—indeed, who actually had opposed them?

117

To do so would be fatal to their own leadership among the people.

But one alternative remained: the Nazarene must be shown to be in league with Satan, receiving from him the power to work these miracles. Why had they not thought of this before? It was the perfect explanation to the throngs who saw in Him a super-human power above that of even the prophets. Quickly the word was passed from lip to lip, "The leaders declare that this fellow, Jesus of Nazareth, casteth out devils by the power of Beelzebub, the prince of devils!" Immediately consternation broke out among the people, some agreeing and some dis-agreeing. With one consent all turned to Jesus for His answer to the charge.

Calling His accusers unto Him, He said: "Every kingdom divided against itself is brought to desola-tion; and every city or house divided against itself shall not stand: and if Satan cast out Satan, he is divided against himself; how shall then his kingdom stand? And if I by Beelzebub cast out devils, by whom do your children cast them out? Therefore they shall be your judges. But if I cast out devils by the Spirit of God, then the kingdom of God is come unto you. Or else how can one enter into a strong man's house, and spoil his goods, except he first bind the strong man? And then he will spoil his house. He that is not with Me is against Me; and he that gathereth not with Me scattereth abroad. Wherefore I say unto you, All manner of sin and blasphemy shall be forgiven unto men: but the blasphemy against the Holy Ghost shall not be forgiven unto men. And whosoever speaketh a word against the Son of man, it shall be forgiven him: but whosoever speaketh against the Holy Ghost, it shall not be forgiven him, neither in this world, neither in the world to come."[1]

What a solemn and fearful warning! It fell from the lips of the Lamb of God Himself! Knowing therefore the terror of the Lord, we do well to ponder these awful words for our own admonition, and to persuade men to beware lest they blaspheme against the Holy Ghost and thus cause the threat to become a dreadful and eternal reality.

The Pentecostal people of today receive much the same treatment as that accorded to Jesus of Nazareth: some accept us and our full gospel message as of God; others consider us as Christians but entirely too enthusiastic, fanatical, "beside ourselves" (Mark 3:21); and others (though they be few, they are not silent), unable to explain the manifestations of the miraculous in our midst—perhaps an instantaneous healing of the body, or an utterance in a known tongue which cannot be called an incoherent gibberish—assert that the whole Pentecostal Movement is of satanic origin. This last view is the subject of our discussion in this chapter.

It is a bit difficult for us to understand how the advocates of this view, who for the most part have made only a superficial investigation of the movement, can without hesitation label the whole thing as of the devil. We know that sometimes it is easier to label than to investigate, but we also know that it is exceedingly dangerous to label as devilish that which may possibly be of the Holy Ghost. And this Pentecostal Movement may possibly be of God! Why then do our accusers run such a risk—condemning the speaking in tongues, the healings, etc.,

---

[1] Matthew 12:25-32.

as "lying wonders," and "snares of Satan"—when they possess so little valid information about us? Can it be that they fail to realize the awfulness of attributing to Satan that which is of the Holy Spirit? As for ourselves, we should hesitate to issue such a grave indictment even after securing all the facts of the case, much less before. We sincerely hope that those who have thus condemned us will examine very closely every argument which we now present in our defense; and we entreat all to think long and carefully upon these pages before reaching a verdict in this case.

1. PENTECOSTAL TONGUES COMPARED WITH PAGAN, MORMON AND SPIRITISTIC TONGUES

A popular method of dealing with Pentecostal tongues of today is to compare them with the ecstatic utterances of ancient and modern heathendom, and also with the ejaculations of Mormonism and Spiritism, which, like the Pentecostal Movement, claim the recurrence of New Testament tongues. Some writers even go so far as to attempt to establish a similarity between the phenomenon present in the early church and all the other manifestations of that nature through history, regardless of the beliefs and practices which characterized those thus exercised. Such an attempt only reveals the inability to distinguish between the true and the false. The early Christians spoke with other tongues as the Spirit gave them utterance, but such obviously has not been true in every ecstatic utterance since that time. Unless a proper distinction is made between the tongues inspired by the Holy Ghost and the tongues inspired by Satan, all such utterances must fall under the condemnation reserved for just a part. Any examination to be effective must be thorough, for on the surface the genuine and the counterfeit appear to be similar.

Suppose we illustrate the necessity for thoroughness in this matter by calling your attention to the somewhat analagous cases of Babel (Genesis 11:1-9) and Pentecost (Acts 2:1-12). There are a number of similarities between these two events: (1) in each case all were gathered together with one accord: (2) God Himself came down into their midst; (3) as a result of God's presence, they spoke with hitherto unlearned tongues. Applying the superficial methods employed by some writers on the subject of tongues, we might conclude that these three similarities indicate that the experiences of Babel and Pentecost were identical. The real student of the Word, however, would readily see that such apparent likenesses are easily distinguishable. True, they were gathered together in one accord at Babel, but it was in an accord of defiance and rebellion against God; whereas at Pentecost the disciples were in one accord of surrender and supplication. God did come down at Babel, but it was to judge the guilty rebels; whereas at Pentecost the Holy Spirit came down to bless and fill the obedient one hundred and twenty. The tongues spoken at Babel brought confusion to the speakers themselves; whereas the tongues spoken at Pentecost released the praises of the believers, and provided a miraculous background for the message which brought three thousand souls into the kingdom.

How different Babel and Pentecost! And how different New Testament tongues and the frenzied ejaculations of idol worshipers, Mormons and

Spiritists! In fact, any attempt to establish a similarity between the New Testament phenomenon and the utterances common to these groups is perilously close to blasphemy. We know positively that the Holy Spirit who inspired the teachings which the disciples believed, also inspired the speaking with tongues; on the other hand, the same spirit which inspired the diabolical doctrines which the pagan, Mormon and Spiritist followers have embraced, also was responsible for any supernatural utterances which may have occurred in their midst. Cannot we reckon with certainty that the devotees of "another gospel" must be led by another spirit?

Let us take a brief glance at the beliefs of these three groups in regard to the Scriptures and the Lord Jesus Christ. Time and space will not permit a detailed discussion of their views on these two fundamental points, but since their views are already well known, we feel that these few remarks will be sufficient for our purpose. Paganism denies the infallibility of the Holy Scriptures; they have their own "sacred" writings. Paganism also refuses to recognize the deity of the Lord Jesus Christ. Mormonism pretends to accept the Scriptures as the Word of God, but contends that the Book of Mormon must be given equal credibility, thus bringing the curse of God upon the whole system (Galatians 1:6-9; Revelation 22:18). Its beliefs about the Lord Jesus are accordingly un-Scriptural. Spiritism lays claim to being in the Word: it is in the Word all right, but is completely forbidden, abhorred and condemned by that Word! Its teachings about Christ are also false, as any true Bible student will declare. How then could the Holy Spirit ever give an utterance in tongues to those whose cardinal beliefs are contrary to the Word? The Spirit and the Word agree!

The Pentecostal Movement of today clearly differs from these three groups in that it takes the Scriptures as the only rule of faith and practice, and in that it recognizes unquestionably the deity of the Lord Jesus Christ. Upon the Written Word and the Living Word we are built, and the gates of hell shall not prevail against us! We have nothing in common with un-Scriptural groups which lay claim to a recurrence of speaking with tongues in their midst. And yet, because of our belief in the continuation of the miraculous signs and gifts of the early church, we are classified as "one of the false cults of these latter days." We protest such a classification as unfair to the facts, and utterly lacking in discrimination between the true and the false. D. M. PANTON has made the statement: "Arguments are always useless in supernatural movements for those already convinced; for, however irresistible, they are at once put aside, by a reference to what is assumed to be the voice of God."[1] But such an indictment does not apply to us, for, as is evident from this volume on tongues, we gladly submit all our teachings and practices to comparison with the Scriptures. "To the law and to the testimony" is our first and final appeal.

2. PENTECOST AND PASSIVITY

Under this topic we shall endeavor to answer one of the most serious and most frequent accusations against the Pentecostal Movement. This accusation concerns the teachings and practices involved in securing the mental attitude necessary for speaking

---

[1] *Irvingism, Tongues, and Gifts of the Holy Ghost*, p. 22.

with tongues. Here is the focal point of much of the opposition to present-day tongues. If a clear and satisfactory answer can be given, it should prove quite helpful to all who have rejected Pentecost on this account.

A. J. POLLOCK has written of the "tarrying" or "waiting" meetings prevalent in Pentecostal circles. To put it mildly, he disapproves of such meetings as can be seen from this quotation: "We are ashamed to have to transcribe an account of such abominations practiced in the name of the Lord. Christians are exhorted to 'let themselves go,' 'not to resist the Spirit,' to 'let their minds become a blank.' This is dangerous advice indeed, laying open the bodies of those who follow it to demoniac influence. Similar advice is given in Spiritist circles."[1]

KEITH L. BROOKS is quoted thus by Pollock (p. 60): "I hear of others who have tarried for a repetition of Pentecostal tongues night after night, letting the mind go blank as they were directed, and agonizing in prayer. Then they have gone into a trance, felt delightful sensations in the body, and mumbled strange things. But some of them have found themselves thereafter frequently subject to these spells. The least excitement brings them on and each time they are left in a weaker physical state. One young man of my acquaintance became insane as the result of these experiences."

BARON PORCELLIS (as quoted by T. B. Barratt) says: "The essential basic root of all these manifestations is what is termed *shibboleth*, 'surrender of self'; or in accurate English, the surrender of one's will to that of another."

---

[1] *Modern Pentecostalism, Foursquare Gospel, "Healings" and "Tongues,"* p. 60.

By the Power of Beelzebub

F. J. HUEGEL gives us, in *Bone of His Bone* (p. 79, 84, 85), his reasons for objecting to any kind of Christian passivity:

"Witness the 'isms' springing up, all under the eaves of the Church. Strange doctrines that have to do with the gifts of the Spirit, and that seem sound enough, and sufficiently grounded in the Scriptures, are causing fatal convulsions in the body of Christ, and plunging earnest Christians, seeking fuller light, into the abyss of fanaticism. 'Doctrines of demons' which according to Paul would, in the latter days, come as a flood upon the church. . . .

"Many have unconsciously come under the oppressive thralldom of the enemy. They have given ear to his lies; they have become passive. Passivity lays us liable to demon intrusion. It is fundamental to Spiritism. The medium is passive—the 'spirit' takes control. 'Awake thou that sleepest, and arise from the dead, and Christ shall give thee light.' We are not to let go of a single faculty and expect God to control us as if we were machines. Union with Christ does not signify any such things. After coming into deepest union with Christ, so that like Paul we say: 'I am crucified with Christ, . . . Christ liveth in me,' we do not become passive. We do not give up self-control. As never before we live. Personality is vastly enhanced. The will is greatly fortified. The mind is marvelously illumined. The memory is gloriously strengthened. We are free as never before to choose, to will, to reason, and to act. We are now to act in perfect harmony with God, every faculty energized by the Holy Spirit. No, it does not lead and never should to passivity. If a single faculty has fallen into disuse and through passivity has come under Satan's baneful sway, let us in Christ's name break the shackle, take back the ground ceded, and in full possession of our God-given faculties be free."[1]

We believe that these four quotations present fully enough the attitude of most non-Pentecostalists toward passivity. There are several important aspects of the question, however, which the authors of these quotations have failed to consider, and consequently their conclusions are only partially correct.

It is true that the Lord Jesus, upon entering the human heart, does not make of man a mere machine, but instead He enriches, ennobles and enlarges all his faculties, and gives to him great freedom in the exercise of those faculties. Nevertheless, one point should be made clear: each faculty operates only in its appointed sphere: it does not attempt to do the work assigned to another. And, of necessity, there are times when one of these faculties will predominate, causing the others to remain temporarily in the background. They are not set aside in any permanent sense, nor are they entirely excluded from the activity which is the prerequisite of one particular faculty. All are blended together in perfect harmony, as God works in the new man "both to will and to do of His good pleasure." Still there is a distinctiveness of activity in each faculty.

As an illustration of this, we might consider the case of a man concentrating on a mathematical problem. At such a time his mental powers—memory, reasoning, deduction, etc.—are actively engaged in finding a solution to the problem, while his spiritual, emotional and physical powers are, in a large degree,

---

[1]Reprinted by permission of Zondervan Publishing House, Grand Rapids, Mich.

inactive. These faculties have not "fallen into disuse," or been "let go"; they are simply superseded by the mental powers whose duty it is to perform a particular task for the man. Now this is the kind of passivity we endorse in our relationship with God. Our critics have been so disturbed over our "letting go" of faculties that they have overlooked the fact that it is necessary at times that one faculty predominate while other powers are more or less quiescent.

But some may ask, "When is there ever an occasion for the mental passivity which you Pentecostalists advocate?" We have discovered that our critics object most to passivity when it relates to the intellect. They insist that any practice which requires the intellect or mind to be even partially inactive is bound to be harmful to the whole man. And unquestionably, it would be injurious for anyone to assume a constant state of mental passivity. This fact, however, does not necessitate the belief that mental passivity is a horrible blight on all occasions. We note that it occurred in the experience of a number of Bible characters, and there is every indication that these occurrences were in the will of God.

For example, consider the manner in which the prophecy of Scripture came to holy men of old. Peter tells us (2 Peter 1:20, 21): "Knowing this first; that no prophecy of the Scripture is of any private interpretation. For the prophecy came not in old time by the will of man: but holy men of God spake as they were moved by the Holy Ghost." Certainly this is a description of yielding one's will to another, receiving truths and speaking them forth at the behest of Another. Moreover, at times these men were caused to utter prophecies which were foreign to their own thoughts, and even incomprehensible to them except through a special revelation. Is this not what Peter says in his First Epistle (1:10-12): "Of which salvation the prophets have inquired and searched diligently, who prophesied of the grace that should come unto you: searching what, or what manner of time, the Spirit of Christ which was in them did signify, when it testified beforehand of the sufferings of Christ, and the glory that should follow. Unto whom it was revealed, that not unto themselves, but unto us they did minister the things, which are now reported unto you by them that have preached the gospel unto you with the Holy Ghost sent down from heaven; which things the angels desire to look into"?

Nor was this type of experience limited to the exclusive group to whom the infallible prophecy of Scripture came. Some of the extraordinary experiences which occurred in the lives of other of God's servants can be explained only as a voluntary yielding of the individual's entire being to God.

We call your attention especially to the speaking with tongues in the early church. Everyone knows that words are formed in the mind before they are spoken. Yet at Pentecost, and in other similar cases, the disciples were speaking words which their minds could not possibly form, because they knew not those words! Was this, or was it not, an instance of passivity?

And there is no escaping the fact that Paul recognized mental quiescence in the exercise of tongues. His statement in 1 Corinthians 14:14 is conclusive on this point: "For if I pray in an unknown tongue, my spirit prayeth, but my understanding is unfruitful." What did you say, Paul? Your understanding was unfruitful when you spoke with a tongue? Do you mean that in your Spirit-filled life you actually experienced times when your "marvelously illumined" mind was passive? What else could Paul mean but that? Could he be more explicit? Undoubtedly, those who are opposed to passivity, such as is found in the Bible, have difficulty with this clear-cut statement of the apostle.

HAROLD HORTON gives this splendid note on the nature of tongues: "It is a supernatural utterance by the Holy Spirit in languages never learned by the speaker—not understood by the mind of the speaker —seldom understood by the hearer. It has nothing whatever to do with linguistic ability, nor with the mind or intellect of man. It is a manifestation of the mind of the Spirit of God employing human speech organs. When man is speaking with tongues, his mind, intellect, understanding are quiescent. It is the faculty of God that is active. Man's will, certainly, is active, and his spirit, and his speech organs; but the mind that is operating is the mind of God through the Holy Spirit."

We should not infer from this quotation that we are to "let our minds go blank" so that we speak with tongues. The Word of God teaches us to keep our minds constantly stayed on the Lord Jesus Christ, no matter what our immediate occupation. In this sense, our mental faculties must always be active, but they are not directly operative in the exercise of tongues. CONYBEARE AND HOWSON concur with this Scriptural view, as is evident by this comment about speaking with tongues: "It was the result of a sudden influx of supernatural inspiration which came upon the new believer immediately after his baptism, and recurred afterwards at uncertain intervals. . . .

Under its influence, the exercise of the understanding was suspended while the spirit was rapt into a state of ecstasy by the immediate communication of the Spirit of God. In this ecstatic trance the believer was constrained by an irresistible power to pour forth his feelings of thanksgiving and rapture in words; yet the words which issued from his mouth were not his own; he was ever (usually) ignorant of their meaning."

It appears to us that four mistakes are generally made by those who so emphatically reject the idea of any kind of mental passivity in the experience of the believer:

(1) They overestimate the value of the mental faculties. While it is true that the mind of the believer has been enriched and enlarged, still it has not become infinite in its grasp of the mysteries of God. Who among us can fully comprehend the Trinity, the Virgin Birth, the Resurrection, or, for that matter, any divine truth? Paul, the greatest human expositor of the mysteries of God, included himself in his confession, "We know in part, and we prophesy in part." And what is true of our limited knowledge of objective truth, is also true of our limited knowledge of the subjective experiences of the spiritual life. From our very entrance into the kingdom of God through the new birth (see John 3:3-12) we are surrounded by mysteries which the human reason cannot fathom. Do we therefore reject all the doctrines and experiences which we cannot fully comprehend? Of course not! We recognize the value of our intellectual powers in their proper sphere, but we also recognize the fact that our finite minds are grappling with the infinite, and therefore accept by faith what we cannot fully understand. How humbling,

and yet how healthful, to conclude with Paul, "O the depth of the riches both of the wisdom and knowledge of God! How unsearchable are His judgments, and His ways past finding out!"

(2) By limiting our search after God to the intellect alone they deny to the human spirit its rightful place as the highest element of man in his relationship with God. The spirit of man, according to 1 Corinthians 14:14, sometimes makes direct contact with the Lord, unaided by the reasoning and understanding of the mind. Through the quickening of the spirit out of death into divine life, the whole being is made alive unto God. Revelations of truth are grasped first by the spirit, and then translated to the intellectual, emotional, and physical natures. While we know little of the spirit, that part of man which is perhaps most truly in the image of God, we do know that the spirit is not secondary but primary.

(3) They fail to realize that contact with God in the lives of Bible characters was a tremendous, and sometimes an overwhelming, experience. Almighty God was a constant, living reality to His servants in those days. The things that are quibbled about by those to whom the Lord is a distant and far-off Creator were accepted without question by these godly men of old. The great fact of their lives was "God, before whom I stand"; God, to whom "all things are possible." How then could they think it strange if, when they yielded themselves to Him, He "moved in mysterious ways, His wonders to perform"? Extraordinary happenings must of necessity take place, they felt, when man was brought into the conscious presence of God. To them it was a simple thing for the Spirit of God to inspire their

own spirit in a manner transcending the understanding, and to give miraculous utterance through
the organs of speech. And has God ceased to reveal
Himself to man, and ceased to dwell within the
believer? Has the passing of the centuries decreased
His majesty and power, or increased the stature of
man to such an extent that we should no longer
expect the miraculous as a result of direct contact
with God?

(4) They do not distinguish between the yielding
to the Spirit and the losing of self-control. We agree
with Mr. Huegel that man is free "as never before
to choose, to will, to reason, and to act." We also
agree with the apostle Paul: "What? know ye not
that your body is the temple of the Holy Ghost
which is in you, which ye have of God, and ye are
not your own? For ye are bought with a price:
therefore glorify God in your body, and in your
spirit, which are God's" (1 Corinthians 6:19, 20).
Our will is greatly fortified, but not fortified so that
we can resist the Spirit of God. On the contrary, we
are commanded to make a complete, trusting surrender of body, soul, mind and spirit unto the Lord
Jesus Christ, until "all our ransomed being captive
is to Him." Paul exhorts us, "Yield yourselves
unto God" (Romans 6:13). So in one sense, we are
independent; yet, in another sense, we are absolutely
subject to the supreme will of God. "The spirits of
the prophets are subject to the prophets"; and yet,
we "quench not the Spirit" but permit His phenomenal workings in us and through us. We do not lose
our individuality while we live and move and have
our being in Him; for in the ecstatic state "self-con-
sciousness is united with the consciousness of God's
presence without being completely absorbed by that.

The inspired person has as clear a consciousness of his own existence as he has of the mighty power that lies over him."[1]

In conclusion, let us say that it is un-Scriptural to be extreme in either activity or passivity of any kind. When there is only activity, there is a barrenness of the supernatural in our lives; when there is only passivity, there is a barrenness of the proper and normal exercise of sanctified human faculties. A combination of activity and passivity will result in an experience like Paul's: "I will pray with the spirit [i.e., in a tongue] and I will pray with the understanding also: I will sing with the spirit, and I will sing with the understanding also"[1] (1 Corinthians 14:15).

3. PENTECOST AND DEMONISM

In the four quotations of the foregoing section, one reason for the opposition to passivity stood out above all others—"it lays us liable to demon intrusion." Most of our critics who thus speak are perfectly sincere in this belief; they consider it their duty to warn all non-Pentecostalists of this "snare of delusion," and if possible, to rescue some Pentecostalists from it. Of course we must disagree with their conclusions, or else repudiate our spiritual experience; but aside from this, we feel that we have Scriptural grounds for disagreement.

The Word of God abounds with warnings against the snares of Satan and his demonic satellites. We read that this archenemy of our souls is a very

---

[1]Pastor Ernst Lohman, as quoted by T. B. Barratt.

cunning and subtle foe, transforming himself into "an angel of light" when through that means his diabolical purposes can best be served. We also read that he would fain deceive the very elect by "signs and lying wonders." And since demonic activity begins in the spirit and mind before entering the body,[1] it is logical to conclude that there is a spiritual and mental passivity which is conducive to such activity. All this must be admitted, if we are to be true to the Word. Nevertheless, we are not forced to admit that the passivity which we have advocated in this chapter is conducive to demonic influence and possession.

Is it not a fact that a multitude of the hellish hosts surrounded the First Century church? If ever their number was legion, if ever their power was strong, it was then. Accordingly, the church was cautioned by the apostles and others to be constantly on her guard against the ten thousand foes who would arise to tear her from the skies. And yet, not once was the church exhorted to refrain from the passivity which, as we have shown, was necessary for some of the supernatural workings of God! Not once was the devilish counterfeit exhibited to frighten true believers away from the divine reality! The same Paul, who enjoined forgiveness upon the Corinthians, "lest Satan should get an advantage of us; for we are not ignorant of his devices" (2 Cor. 2:11), also instructed the Corinthians on this wise: "Now concerning spiritual gifts, brethren, I would not have you ignorant" (1 Cor. 12:1).

Why must the critics of present-day tongues discuss only "lying wonders"? Why must they, in their

---

[1]Ephesians 6:11, 12; 2 Corinthians 10:4-5.

efforts to establish the presence of the counterfeit, forget the genuine? Why must they use the fact of demonic activity as a weapon of fear to keep earnest Christians from the good and perfect gifts of the Holy Spirit? Why do they not, rather, follow the course of the spiritual counselors of the early church? Why do they not distinguish between the spurious and the true, rejecting the spurious but rejoicing in the true? It cannot be that they consider that all phenomena are satanic. Nor can it be that they consider that it is impossible to distinguish between "lying wonders" and divine miracles. What, then, is their purpose in presenting only one side of the story, when the Bible presents two? They are desperately afraid of demon influence and possession. But does this justify their one-sided teachings with respect to the supernatural?[1]

And perhaps another question should be asked here: Is it possible for a demon spirit to enter and to possess a Christian believer? D. M. Panton thinks so: "The idea that no believer can experience the onfall of an evil spirit is not only in itself deeply erroneous, and contrary to actual cases unnumbered, but establishes the error that whatever spirit does actually fall must be the Holy Ghost if only the recipient is truly converted." However, those who take the opposite position point out that if the demons had to beg Christ's permission to enter swine

---

[1] 2 Timothy 3:8 tells us that "Jannes and Jambres withstood Moses;" and in Exodus 7 and 8 we read how they withstood him, matching miracle for miracle, opposing devilish power to divine power. But does the Word leave any doubt as to the source of these sorcerers' power? No, thank God! On the other hand, these false miracle workers had to confess that the miracles of Moses were "the finger of God."

(Mark 5:12-13), surely demons would also have to beg His permission to enter the saints; and who would dare to say that He would ever allow them to enter His very elect?

In one sense this controversy seems to resolve itself into the ancient battle between Arminianism and Calvinism, between the view of man's responsibility and the view of God's power to secure the believer. And just as there is wide divergence of opinion in regard to these two great doctrinal views, so there is much disagreement on the question of satanic invasion of the child of God. We should like to sketch briefly both sides of the controversy before giving our own conclusion.

The statement of the Lord Jesus in Luke 11:24-26 is cited as definite proof of the ability of evil spirits to enter the life of one who has once been cleansed and delivered from their dominion.[1] Indeed, every warning of this kind in the Scriptures is meaningless, if the possibility does not exist. The Word also shows that God has made man responsible for every one of his thoughts, words and actions. When man deliberately steps aside from the divine will (either in moral conduct or un-Scriptural passivity), God must not be held accountable for the tragic results. Divine protection from satanic intrusion and control is dependent upon man's choice to remain in the will of God.

---

[1] "When the unclean spirit is gone out of a man, he walketh through dry places seeking rest; and finding none, he saith, I will return unto my house whence I came out. And when he cometh, he findeth it swept and garnished. Then goeth he, and taketh to him seven other spirits more wicked than himself; and they enter in, and dwell there: and the last state of that man is worse than the first."

But the opposite view is not without arguments in its favor too. All the great promises of divine protection are quoted in support of this position. Biblical instances of the refusal of God to permit Satan's designs upon His children are advanced as definite proof that evil spirits are subject to God's permission. (See Job 1:6 to 2:7; Luke 22:31, 32.) Furthermore, though there are Scriptural examples of demon spirits entering into some whose spiritual experience was exceedingly doubtful, there are no concrete examples of any such entrance into the lives of those who were clearly and unmistakably the children of God.

As for us, while we realize that only an infinite God can fully reconcile opposites, we can see enough to know that there is a great deal of truth in both of these views. Why should we look upon them as mutually exclusive when both are taught in the Word? Why should we try to force one Scriptural truth to cancel another Scriptural truth? Ours is but to read and believe. Otherwise, in eternity we shall discover that in our extreme conceptions and contentions for truth here on earth, we were betrayed into an exceedingly subtle "taking away" from that which is written.

It cannot be denied that definite warnings have been given to the Church regarding the possibility of demon intrusion. On the other hand, it cannot be denied that these warnings are directly and immediately applicable only to the believers whose sin has made them liable to this terrible fate. To such the solemn exhortations are directed in a special sense and with all the intensity of divine love. Be awakened! Be alarmed! Speak not of God's promises of protection while you openly defy His will! Dare not to become passive as long as you persist in your sinful, backslidden state! Like a sow that was washed, have you turned again to your wallowing in the mire? Fear, lest in taking upon you again the nature of swine, you discover that wicked spirits are permitted to enter into you, even as at Gadara of old!

But surely, if we read our Bibles aright, we cannot believe that such dreadful admonitions come with the same force to the obedient child of God. "Knowing this, that the law is not made for a righteous man, but for the lawless and disobedient" (1 Tim. 1:9). To the obedient child "God has not given the spirit of fear; but of power, and of love, and of a sound mind" (2 Tim. 1:7). To him, as he walks in this positive spirit, come not the negative warnings, but the positive assurances of divine blessings and protection. True, the warnings are given to all, but their primary application is to the lawless and disobedient and not to those whose sin has been covered by the Lamb of God, whose delight is to do the will of the Father in heaven.

Why should anyone wish to disturb the trust of the obedient child in the ever-watchful care of his heavenly Father? Why should anyone desire to cause him to doubt the protecting power of the Good Shepherd? To whom else can he go? If he is robbed of his simple trust in the veracity of God's promises to them that obey Him, he is of all men most miserable. If he cannot have confidence in the blessed assurance of the God who spared not His only Son, everything is lost. He must believe! He must be as Abraham, who "staggered not at the promise of God through unbelief; but was strong in faith, giving glory to God; and being fully persuaded that what

He had promised, He was able to perform" (Rom. 4:20, 21).

What assurance do we have when we seek Him with all our heart? "I will be found of you" (Jer. 29:13, 14). What protection can we claim when we ask for the Holy Spirit? "If a son shall ask bread of any of you that is a father, will he give him a stone? Or if he ask a fish, will he, for a fish, give him a serpent? Or if he should ask an egg, will he offer him a scorpion? If ye then, being evil, know how to give good gifts unto your children: how much more shall your heavenly Father give the Holy Spirit to them that ask Him?" (Luke 11:11, 13). To these words we must cling, regardless of what men may say. "For what if some did not believe? Shall their unbelief make the faith of God without effect? God forbid: yea, let God be true, but every man a liar" (Rom. 3:3, 4).

Some may object to the belief to which we have just subscribed. To them it may seem that we are guilty of the error of which Mr. Panton spoke; viz., the belief "that whatever spirit does actually fall must be the Holy Ghost, if only the recipient be truly converted." But, mark you, we have not taken as the basis of our belief the mere fact of conversion; rather, in addition to that fundamental fact, we have insisted upon clean hands and a pure heart as the basis for divine protection against demon invasion. This is an all-important qualification. We have also shown that passivity in an individual who at one time was truly converted but now practices sin is conducive to demon activity. It does not follow, however, that Scriptural passivity in the life of an overcomer falls in the same category. Our firm conviction is this: if, as seems evident, the Lord protected even the carnal Corinthian believers in their states of ecstasy from invasion by demons who were ever present in idolatrous Corinth, we have every right to believe, from this and the other evidence which we have presented, that the overcomer shall also be kept safe from demonic power.

Our trust in the all-powerful blood of the Lord Jesus Christ and the promises of His Word is reinforced by certain safeguards which God has provided for us in our dealings with the supernatural. *What are the purposes of these safeguards?* First, to forewarn us and to insure the safety which He has promised to us as obedient children. Second, to increase our confidence. The unknown has always brought fear to the heart of man (and what is more unknown than the supernatural realm?). Added to this instinctive fear is the doubt resulting from the excessive warnings of extremists about the possibility of demon possession. Because of these warnings, many Christians, despite their trust in the Blood and the Word, are afraid to open their spiritual nature even to the Spirit of God. How necessary, then, that God in His grace should provide means whereby we can distinguish between good and evil spirits. The third purpose is to enable us to detect the false spirit which may have seized some unfortunate person who could not claim the Lord's protection; and, subsequently, to cast out that spirit in the name of the Lord Jesus Christ. Fourth, to keep the work of God free from false prophets who would deceive the very elect if possible.

Let us look at the five most important safeguards:

(1) Every revelation, impulse and utterance must be subjected to the teaching of the Scriptures. The

Holy Scriptures must be the rule of faith and practice here as well as in all other realms.

(2) We must observe the reaction of the Holy Spirit within us. Generally speaking, every true believer knows the leading of the Spirit and can tell by the impulses and checks of the Spirit what is the will of God for his life. "For as many as are led by the Spirit of God, they are the sons of God" (Rom. 8:14).

(3) Two tests, involving the lordship and incarnation of Jesus Christ, can be applied to those under the control of supernatural spirits. The first of these is found in 1 Cor. 12:1-3: "Now concerning spiritual gifts, brethren, I would not have you ignorant. Ye know that ye were Gentiles, carried away unto these dumb idols, even as ye were led. Wherefore I give you to understand that no man speaking by the Spirit of God calleth Jesus accursed: and that no man can say that Jesus is the Lord, but by the Holy Ghost." The second test is given to us by John in his First Epistle (1 John 4:1-3): "Beloved, believe not every spirit, but try the spirits whether they are of God: because many false prophets are gone out into the world. Hereby know ye the Spirit of God: every spirit that confesseth that Jesus Christ is come in the flesh is of God: and every spirit that confesseth not that Jesus Christ is come in the flesh is not of God: and this is that spirit of antichrist, whereof ye have heard that it should come; and even now already is it in the world."

It is easy to see how these two tests could establish without question the source of supernatural inspiration. How could the Holy Spirit, who is come to glorify Jesus, ever deny His lordship. or call Him accursed? Such a denial, such a blasphemous utterance, must come from another spirit. And how could the Holy Spirit, who inspired Paul to write of Jesus: "God was manifest in the flesh, justified in the Spirit, seen of angels, preached unto the Gentiles, believed on in the world, received up into glory" (1 Tim. 3:16); who moved John to say: "The Word was made flesh, and dwelt among us (and we beheld His glory as of the only begotten of the Father) full of grace and truth" (John 1:14), deny that "Jesus Christ is come in the flesh"? This denial, like the first, can proceed only from the spirit of antichrist.

Thus, on these two fundamental points, the tests are to be made, and they should be made with divine authority, for Satan and demons are under divine constraint to answer these questions. ("Is Jesus Lord?" "Did Jesus Christ come in the flesh?") Therefore, straightforward, unequivocal answers should be demanded (in fact, must be demanded) if the tests are to prove effective. And remember, that since Jesus is Lord over demons, we should expect His power to cast them out, once they are identified.

As far as we can see, these tests were not applied promiscuously in the New Testament church. Not once, as far as the record is concerned, was a believer subjected to such questionings, though many Christians were under the control of a supernatural spirit. The word does not give a single instance of the exercise of these tests upon Christian or non-Christian. We believe, of course, that they were made, but it does appear from the lack of mention that they were not made on every instance of supernatural experience. The logical conclusion is that the tests were applied only when the saints detected a wrong spirit.

By the Power of Beelzebub

May we call your attention again to the fact that while the apostles recognized the fact of demon activity, they did not discourage contact with the Spirit of God in supernatural gifts. Paul taught the Corinthians how to distinguish between true and false spirits, and then gave them three chapters on the purpose, motive, and use of spiritual gifts. John likewise followed his warning with the encouraging word, "Ye are of God, little children, and have overcome them: because greater is He that is in you, than he that is in the world" (1 John 4:4).

Are these tests ever applied in the Pentecostal Movement today? Yes. It is apparent, however, that a universal test of Pentecostal people under the influence of a supernatural power cannot be made. Nevertheless, we are confident that, if such a thing could be done, virtually the same results would be obtained today as in apostolic days: the vast majority, being filled with the Holy Spirit, would answer, "Jesus is the Lord," and, "Jesus Christ is come in the flesh." Contrariwise, there are some who, because of their love and practice of sin, are in league with Satan, and would answer, "Jesus is accursed," "Jesus Christ is not come in the flesh." In a movement so large it is impossible to keep out entirely the latter— but neither was it possible in the early church, else why the necessity of tests then? At least it must be admitted that our claim to equality with the early church concerning the results obtained by the tests is just as valid as any contrary claim of our opponents, until proved otherwise.

One last thought on these tests: We are more than willing that our fundamentalist friends should come among us and make the tests for themselves. Those who are godly and sincere men will discover

to their own satisfaction the truth of our above assertion. We are not so sure, however, that some of our
critics would believe even if the tests proved satisfactory. Repeatedly, in their writings upon the
subject, they have emphasized the fact that demons
confess that Jesus is the Son of God, implying that
the tests would not be conclusive proof of the spirits.
We, too, believe that at times demons do make such
confessions (Mark 5:7), but we prefer to believe
that these Scriptural tests will enable us to distinguish between the Spirit of God and the spirit of the
enemy, even as the apostles have declared!

(4) The supernatural gift of discerning of spirits
(1 Corinthians 12:10) is the fourth God-given
safeguard to His children. This gift should be
resident in every congregation whose members manifest the other gifts of the Spirit.

(5) Finally, there is the fruit in the lives of those
in whom spiritual phenomena occur. The Lord
Jesus said, "Ye shall know them by their fruits"
(Matthew 7:16). If, as some assert, we Pentecostal
people, in our speaking in tongues and exercise of
other supernatural gifts, are really under the dominion
of demons, our lives should be filled with the type of
activity common to demons. A few critics do their
best to show that this is true, but for every isolated
case which they can produce there are an overwhelming number of Pentecostalists who have the respect of
the world (and of many fundamentalists) as good,
honest, God-fearing Christians. Other critics, recognizing this fact, try to discredit the Movement
through just the opposite means. They inform all and
sundry that Satan, as an "angel of light," allows
us to lead a moral life so that we ourselves shall be
deceived, and that others might be caught in his

snare. Our accusers will not give us a chance, will they? Failing to prove that we are in heresy and immorality, they attribute our orthodoxy and morality to Satan! May the Lord forgive them, and may the Lord convict them of their bigoted attitude!

DR. ERNEST GOODE of Shoeburyness Presbyterian Church, Essex, England, says: "Let critics and cavilers say what they like—and they ought to be very careful what they say, lest they commit the awful, unpardonable sin of blasphemy against the Holy Ghost—the Pentecostal Movement of these last days is of God. It was started by God; it was empowered by God; it is filled with God. The Word is preached in the power of God; the prayers that are offered are inspired of God; the joy that lights up all faces is the joy of God; the purity and power that so many receive is the baptism of God; the miracle-working power that banishes disease is the work of God. The writer has never been in meetings where there has been so much of God, so much of joy, so much of power, so much of glory. He has witnessed scenes, heard testimonies, listened to messages, shared in outpourings that have almost bewildered him and made him feel that surely he must be dreaming. It was so novel, so unusual, so glorious. It seemed too good to be true. And yet there it was right before his very eyes. The writer cannot conceive it possible for any man, be he minister or layman, to sit in the meetings of the Pentecostal Movement without feeling, 'Here is the real thing—that for want of which pulpits are futile, powerless and voiceless, and congregations are languishing and dying.' "[1]

_____

[1] *With Signs Following*, by Frodsham.

Beloved, much more could be said in behalf of the Pentecostal Movement against the charge of Satanic inspiration, but we desist. Enough facts have already been presented to convince the honest critics. To those who through ignorance (see 1 Timothy 1:13) have thus accused us, we would say, Satan is not casting out Satan any more today than in Christ's day. To them we would repeat the words of Jesus to His disciples, when on two occasions they thought Him to be another spirit, "Fear not, it is I" (Matthew 14:25-27; Luke 24:36-43). And to all of our accusers we would repeat the fearful warning of Jesus to the Pharisees and Scribes, *"Wherefore I say unto you, all manner of sin and blasphemy shall be forgiven unto men: but the blasphemy against the Holy Ghost shall not be forgiven unto men"* (Matthew 12:31).

CHAPTER 9

Disparaged by the Apostle Paul

MANY Christians today are willing to concede that the Pentecostalists do speak supernaturally in tongues other than their own; that their utterances are genuine manifestations of the *glossolalia* of the early church, and not incoherent gibberish, nor satanic counterfeit. Having conceded this, these friends are still of the opinion that the Pentecostalists overestimate the value of this gift, which is not accorded a prominent place in the Scriptures, and which is frowned upon by the sacred writer who wrote most about it—the apostle Paul.

We have observed before that speaking in tongues is perhaps the most spectacular feature of the Pentecostal Movement and the one which distinguishes its adherents from all other Christian believers. It receives more attention from those outside the Movement than other more familiar teachings and practices, and Pentecostal people are required to answer more questions about it. This fact has brought forth the charge that speaking with tongues is given a prominence which is not warranted by the Word. Such is not the case. We Pentecostal people neither overestimate the value of tongues nor do we under-estimate it. Our constant aim as Bible-loving Christians is to conform every belief to the teachings of the Bible, no more and no less! We trust that this chapter will be read very earnestly and carefully. since we shall endeavor to answer many of the objections to the Pentecostal belief about tongues.

1. ABSENCE OF MENTION OF TONGUES IN ALL BUT THE CORINTHIAN EPISTLE

We are told that if Paul had placed the emphasis upon the gift of tongues accorded to it by Pentecostalists today, he would have written of it in more than one Epistle. And the fact that it is mentioned in only the Corinthian Epistle, which was written to carnal Christians, proves that the apostle did not highly regard the gift. Furthermore, it is pointed out that this epistle is the most corrective of all the Pauline Epistles. To base a principal doctrine upon it surely reveals a lack of wisdom in Scriptural exegesis, we are told.

It may surprise some good folk to know that all Bible students do not agree that the subject of tongues is confined to only one Pauline Epistle. A number of authors consider that the "spiritual songs" in Ephesians 5:19 and Colossians 3:16 are an indirect reference to the *glossolalia*. That the gift did assume the form of song is clear from 1 Corinthians 14:15, where Paul says, "I will sing with the spirit,"[1] GEORGE BARTON CUTTEN, who is, as you know, a non-Pentecostal writer, referring to these two verses (Ephesians 5:19; Colossians 3:16) and

---

[1]See further discussion of "singing in tongues" in Chapter 20.

also a third passage, 1 Thessalonians 5:19-20 ("Quench not the Spirit. Despise not prophecyings"), makes this comment: "If these are references to tongues, as seems likely, then the gift of tongues was not confined to Corinth, but was somewhat widespread, as indeed we should expect it to be. All of these cases were evidently the same kind that Paul knew well at Corinth, and the phenomena were so well known and so well defined as to require no description or comment."[1] *The Pulpit Commentary* adds this note on 1 Thessalonians 5:19: "By the Spirit here is usually understood the miraculous gifts of the Spirit—speaking with tongues or prophesyings; and it is supposed that the apostle here forbids the exercise of these gifts being hindered or checked."[2]

We do not offer these comments as positive proof that Paul was speaking of the gift of tongues to the Ephesian, Colossian and Thessalonian churches. It is our own personal belief that these passages are references to tongues, but since it is not clearly stated as such we should hesitate to enter them as evidence. However, we do wish to make this one point. It is plain that speaking in tongues was not limited to the Corinthian church. Paul tells the Corinthians that "God hath set in the church . . . diversities of tongues." By "the church" he did not mean just the church at Corinth, but the Church everywhere. It is a matter of record that the churches at Jerusalem (Acts 2:4), Caesarea (Acts 10:46), and Ephesus (Acts 19:6) were familiar with this miraculous utterance. Mark tells us that the Lord

---

[1] *Speaking with Tongues*, p. 20.
[2] Vol. 48, p. 105.

promised that "these signs shall follow them that believe; in My name . . . they shall speak with new tongues. . . . And they went forth, and preached *everywhere,* the Lord working with them, and confirming the word with signs following." These statements should be sufficient proof that the *glossolalia* was widespread in the early church. If such were not the case, and if the Epistles were circulated among all the churches, as is commonly believed, how non-plussed must have been all the churches but Corinth by Paul's detailed discussion of tongues!

But even if there be an absence of mention of tongues in all Pauline Epistles but the Corinthian, does this necessitate the belief that the gift was disparaged by the apostle? To be consistent, we would have to believe also that the Lord's Supper was disparaged by Paul. We cannot recall any other Epistle but the Corinthian (1 Corinthians 11:20-34) in which he mentions this ordinance; yet no one questions his appreciation of it. His words in the Corinthian letter reveal his reverence for the sacred table, and forbid anyone to doubt its position in the church. Why, then, should anyone use the same argument to question speaking in tongues?

Nor does the corrective nature of this Epistle constitute an argument against basing our belief upon its teachings. What nonsensical statements have been made by the opponents of Pentecost along this line; take this one for example: "In reading carefully the two Epistles to the Corinthians, one is amazed at the low moral and spiritual tides which prevail. They have ebbed to a low exceeding that of any other New Testament Church. The apostle does not spare. He calls them babes in Christ and carnal (1 Corinthians 3:1); puffed up (4:8); he rebukes them for

[150]

fornication (5:1); for going to law one with the other (6:1-8); for excesses and disorders at the Lord's table, and for drunkenness (11:17-22); for contentions and divisions among them (1:11-12); and for heresy (15:12). And yet in spite of pride and carnality and dissension and disorder and drunkenness and fornication and heresy, *every one of them spoke in unknown tongues when they came together* (14:26). This is the standard of religion held out to us by Pentecostal preachers as being the full gospel."[1]

What utter absurdity! Pentecostal preachers do not hold out such a standard of religion as the full gospel any more than do the ministers of other denominations who base their doctrine of the Resurrection on the fifteenth chapter of this Epistle, or the ministers who reverently read to their people the passage on the Lord's Supper in the eleventh chapter. The Corinthian standard of life is rejected as much by Pentecostal preachers as by any other preachers of today, or as by Paul, whom we follow as he followed Christ. We endorse his corrective teachings to the church at Corinth, and we base doctrinal beliefs on them, but not on the errors of the Corinthians.

It is not necessary, however, for us to defend this first Epistle to the Corinthians; it can defend itself. Admittedly, it does not contain the highest church truth, as the Ephesian Epistle does, but all must recognize the fact that some very wonderful truths are found in it. Time and time again, the apostle takes occasion from the errors and failures of the Corinthians to point out the power and

---

[1] J. Franklin Fisher, in his tract, *Speaking With Tongues.*

beauty of a truth. We do not rejoice in the iniquity of the carnal ones of Corinth, but we do rejoice in the truth which was declared to help them to see clearly and walk circumspectly. And these corrective teachings represent some of the greatest passages in Scripture—the superiority of the wisdom of God over the wisdom of man (ch. 1 and 2); the relationship and reward of those who are "laborers together with God;" the sublimity and eternality of love (ch. 13); the nature and glory of the Resurrection (ch. 15). We do not concur with the belief that one shows a lack of wisdom in Scriptural exegesis in basing Pentecostal doctrine on 1 Corinthians. According to Paul himself, "All Scripture is given by inspiration of God, and is profitable for doctrine, for reproof, for correction, for instruction in righteousness: that the man of God may be perfect, throughly furnished unto all good works" (2 Timothy 3:16, 17).

As we turn to the Letter itself to determine whether or not it supports the claim of non-Pentecostalists regarding the disparagement of tongues by Paul, we have but one request to make of the reader. Please read the twelfth, thirteenth and fourteenth chapters at least two or three times in order to "stir up your pure mind by way of remembrance" as to what the apostle actually says about tongues. It is possible to read into his writings what isn't there!

2. TONGUES LAST IN THE LIST OF THE GIFTS

In the twelfth chapter there are two listings of the gifts of God to the Church. The first is in verses 8 to 10: "For to one is given by the Spirit the word of wisdom; to another the word of knowledge by the same Spirit; to another faith by the same Spirit; to another the gifts of healing by the same Spirit; to another the working of miracles; to another prophecy; to another discerning of spirits; to another *divers kinds of tongues;* to another the interpretation of tongues." The second list is found in verse 28: "God hath set some in the church, first apostles, secondarily prophets, thirdly teachers; after that miracles, then gifts of healings, helps, governments, *diversities of tongues.*" You will notice that in the first list tongues together with its companion gift, the interpretation of tongues, is last. In the second list it again is given the last position. Many Bible teachers are confident that the lowly position of tongues in these two catalogues of the gifts indicates Paul's low estimate of the gift.

We do not contend that the gift of tongues is the best gift. To do so would be to give to it a chief seat reserved for another. All that we do claim for it is that it is one of the nine gifts and as such, deserves proper recognition. Even if it is the least of the nine supernatural gifts (vs. 8-10), it is still a gift, and should not be despised. "But now hath God set the members every one of them in the body, as it hath pleased Him. And if they were all one member, where were the body? But now are they many members, yet but one body. And the eye cannot say unto the hand, I have not need of thee: nor again the head to the feet, I have no need of you. Nay, much more those members of the body, which seem to be more feeble, are necessary" (ch. 12:18-22). The mere fact that it is enumerated last does not mean that it is to be regarded as a non-desirable gift, neither does it mean, necessarily, that it is the least of the gifts.

In 1 Corinthians 13:13 we read "And now abideth faith, hope, love,[1] these three; but the greatest of these is love." And yet, love is last in the list of the three! In 2 Peter 1:5-7: "And besides this, giving all diligence, add to your faith virtue; and to virtue knowledge; and to knowledge temperance; and to temperance patience; and to patience godliness; and to godliness brotherly kindness; and to brotherly kindness love." Here again love is given the last position, but who would say that it does not merit the leading position accorded it in Galatians 5:22-23?

We would call your attention also to two more reasons why we do not believe that the listing of tongues last by Paul was intended as disparagement. Tongues are mentioned first in the discussion in the thirteenth chapter of 1 Corinthians. Employing the same argument, we could say that it is to be preferred before prophecy, and understanding of mysteries, knowledge, faith, philanthropy and martyrdom. Also the two lists in the twelfth chapter do not pursue the same manner of enumeration. Prophecy, for instance, is sixth in the first list, below healing and miracles; but in the second list it is lifted above them. Then, too, the position of healing and miracles is reversed in the two lists.

3. LOVE AND NOT TONGUES TO BE DESIRED.

The latter part of verse 31 in chapter 12 is

---

[1] We shall substitute "love" for "charity" throughout our whole discussion.

[154]

reached with a sigh of relief by most non-Pentecostal teachers. At last they have come to a verse
that will guide them out of all the confusing dilemma
of miracles, healings and tongues! They knew that
Paul could not continue long in that vein. He will
turn now from these showy gifts to the lofty and
invisible virtues, saying, "And yet show I unto you
a more excellent way." In effect they say, "The
phenomenal gifts may attract the attention of Pentecostalists, even as bright colors catch the eye of
peasants; but as for us, who have a loftier appreciation of the gifts of God, may He give us love!" Then
follows a rapturous recital of the thirteenth chapter
with its exaltation of love above all other gifts.

Let us look briefly at the twelfth chapter. Paul
introduces the subject of the next three chapters in
the very first verse, "Now concerning *spiritual gifts,*
brethren, I would not have you ignorant." He
desires to impart some information about spiritual
gifts, and this he does without delay. He reveals
that the Holy Spirit is the source of the gifts, and
that, though they differ in character, they all have
the same purpose; viz., the edification of the Church.
Just why Paul, the master of logic, should spend
thirty and a half verses eulogizing the gifts, and
then with one fell sweep demolish his whole argument with the words, "Yet show I unto you a more
excellent way," the non-Pentecostalists do not explain. Yet if verse 31 is to be interpreted according to
their theory, all the clear, positive statements of
chapter 12 are canceled by it. But Paul just doesn't
argue that way!

You will observe that the apostle, up to this
particular verse, has spent considerable time telling
the Corinthians that the *manifestation of the gifts*

was for the profit of all. They were not given for the sake of their possessors alone, but for the body as a whole. Neither could they exist apart from one another, since each was the complement of the other, supplying the need of the spiritual body as the physical members supply the need of the physical body. In verse 31 Paul further develops his thought by revealing that if the gifts are to be profitable to both the contributor and the recipient, they must be motivated by love.

ELLICOTT agrees with this interpretation of the verse: "The excellent way is not some gift to be desired to the exclusion of the other gifts but a more excellent way of striving for those gifts. That which will consecrate every struggle for attainment and every gift when attained is love." Even DR. IRONSIDE seems to support this view: "We have noticed that in the twelfth chapter of this Epistle we have the gifts which the risen Christ gave to His Church. In chapter fourteen we have the use of the gifts; but in between the two chapters we have the spirit in which they are to be exercised. Someone has said that the thirteenth chapter of First Corinthians is the 'divine smithy,' alluding to the furnace in the blacksmith's shop, where the tools of chapter twelve are heated red-hot to be properly used in chapter fourteen."[1]

---

[1] *Addresses on the First Epistle to the Corinthians.* This admission by Dr. Ironside makes it difficult for us to understand another comment by him concerning the gift of tongues: " 'He that speaketh in a tongue edifieth himself.' He enjoys it but no one else does. . . . Do not covet a gift which makes you as selfish as that." Can a gift be selfish in itself? Is it not true, rather, that the possessor himself by his proper use or by his abuse of the gift determines its nature?

The thirteenth chapter has been immortalized as the "Love Chapter," and without a doubt it is the most beautiful description of love in all literature. Nevertheless, we must not wrest it from the setting in which the Holy Spirit has placed it. The verse and chapter divisions in the Word are helpful for reference, but are not inspired of God. We cannot, therefore, reckon with certainty that a thought has been exhausted, and a new idea is to be introduced, simply because one chapter ends and another begins. Paul does not discuss spiritual gifts in chapter twelve, discard them in chapter thirteen, and take them up again in chapter fourteen. A chapter, as well as a verse, must be considered in the light of its context.

Why should it be thought that the gifts are in competition with love? Why should the Corinthians be forced to make a choice between the gifts and love? Why should the supreme fruit of the Spirit be coveted to the exclusion of the gifts of the Spirit? The apostle does not assume an "elder brother" attitude and demand that they, or we, must choose between the two. The blessed truth is that the same Spirit, who sheds abroad the love of God in our hearts, also divides severally the gifts of the Spirit! God is not impoverished when we aim at and attain love; His inexhaustible coffers are full of every good and perfect gift, and He will lavish them upon all who will covet them earnestly. True, Paul is seeking to impress the gift-conscious Corinthians with the power and permanance of love. He longs for them to see that the greatest thing in the world is love; that all the commandments hang on love; and that "the end of the commandment is love out of a pure heart." By all means follow after, pursue, and possess love which abideth forever! But *please* do not disparage what Paul does not disparage. Do not cast aside as worthless tongues, prophecy, understanding, knowledge, faith, benevolence, and martyrdom. Read again Chapter 13:1-3:

"Though I speak with the tongues of men and of angels, have not love, *I* [not tongues] am become as sounding brass or a tinkling cymbal. And though I have the gift of prophecy, and understand all mysteries, and all knowledge; and though I have all faith, so that I could remove mountains, and have not love, *I* [not prophecy, understanding, knowledge, or faith] am nothing. And though I bestow all my goods to feed the poor, and though I give my body to be burned, and have not love, it profiteth *me* [not the act of bestowal or martyrdom] nothing."

Beloved, the Spirit of God, through Paul, does not spend a whole chapter showing the divine origin, administraton, and operation of these supernatural gifts, just to decry them in the next chapter. There is nothing essentially wrong with any of these gifts. There is no contrast between the gifts and love, save in the matter of permanence (see Chapter 5); the contrast is between the operation of the gifts with love and the operation of the gifts without love. To fail to see this is to miss the entire meaning of this wonderful chapter. Paul sums up chapter twelve in the concluding verse, "But covet earnestly the best gifts: and yet show I unto you a more excellent way." And he sums up chapter thirteen by the first verse of chapter fourteen, "Follow after love, AND desire spiritual gifts." The Corinthians had a zeal for the gifts without love, while many today have a zeal for love without the gifts:

the proper and Scriptural zeal is for love AND the gifts.

4. PROPHECY MUCH TO BE PREFERRED ABOVE TONGUES

Our non-Pentecostal friends are quite fond of the last part of 1 Corinthians 14:1: "Follow after love, and desire spiritual gifts, *but rather that ye may prophesy.*" To them, this verse—indeed, the whole fourteenth chapter, with its plain declarations in favor of prophecy—reveals the wholly unsatisfactory nature of tongues. Paul's exhortation to "covet earnestly the best gifts" is cited as an indirect disparagement of tongues. MR. HAYES says, "We covet the better gifts and are well content with the best. We can do without the least, as long as we have the better and best."[1]

It is evident from their comments on 1 Corinthians 12 to 14 that those who support this view make the mistake of confusing the gift of prophecy with the preaching and teaching of the Word common to the ministry today. While it is true that pastors, evangelists and teachers do prophesy in a sense, still it is clear that the prophetic ministry of which Paul speaks in these chapters was distinct for these other ministries (1 Corinthians 12:28; Ephesians 4:11). We can deduce the following facts about the gift of prophecy from the New Testament: it is one of the nine supernatural gifts (1 Corinthians 12:8-10); it is the speaking forth of a sudden revelation (1 Corinthians 14:25, 30); it would seem

---

[1] *The Gift of Tongues*, p. 102. We would advise Mr. Hayes to read again chapter twelve (especially verses 21 and and 22) of Paul's first Epistle to the Corinthians.

to be of the same ecstatic nature as tongues, except that it is uttered in one's own native tongue (Acts 19:6; 1 Corinthians 14:3, 6, 24). Nevertheless, whether prophecy is looked upon as a natural or supernatural gift, it cannot be exalted to the exclusion of tongues, for this, in reverse, was the error of the Corinthians. Non-Pentecostalists are quick to point out the undue emphasis on tongues in the church at Corinth, but are they not just as unbalanced when they utterly reject tongues in favor of prophecy? Again we ask, why must we accept one and reject the other? According to the Word, God has set them both in the Church. There is no problem in His mind about a choice between these two gifts; He knows that each has its place, and desires to "divide them severally as He will." Why else would He go on record that "diversities of tongues" are a part of His plan for the Body of Christ?

Paul does draw a contrast between prophecy and tongues in 1 Corinthians 14. He reminds these tongues-conscious Corinthians that prophecy is understood by the hearer, and does not require the exercise of another gift to make it edifying to the Church; whereas, tongues are not understood by the hearer, and must be accompanied by the gift of the interpretation of tongues to edify the Church. The believer who speaks in a tongue is edified, but not so the hearer. Therefore, since the primary purpose of the gathering together of believers is the profiting of all, Paul expresses a decided preference for prophecy over tongues, as far as the public exercise of the tongues is concerned. [1] However, he qualifies this

---

[1] See Chapter 20 of this volume for a detailed discussion of Paul's estimation of the devotional use of tongues.

preference by saying, "Greater is he that prophesieth than he that speaketh with tongues, *except he interpret,* that the Church may receive edifying." In other words, when the tongues are coupled with their companion gift, the interpretation of tongues, they are as edifying to the Church as is prophecy.

This equality of interpreted tongues with prophecy may be challenged by some on the grounds of the apostle's emphatic declaration in verse 19: "Yet in the church I had rather speak five words with my understanding, that by my voice I might teach others also, than ten thousand words in an unknown tongue." Paul's statement here, say they, rather than showing an equality, actually shows that prophecy is at least two thousand times as desirable as tongues! But have not these friends failed to see that these "ten thousand words in an unknown tongue" are words which are not afterwards interpreted? This verse must not be construed as contradictory to verse 5. Certainly, it cannot refer to the proportionate value of interpreted tongues and prophecy in the public assembly, for there are definite limits placed upon the number of prophetic utterances in each service as well as tongues utterances. While verse 23 does say that if all speak with tongues they will be called mad, and, contrariwise, verse 31 says that if all prophesy much blessing will result, still we see from verse 29 that the prophets are limited to "two or three" utterances,[1] and from verse 27 that those who speak in a tongue are limited to

---

[1] To believe that verse 31 gives every possessor of the prophetic gift the right to exercise it at each service, would destroy the balance of worship, and leave no room for the operation of the other gifts. Hence Paul's restrictions in verse 29.

"two or at the most three." So really very little difference exists between the two. If the ratio were two thousand to one, as some claim, Paul probably would have written something like this: "If any man speak in an unknown tongue, let it be once every ten years, or at the most once every five years . . . but let the prophets speak two or three at each service."

5. TONGUES ONLY FOR THE IMMATURE

MR. HAYES writes:

"Paul seems to suggest in this immediate context that the gift of tongues had to do with the infancy experience of the Church, and was not to be desired or cultivated in their mature life. He says, 'Brethren, be not children in mind: yet in malice be babes, but in mind be men.' 1 Corinthians 14:20. Pentecost marked the birth of the Christian Church. The disciples at Caesarea and at Ephesus who had the gift of tongues had just accepted Christianity, and the experience marked the first transports of their joy. There is no indication in the Book of Acts that the *glossolalia* formed a part of the regular worship of the Christian Church, or was ever experienced except at the beginning of the Christian life.

"It was a childish transport, not a mature development. It was natural to children and could be excused in them. It was unnatural in maturity; to desire it was childish, and to exercise it was babyish. Men ought to speak understandingly. This seems to be the position of Paul, as far as public services are concerned. He would two thousand times rather have a prophecy in public meeting than a powwow. The church ought to advance out of the kindergarten stage into the more advanced and more self-

controlled and more profitable higher classes. When
the proportionate value of the gift of tongues is
plainly preached and insisted upon, it is not likely
that many will exercise it or that older and mature
Christians will find any attraction in it."[1]

This quotation may represent non-Pentecostal
sentiment toward tongues, but it does not represent
the Scriptures. We have already observed that 1
Corinthians 14:19 refers to uninterpreted tongues;
that the gift is one of the nine spiritual gifts to the
Church. There is no indication at all in any of the
three chapters that tongues are only for the immature.
Paul himself glories in his own personal exercise of
the gift: "I thank my God, I speak with tongues
more than ye all." One could scarcely term the
apostle a "babe"! The fact of the matter is that
the fourteenth chapter was penned to awaken the
Corinthians to the absolute necessity of the interpretation of public utterances in tongues. Unless
they realized this necessity, they were children or
babes in understanding. But to conclude from 1
Corinthians 14:20 that all who speak in tongues are
immature, is plainly a wresting of the verse out of
the whole thought of the chapter.

As for the absence of mention of tongues in
Acts following its attendance upon the infilling of
the Spirit, we must remember that Luke's purpose
was the tracing of the spread of the gospel and not
so much the describing in detail of church worship.
Paul alone has drawn back the curtain and given us
in 1 Corinthians 12 to 14 a glimpse of early church
worship. What he has pictured for us there, we have
no doubt, was representative of every established
church in those days.

------

[1] *The Gift of Tongues*, p. 108.

6. RESTRICTIONS REVEAL PAUL'S DEPRECIATION OF TONGUES

J. FRANKLIN FISHER does not seem able to perceive the difference between restriction and rejection, for he writes: "Instead of encouraging the use of tongues, the apostle puts their employment under the most careful regulation. . . . In the light of all these limitations, the conviction comes that Paul permitted tongues only as a concession to the church because of their carnal state until they should become spiritual. . . . If the speaking in tongues of the Corinthians was all of God, how then would the apostle dare to discourage and limit its use? Would he not become guilty of opposing and quenching the Spirit?"

This good brother needs to realize that every gift of God can be the subject of abuse! DR. IRONSIDE says, "It is rather a sad commentary upon our fallen human nature that everything God has given us has been abused by man."[1] He then tells of the abuse of the physical appetites, of the Sabbath, and of the Lord's Supper (1 Cor. 11:17-26). Because God in His wisdom asks His people to submit their spiritual gifts to certain regulations, even as He asks them to submit their natural gifts to certain regulations, it is not necessary to conclude that those gifts are not of God or that they should be rejected as unprofitable. Do we reject automobiles because their manufacturers have equipped them with brakes? Of course not! We are grateful for the brakes; we use them when necessary, and keep right on driving the automobiles.

But can a miraculous gift be abused? JOHN R.

---

[1] *Addresses on the First Epistle to the Corinthians.*

RICE, an outstanding fundamentalist evangelist and author, does not believe so. According to him, "The Scripture does not say that they (the Corinthians) were speaking in miraculous tongues, but rather that they were simply speaking foreign languages, showing off in church. The rebuke and the rules for control of tongues in 1 Corinthians 14 would apply to foreign languages in the church, even though they were not given by the Holy Spirit. . . . First Corinthians 12:10 plainly tells us that the Holy Spirit did, in some cases, give the gift of tongues to people and the gift of interpretation. But this is not what Paul was rebuking in 1 Corinthians 14. Paul would not have had to rebuke them if what they had was a miracle from God. God does not give miracles and let people use them wrongly. Not one time in the Bible is there a record of anybody who was given by God the power to work a miracle and then used it wrongly. God gives miracles only according to His own honor and glory, and what the people at Corinth had when they were having their various languages in the church and Paul had to rebuke them in the fourteenth chapter of 1 Corinthians, was not miraculous at all and not a gift of the Spirit."[1]

It seems strange that Paul should write of miraculous tongues in the twelfth and thirteenth chapters of 1 Corinthians, and then turn abruptly to a discussion of mere linguistic ability in the fourteenth chapter. And who could believe that the apostle would approve the display by two or three members of the congregation of their knowledge of foreign languages in every service? Common courtesy would forbid such ostentation! Unless the speaking in tongues

---

[1] *The Sword of the Lord*, p. 8. June 14, 1946.

and their interpretation are miraculous, they have no place whatsoever in the church: for though Paul, in recognizing the ability of the gifted one to speak or to keep silent (1 Cor. 14:27, 28), discloses that the initiative rests with the *glossolalic* one, the whole context reveals the miraculous character of the gift. (See Chapter 3.)

Then, too, it is evident that Dr. Rice has overlooked the record in Numbers 20:7-12 of the second striking of the rock by Moses. Miraculous power was certainly operative on this occasion, despite the fact that God had commanded Moses only to *speak* to the rock. For this act of disobedience, this wrong use of miraculous power, Moses was excluded from the Promised Land. If one of the greatest of God's servants could and did fail to properly use miraculous powers, why should anyone be quick to condemn a similar failure in the least of the saints, even the Corinthians, or the Pentecostalists?

DONALD GEE has an excellent comment in this connection: "It is a pleasant dream held by some people that all exercise of the gifts of the Spirit is necessarily perfect, and beyond abuse or mistake. Such an idea can only come from a very careless reading of the New Testament. Unfortunately it may have serious results. In those who are prejudicial against the subject it makes them label the slightest error or imperfection they may run up against as a sure sign of a counterfeit that justifies them in condemning the whole. In those who delight in the Gifts of the Spirit, it places them beyond the realm of teaching and correction; they regard their experience as infallible.

"Now nothing can be more certain than that the New Testament reveals the exercise of spiritual

[166]

gifts can be imperfect. Paul's treatment of the subject in 1 Corinthians 12, 13, and 14 arises solely out of the Corinthian assembly using certain gifts wrongly.

"Note particularly that he never questions the genuineness of their gifts. There is not one single line in which he suggests (as so many hastily do today) that they had counterfeit gifts inspired by deceiving spirits. All through the three chapters he proceeds on the assumption that they had right gifts but used them wrongly. The fact that this not only is possible, but actually occurred in the early church, is thus established beyond argument.

"What are the reasons for these abuses? They are admittedly not in the Spirit of God. Neither are they in the nature of the gifts themselves, for coming directly from the Lord they would necessarily share His perfection. We are shut in to the obvious fact, which is exactly what the Scripture teaches, that the imperfections in their exercise spring from the 'earthen vessels' through whom the manifestation flows."[1]

In the case of the Corinthians, we have seen that they gave entirely too much prominence to tongues in the public assembly, placing the gift under no restraint in regard to interpretation or number of utterances. To counteract this unwise practice, Paul was forced to adopt almost a negative attitude toward the gift. Nevertheless, as we have said elsewhere in this chapter, the apostle took occasion from the mistakes of the Corinthians to point out the power and beauty of the gift which was being abused. From the fourteenth chapter, so filled with corrective measures in regard to tongues, we have compiled the

---

[1] *Concerning Spiritual Gifts*, pp. 71, 72.

following list of his declarations in favor of the gift. These positive statements should not be overlooked any more than the regulations and restrictions, in judging his attitude toward tongues.

(1) "Desire spiritual gifts"—verse 1.

(2) "He that speaketh in an unknown tongue speaketh . . . unto God"—verse 2.

(3) "In the Spirit he speaketh mysteries" (sacred secrets)—verse 2.

(4) "He that speaketh in an unknown tongue edifieth himself"—verse 4.

(5) "I would that ye all spake with tongues"—verse 5.

(6) "For greater is he that prophesieth than he that speaketh with tongues, except he interpret, that the church may receive edifying"—verse 5.

(7) "If I pray in an unknown tongue, my spirit prayeth"—verse 14.

(8) "I will pray with the spirit" (i.e., in a tongue)—verse 15.

(9) "I will sing with the spirit" (i.e., in a tongue)—verse 15.

(10) "Thou verily givest thanks well"—verse 17.

(11) "I thank my God, I speak with tongues more than ye all"—verse 18.

(12) "In the law it is written, with men of other tongues and other lips will I speak to this people"—verse 21.

(13) "Wherefore tongues are for a sign . . . to them that believe not"—verse 22.

(14) "If any man speak in an unknown tongue, let it be by two, or at the most by three, and that by course: and let one interpret"—verse 27.

(15) "Forbid not to speak with tongues"—verse 39.

We can see from all these statements that Paul, under the inspiration of the Holy Spirit, did say some favorable things about tongues,[1] even while he sought to bring the Corinthians back to the correct balance. And need we remind our non-Pentecostal friends that prophecy is also restricted in chapter fourteen? If we reject tongues because Pauline restrictions were imposed upon them, by the same token we must reject prophecy.

7. "FORBID NOT" REALLY MEANS TO FORBID TO SPEAK WITH TONGUES

Quite a number of years ago in one of the Midwestern states a young man was converted from a very ungodly life and led into the Pentecostal Movement. There was a minister in the community who came to him one day and sought to convince him that speaking with tongues was not of God, even going so far as to quote incorrectly 1 Corinthians 14:39, declaring that the verse read, "forbid to speak with tongues." The young fellow was stunned upon hearing this, but only for a moment, for the Spirit of God caused him to exclaim, "That is not what the Word of God says!" He knew practically

---

[1]H. L. Crockett (*Conversations on "The Tongues"*, p. 42) would have us to believe that Paul was carrying on an indirect dialogue in chapter 14, all the remarks favorable to tongues coming from the Corinthians, and only the corrective words coming from Paul. This is a most ingenious theory and should prove highly satisfactory when applied to many other difficult passages. But by the time all of us Bible readers have had an opportunity to apply this novel form of exegesis, how much of the Bible would be left? Personally, we prefer to believe that the statements approving tongues came from Paul as much as those which limited tongues. And we are persuaded to believe that every true student of the Word will agree with us.

nothing of the Bible, but was supernaturally led by the Spirit to open his Bible to just the right place, 1 Corinthians 14. There he discovered what the Word actually says on the subject, and read verse 39 aloud to his adviser: "forbid NOT to speak with tongues." Needless to say, the misquoting minister retired from the scene, post haste!

Though most of the opponents of tongues do not employ such a crude method as this, their motive is nonetheless the same—to put an end to all speaking with tongues in the church today. We do not charge them with deliberate misrepresentation of the truth, for we believe that many of them are honest and sincere in their efforts to forbid tongues. Still, there is no escaping the fact that, despite their honesty and sincerity, prejudice and a lack of thorough study of tongues in the Scriptures have combined to distort their teachings on the subject. How else can we explain their use of little technicalities to evade the evident meaning of the Word, even as some lawyers employ certain loopholes in the law whereby they defeat the very purpose of the law?

For instance, some teach that 1 Corinthians 14:39 really means to forbid to speak with tongues! Not that they deny that the verse says, "Forbid not to speak with tongues." No, their argument is much more subtle and appealing than that. What they say is that the very negative aspect of Paul's admonition was a bit of "inspired psychology." If he had instructed the Corinthians not to speak with tongues at all, human nature being what it is, those carnal believers would have increased rather than diminished their exercise of the gift. Hence, the apostle did permit a limited exercise of tongues rather than provoke an even more extravagant display. His one hope was that the discriminating ones among the Corinthians would take note of his positive exhortation in favor of prophecy ("covet to prophesy") and recognize his low estimation of tongues through his use of a negative exhortation ("forbid not to speak with tongues"). By their seeing the difference, Paul felt that it would not be long before the tongues would lose their charm and be discarded by all the saints at Corinth.

Before we attempt to refute this argument, we would make a few observations concerning the dangers of such un-Biblical exegesis. The most generally accepted law of Scriptural interpretation is to interpret the Scriptures, whenever possible, according to their simplest and most evident meaning. What a radical departure from this law is this explanation of 1 Corinthians 14:39! These teachers would not only modify the command but entirely obliterate it. They would accomplish this by giving to it a meaning which is exactly opposite to that which is apparent. Can we in the interest of Scriptural interpretation as a whole permit this treatment of this verse? Obviously, if we allow it here, we must allow it in other passages, for other teachers would insist that we allow them the same privilege of voiding other commands in the Word. And who could not readily see the results of such a policy? Even the unqualified commandments would be imperiled; a chaotic condition would exist in which every man could interpret the Word according to that which was right in his own eyes, regardless of how fanciful or artificial his interpretation might be; every declaration could be twisted until it gave an exactly opposite meaning.

That this practice has been in vogue throughout the

centuries does not guarantee its correctness. It is a matter of fact that at the dawn of civilization Satan first advanced this method of wresting the Word of God. Genesis 3:1-5. Through his subtle and seemingly plausible reasoning, Eve was deceived, only to make the awful discovery that God had meant exactly what He said! And is it altogether irrelevant to say that the negative quality of that particular command did not lessen God's insistence upon its being obeyed, or diminish His judgment upon its violation? Surely, we must insist upon the rule that every statement in the Word, unless qualified elsewhere, must be interpreted according to its simplest and most evident meaning.

To say that 1 Corinthians 14:39—"forbid not to speak with tongues"—really means to forbid to speak with tongues, is in flat contradiction to the language of the verse itself. Such perverse reasoning can only produce direct disobedience to Paul's commandment. Let no man deceive you with vain or subtle words; the apostle meant precisely what he said—"forbid *not* to speak with tongues"! Because of his preference for prophecy to uninterpreted tongues, and his restrictions even on interpreted tongues, Paul was fearful lest some extremists should attempt to abolish tongues altogether; hence his emphatic declaration, "Forbid not to speak with tongues." Why did the Holy Spirit inspire him to express this command in the negative? Because He knew that there would be need for a strong deterrent to the divers and sundry efforts to exclude tongues not only at Corinth but also throughout Church history.[1]

---

[1] It is apparent that disorderly tongues can be forbidden with-

Let us see what MR. HAYES' conclusion is in regard to tongues:

"The best attitude toward them will be one of consistent tolerance and persistent testing, a recognition of their occasional and individual and proportionate value, together with a constant insistence upon their orderly and edifying use." (So far Mr. Hayes seems to reflect a tolerant attitude toward tongues, but we find later that he qualifies—in fact, cancels—these remarks.)

"On the whole, then, our conclusion must be that the gift of tongues is of comparative insignificance, that no one need covet it in these days, and that it is a gift belonging to the immature rather than the mature development of the Church. As it is an ecstatic experience it ought not to be cultivated because of the nervous disorders that will inevitably ensue in any prolonged indulgence in it, and whenever it occurs in any religious meeting the responsible leader of the meeting ought to see to it that it is submissive to discipline and subject to self-control.

"It is an interesting fact that when physical prostrations were frequent in John Wesley's meetings, Charles Wesley preached upon one occasion, and quietly informed his audience before he began that anyone who was stricken down during the service would be removed from the room just as quietly and expeditiously as possible; and after that

out disobedience to 1 Corinthians 14:39. When the exercise of tongues is not according to the apostle's regulations, it should be checked, or else the leaders of the service become as guilty of disobedience as those who would forbid the exercise of all tongues, whether Scriptural or un-Scriptural.

announcement no one was stricken.[1] Usually a few quiet words of suggestion from the leader will dispose of all such phenomena.

"When the possessors of the gift of tongues refuse to recognize any church authority, and are inclined to ignore the injunction that all things be done decently and in order, and are unwilling to submit to the Pauline restrictions of the gift, they brand THEIR gift at once as un-Christian, and its exercise as un-Scriptural; and they should be disciplined accordingly. The gift of tongues must be recognized as a possible accompaniment of any Christian or pagan experience. It should never be allowed to become the prominent feature of any Christian movement. It should be discouraged under all normal conditions anywhere. It is doubtful whether it ought to be encouraged under any conditions anywhere. In the church of today it is less a blessing to be desired than an affliction to be endured. Let it cease as soon as may be; but let love abide in all our dealing with it. 'Whether there be tongues, they shall cease . . . and now abideth faith, hope, love, these three; but the greatest of these is love'!"[2]

We have quoted at length from Mr. Hayes because his conclusion is so similar to that advanced by many of our fundamentalist friends. One thing we would point out to all who concur with this view: there are more ways than one to forbid to speak with tongues. Some prefer absolute opposition

---

[1] We do not possess all the facts about this case, and therefore cannot pass judgment upon Charles Wesley's action. We do know, however, from John Wesley's statement concerning physical manifestations (see Chapter 7), that he (John) recognized their worth in their proper sphere.

[2] *The Gift of Tongues*, p. 117.

to the gift, while others prefer the method advocated by Mr. Hayes, for they feel that it more nearly conforms to the letter of the Word. But what is the difference between determined bigotry and disapproving tolerance, since both accomplish a cessation of tongues?

Is it necessary for Mr. Hayes to declare explicitly, "I forbid anyone to speak with tongues in my meetings"? Has he not stated virtually those very words in his conclusion? Would any possessor of the gift of tongues feel at liberty to manifest his gift in a service in which the leader depreciates that gift as productive of "nervous disorders," "a possible accompaniment of any Christian or pagan experience," "less a blessing to be desired than an affliction to be endured"; and especially, if the leader gives "a few quiet words of suggestion" to "dispose of all such phenomena"? And what about Mr. Hayes' reference to "church authority and Pauline restrictions of the gift"? Doubtless he is speaking of 1 Corinthians 14:28—"If there be no interpreter, let him keep silence in the church." This is just another way of utterly silencing tongues, for no one is encouraged to pray that he may interpret the tongues which "should never be encouraged under all normal conditions anywhere." And even if there were an interpreter in the church (and one is rare indeed outside of Pentecostal ranks!), he would not be given an opportunity to interpret, for just as soon as the utterance in tongues began, in most non-Pentecostal churches an usher would escort the tongues person out of the room "as quietly and expeditiously as possible"!

We might as well face the facts: speaking in tongues is not acceptable anywhere except in the

Pentecostal Movement. It may be rejected on the ground that it is not in decency and in order, but the real reason is that it is not in harmony with the formal worship so prevalent today. And what a mistake the leaders make when they insist that all exercise of tongues, which is not in line with their conceptions, is therefore "un-Christian[1] and un-Scriptural!" Beloved, if these men are to deserve respect for their authority concerning tongues, then their authority must be based upon the Scriptures. There is a wide difference between submitting to the autocratic authority of ecclesiastical leaders and submitting to the authority of the Scriptures. Paul did not tell the Corinthians to "dispose of all such phenomena," but "if any man speak in an unknown tongue, let it be by two or at the most three." This was his restriction. "Forbid not to speak with tongues," was his command. And to those who question his authority, Paul says, "If any man think himself to be a prophet, or spiritual, let him acknowledge that the things that I write unto you are the commandments of the Lord."

Is there any wonder that a Pentecostal Movement has become a necessity? Subjected to un-Scriptural discipline in the established churches, forbidden any exercise of the gift of the Spirit whatsoever, many precious saints have been forced to withdraw from such an antagonistic atmosphere, and band themselves together with those of like precious faith. (Paul him-

---

[1]The charges of Corinthianism—megalomania, carnality, sensuality, and insubordination—which are hurled against Pentecostal people today, are not new. So the Pope branded Luther; so the State church labeled the Wesleys and Whitefield; and so religious leaders have always branded anyone who has not submitted to their authority.

self would find difficulty in remaining in circles where all speaking with tongues is excluded.) Many, with heavy hearts, have left their former groups; they had no desire to leave, but it was either that or else relinquish their convictions. It was not a case of departure because their former associates had departed from the fundamental doctrines, or had been utterly forsaken of the Lord, for they still cling tenaciously to the faith and have the blessing of God upon them and their labors. The disagreement has come because of the total rejection by the denominational leaders and groups as a whole of the exercise of tongues and other spiritual gifts.

To conclude this chapter and this section we ask you to consider some "Words of Advice" by non-Pentecostalist T. J. McCROSSAN:

"1. To the scores of dear brethren who are bitterly opposed to speaking with tongues: listen to Paul's words in 1 Corinthians 14:39, 'Wherefore, brethren, covet to prophesy, and forbid not to speak with tongues.'

"(a) All will in reality be forbidding others to speak with tongues, who declare most emphatically that there is no genuine speaking with tongues today. From our own experience already narrated, and from the experience of many other reliable witnesses, we know that speaking with genuine tongues today is a blessed reality. Instead of opposing this gift of tongues, we ought to praise God for again bringing this gift back to His church.

"(b) Again all will forbid others to speak with tongues who declare, as hundreds do today, that all speaking with tongues is of the devil.

"1 Corinthians 12:10 informs us that 'speaking

with tongues' is one of the gifts of the Holy Ghost. Now the Holy Spirit is here today with all the power and authority which He had in the apostolic days. See 1 Thessalonians 1:5 and Romans 15:19. Why then should not all His gifts be in the Church today?

"Many dear saints have the gift of tongues today. We have heard some of them pray in a foreign tongue, when God has put some great burden on their hearts for lost and perishing souls. As the Holy Spirit pleaded through them, you detected the very presence and power of God. Oh, what heart-thrilling appeals were those. You felt, as you listened, a spirit of awe, and you realized the very presence of God. We have known such saints, after being on their faces before God for an hour or more pouring forth their petitions (or letting the Holy Ghost pour forth His petitions through them), to be unable to speak English for another hour or so.

"Brother, this gift of tongues has come back to the Church, and will be more and more prevalent until Jesus comes. If you say this is all of Satan, you will surely offend the Holy Ghost, and He may forsake you, and leave you as powerless as He has left many others.

"Friend, we had better obey Paul's word and 'Forbid not to speak with tongues.' Let us take 'the middle of the road' attitude on this subject. Let us realize that this gift has come back to the Church, and if God should give some saint a message in tongues in your congregation—and He might— let him deliver it without interruption, but pray God to give the interpretation to some one. If, after the message has been delivered, there is no interpreter present, then remember Paul's words (1 Corinthians

14:28), 'But if there be no interpreter, let him keep silence in the church; and let him speak to himself, and to God.'

"Sometime some one may speak with tongues in your meeting, and you will feel at once that it is not of God. It will be harsh and repelling; your spiritual nature will revolt. Then just quietly place your hand upon such an one and ask God to rebuke the evil spirit, and you will have very little trouble. By this mode of procedure you will keep out all fanaticism, and yet will not interfere with the genuine working of the Holy Ghost; for never forget that the gift of tongues is back in the Church today. If ever God needed wise and firm spiritual leaders it is now."[1]

---

[1]*Speaking With Other Tongues, Sign or Gift—Which?* pp. 41-43.

SECTION III

WHAT "THIS" IS

"But this is that which was spoken."
Acts 2:16.

PART A

The Initial, Physical Evidence of the Baptism With the Holy Ghost

INTRODUCTION TO PART A

"The baptism with the Holy Spirit," according to the late DR. R. A. TORREY, "is an operation of the Holy Spirit distinct from and subsequent and additional to His regenerating work, . . . an impartation of power, and the one who receives it is fitted for service, . . . not merely for the apostles, nor merely for those of the apostolic age, but for 'all that are afar off, even as many as the Lord our God shall call,' as well; i.e., it is for every believer in every age of the Church's history."[1]

---

[1] *What the Bible Teaches*, p. 271, 278.

[183]

This definition of the baptism also represents the basic view of the Pentecostal Movement toward the experience. However, in addition to the three fundamental points cited by Dr. Torrey, we believe that this baptism can be described as a charismatic experience; i.e., it is of a transcendent and miraculous character, producing extraordinary effects which are visible to the onlooker, its initial oncoming being signalized by an utterance in other tongues.

It is not within the scope of this volume to deal with all the aspects of the baptism with the Holy Ghost. We can consider the experience here only in its relationship to speaking with tongues. We realize that this will leave many questions and contrary opinions unanswered, but it is impossible to include a full discussion of the baptism in this particular work. The Lord willing, we expect to publish at a later date a volume which will provide a comprehensive treatment of the subject. Until then, we can but ask you readers who disagree with the statements by Dr. Torrey to withhold final judgment on them. On the other hand, you who do agree with Dr. Torrey that there is an enduement of power for all Christian believers subsequent to regeneration should find no serious doctrinal barriers between you and a consideration of the Pentecostal view of the charismatic aspect of the baptism with the Holy Ghost.

One of the first things to do in determining the nature of this experience is to examine it in the Scriptures. When we know definitely what kind of baptism the New Testament believers received, we can be assured that THAT is the kind of baptism God desires to give us; we can compare our experiences with THAT, and rest content only when we have

THAT. Now, where in the Scriptures is the logical place to find THAT? There are a number of prophecies in the Gospels and even in the Old Testament concerning the baptism, and there are numerous references in the Epistles to the Spirit-filled life, but neither the prophecies nor the explanations of the Spirit-filled life (which life presupposes an initial filling) contain a description of the experience itself. Hence, if we are to discover what definitely took place when one was baptized or filled with the Spirit in the early church, we must turn to the Book of Acts, the experience book of the New Testament Church. There alone can we find a detailed description of the baptism or filling[1] with the Spirit which was experienced by those early believers. Surely, what we find there should be THAT which is the pattern for all future baptisms or fillings with the Holy Ghost.

Is not this our practice when dealing with any other historical event in whose details we are interested? We study the background and the aftermath of the event in order to gain a full perspective, but for exact information on the event itself we turn to the historical record. For example, if we desire minute knowledge concerning the baptism and anointing of the Lord Jesus at Jordan, we may read Isaiah 61:1-3; Luke 4:17-19; and Acts 10:38; but for the actual account we would turn to the historical record of the Gospels—Matthew 3, Mark 1, Luke 3 and John 1. The former passages give us a clear understanding of the purpose of that baptism and

---

[1]Both of these words are used to describe this experience. *Filling* refers more to the inward and invisible phase of the work; whereas, *baptism* seems to indicate the outward and visible phase. See Matthew 3:11; Acts 1:5; 2:4; 11:16.

anointing, but only the Gospels contain a description of His conversation with John, His baptism in water, the descent of the dove and the voice from heaven. And so we must deal with this baptism with the Holy Ghost, for it too is a definite experience, something which one undergoes personally, an actual living through of an event. To discover its precise nature we must examine the record left to us in Acts by Luke, the historian of the early church.

Some have raised the objection that doctrines should be based upon Biblical teachings, rather than upon Biblical experiences. They reason that any attempt to make all conform to a certain type of Biblical experience will produce nothing but vain imitations of that which is not clearly taught to be for all.

It is true that the experiences of the disciples should be studied in the light of the clear teaching of the Word, and it is also true that there are some Biblical experiences in which all believers obviously cannot share; for example, the sovereign dealings of God in the lives of the apostles (see Chapter 5). Nevertheless, there are certain spiritual experiences related in the Scriptures which have served as a standard for all believers throughout the centuries of Church history. It stands to reason that the Scriptural examples of conviction for sin, repentance, regeneration, etc. are the best possible standard for measuring those experiences today. They were a part of the lives of not just a privileged few but of all believers in the early church; they were not exceptional, but normal and expected. And it is our conviction that the baptisms or fillings with the Holy Spirit, as recorded in Acts, should likewise be the standard for believers today.

But we do not build our doctrine wholly on these experiences. There are some statements by the inspired writer which are so definite in their teaching that they approximate an exact declaration of Pentecostal doctrine. It has been through a combining of these statements with the experiences in Acts that we have come to the conclusion that in apostolic days speaking with tongues was a constant accompaniment of the baptism with the Holy Ghost, and should be in these days as well.

Occasionally, we have been accused of coining an un-Scriptural term in referring to the relationship of tongues to the baptism as the "initial, physical evidence." It must be conceded that the words, "initial, physical evidence," do not appear in the Scriptures. However, we would remind our critics that the word "Trinity" also does not appear in the Scriptures, yet who would dare to say that "Trinity" is an un-Scriptural term? Must a theological term be actually inscribed upon the sacred pages before we can be permitted to use it in reference to a Scriptural doctrine?

And we would be clearly understood on one point: the Pentecostal Movement does not teach that the *glossolalia* is the only evidence of the baptism with the Holy Spirit. As in apostolic days, so today there are other evidences of this experience. Our position is that He who desires to endue us with power from on high has also provided an immediate means by which we can know whether or not we have received that enduement; i.e., by speaking with other tongues as the Spirit gives utterance.

The propagation of this doctrine has provoked a fierce, theological controversy in the ranks of Fundamental Christianity. Many have urged us

Pentecostalists to cease to spread such a controversial doctrine, since it provokes so much strife, division and unrest in the Body of Christ. But these friends fail to realize that in our insistence upon tongues, we are not contending for a pet doctrine, nor even for the *glossolalia* itself (blessed though it is!), but for that wonderful experience of which speaking with tongues is the initial, physical evidence. It is our sincere belief that without this evidence there can be no fully Scriptural baptism with the Holy Ghost. Thus, to us, the value of speaking with tongues is, in one sense commensurate with that of the baptism itself; though in another sense, it is of but relative importance, being simply a marvelous evidence of a marvelous experience. Now whether we are right or wrong in this belief—you will have ample opportunity to decide this as you read the next ten chapters—it can readily be seen why we cannot dismiss as inconsequential the relationship of tongues to the baptism.

Still, though we feel that we must continue to preach the doctrine, we honestly desire in every way possible "to endeavor to keep the unity of the Spirit in the bond of peace." The Pentecostal Movement has striven to co-operate with every evangelical group in furthering the kingdom of God. Whenever an opportunity has been afforded us to be laborers together with non-Pentecostal brethren in a soul-saving effort, we have been more than willing to lay aside doctrinal differences. Even so, we believe that there is a legitimate place in the Church for difference of opinion,[1] and while we do not believe in con-

---

[1]"The object of controversy should be to clear away all prejudice, all ignorance, all passion, every groundless opinion and prepossession, which stand in the way of acceptance of truth.

tention for contention's sake, we intend to speak forth boldly the full gospel message.

And may we suggest that if it is possible to establish as Scriptural truth the teaching that speaking with tongues is the initial, physical evidence of the baptism, the argument of some non-Pentecostal brethren that the teaching causes unrest among their followers is worthless. Where has truth not brought unrest? Have not we all found from our study of history and from personal experience that truth always brings rest or unrest, depending upon its acceptance or rejection?

And controversialists should be ready to admit the probability that those who differ most widely from them may, for that very reason, see some side of truth which is hidden from their own eyes, and therefore should be ready to give a candid consideration to their arguments." *Pulpit Commentary*, vol. 42, p. 7.

CHAPTER 10

The Pattern at Pentecost

LUKE has recorded for us in the second chapter of Acts the first baptisms or fillings with the Holy Ghost. To refresh your memory, we suggest that you turn to that passage and read it very carefully. We need not remind you of the importance attached to this record by the Pentecostal Movement of today. The late T. B. Barratt, Pentecostal pastor of Oslo, Norway, has made this statement: "Regarding salvation through justification by faith, we are Lutherans. In water baptism formula, we are Baptists. In regard to sanctification, we are Methodists.[1] In aggressive evangelism, we are as the Salvation Army. But in regard to the Baptism of the Holy Spirit, we are Pentecostal!" In other words, we believe that the experience of the one hundred and twenty in Acts 2:4—"And they were all filled with the Holy

---

[1]Though there is some difference of opinion among Pentecostalists in regard to the exact method of sanctification, all believe in a holy, separated life.

[191]

Ghost, and began to speak with other tongues, as the Spirit gave them utterance"—is the Scriptural pattern for believers of the whole Church age.

In our consideration of this experience we ask you to observe with us that

A. THIS DAY OF PENTECOST WAS A DISPENSATIONAL DAY

1. THE TIME

The feast of Pentecost was instituted by the Lord so that the children of Israel could offer thanksgiving for the wheat harvest. It is significant that this festival day was celebrated just fifty days after Passover. Since the giving of the Law at Sinai (Exodus 19 and 20) occurred fifty days after the first Passover in Egypt (Exodus 12), it was only natural that the Hebrew nation associated Pentecost with Sinai. The giving of the Law was the event which put Israel on a national basis, and, of course, was held in high esteem by the Jews.

It was not an accident that God chose Pentecost as the day upon which to send the Holy Spirit, to make manifest the merits of the atoning work of the Lord Jesus Christ, and to reveal that the time for dealing with Israel as a nation was now supplanted by the dispensation of the Church. This day, fraught with its memories of new beginnings, provided a perfect background for the birthday of the Church. The types and shadows of the Old Testament found their perfect and timely fulfillment. Hence, the tarrying of the disciples was primarily imposed upon them so that all things could fit into the divinely arranged plan.

2. THE PLACE

The outpouring of the Spirit took place in Jerusalem. We are all familiar with the command of the Lord concerning the place where the disciples were to await the Heavenly Gift: "And, behold, I send the promise of My Father upon you: but tarry ye in the city of *Jerusalem* until ye be endued with power from on high" (Luke 24:49). "And being assembled together with them, commanded them that they should not depart from *Jerusalem,* but wait for the promise of the Father, which, saith He, ye have heard of me" (Acts 1:4). It may be that Joel and Zechariah also spoke of this city in connection with the initial outpouring of the Spirit, as well as in connection with the last-days fulfillment of their prophecies (See Joel 2:32 and Zechariah 12:10). We know that Jerusalem, the political and religious capital of Israel, did prove to be the ideal location for the outpouring of the Spirit. It is doubtful if the Church and its message would have found any acceptance at all among the Jews if its Founder in His life and death had not been intimately associated with Jerusalem, or if the Church had started its activities elsewhere.

3. THE NUMBER

Some Bible teachers make persistent efforts to limit the recipients of the Holy Ghost on the day of Pentecost to the apostles. Here are a few brief reasons why we reject this reasoning.

The "all" of 2:1 (chapter 2, verse1) must refer to the same company described in 1:15-26. It is also quite clear in 2:15 that Peter and the eleven (verse 14), standing up separate from the body of the disciples, said of them, "These (*men* is in

italics, indicating that it was supplied by the translators) are not drunken as ye suppose"; which is a
demonstration that those of whom they thus spoke
had been speaking with tongues. To limit the outpouring and subsequent speaking with tongues to the
twelve would be an Old Testament conception. It
is not in harmony with the prophecy of Joel, quoted
by Peter, "I will pour out My Spirit upon ALL
flesh." Lange says, "Not only the apostles, but all
the disciples, were filled with the Holy Ghost. . . .
There is a universal priesthood of ALL believers, and
the Holy Ghost is the anointing which consecrates
and qualifies for this priesthood." Note, too, that
Joel's prophecy specifies "daughters" and "handmaidens" as well as "sons" and "servants"; this
part of the prophecy would be totally irrelevant if
only upon twelve men was poured out the Spirit.
Why should the Pentecostal outpouring and tongues
be limited to the twelve, when throughout the Book
of Acts all disciples who met the conditions (Acts
2:38), whether men or women, leaders or followers,
received the Spirit?

Then, too, the number of *one hundred and twenty*
is in accord with the Scriptural type found in 2
Chronicles 5:11-14. There we find a description of
another wonderful day in Israel's history; viz., the
dedication of the Temple of the Lord. "And it
came to pass, when the priests were come out of the
holy place: (for all the priests that were present
were sanctified, and did not then wait by course:
also the Levites which were the singers, all of them
of Asaph, of Heman, of Jeduthun, with their sons
and their brethren, being arrayed in white linen,
having cymbals and psalteries and harps, stood at the
east end of the altar, and with them *an hundred and*

twenty priests sounding with trumpets:) it came even to pass, as the trumpeters and singers were as one, to make one sound to be heard in praising and thanking the Lord; and when they lifted up their voice with the trumpets and cymbals and instruments of music, and praised the Lord, saying, For He is good; for His mercy endureth for ever: that then the house was filled with a cloud, even the house of the Lord; so that the priests could not stand to minister by reason of the cloud: for the glory of the Lord had filled the house of God." It is difficult for us to believe that the number of priests sounding the trumpets was inserted in the record without a purpose. Certainly, there is a connection between the glory of the Lord filling the material Temple of those ancient days and the filling of the spiritual temples in this new dispensation.

4. THE GIFT

In John 7:37, 38 the Lord Jesus said, "If any man thirst, let him come unto Me and drink. He that believeth on Me, as the Scripture hath said, out of his innermost being (or, from within him) shall flow rivers of living water." John adds this note, "But this spake He of the Spirit, which they that believe on Him should receive: for the Holy Ghost was not yet given, because that Jesus was not yet glorified." These verses definitely point to Pentecost, as the apostle Peter declared: "Therefore being by the right hand of God exalted, having received of the Father the promise of the Holy Ghost, He hath shed forth this, which ye now see and hear" (Acts 2:33).

It was to be expected that when the Holy Spirit was given in a way that could never be repeated—

when He, the Third Person of the Trinity, became the Active Agent of the Godhead in performing the Father's will in the Church—that inaugural ceremonies, distinct and superior to all others, should attend this special Gift. Accordingly we read: "And suddenly there came a sound from heaven as of a rushing mighty wind, and it filled all the house where they were sitting. And there appeared unto them cloven tongues like as of fire, and it sat upon each of them. And they were all filled with the Holy Ghost and began to speak with other tongues, as the Spirit gave them utterance." [1]

B. THE PENTECOSTAL EXPERIENCE IS A PATTERN

And yet, despite the fact that there were many aspects of Pentecost which were peculiar to that day alone, never to be repeated, there were some things

---

[1] Acts 2:1-4.

[2] "The day of Pentecost is emphatically the complement of the great days of the New Testament. The visible glories of this day are the fitting sequel, the almost natural sequel, of the more veiled glories of certain days that had preceded it. The heavenly luster and music of the day of incarnation, unique as they were, reached the eye and ear of but few. The world was asleep! The dread, tremendous glory of the day of crucifixion, charged though it was with fullest significance, was not seen to be such at the time. The glories of the day of resurrection undeniably opened eyes and hearts to the keenest and most thankful appreciation of them, but their appeal was to a very limited number. When the calm, sweet, strange glory of ascension day revealed a vision of literally endless light, the scene undoubtedly began to widen, if only that it so heightened. And now but a short interval has passed, and there is a certain manifestation given to this day of Pentecost which reflects floods of glory upon the Giver, and pours light and hope, new and amazing, upon a world well-nigh prostrate." *Pulpit Commentary*, Vol. 41, p. 74.

about the day that were established as a pattern for future believers.

1. THE PERSONAL NATURE OF THE BAPTISM

This was a direct communication between God and man. John the Baptist showed the personal nature of this experience by saying, "He shall baptize YOU with the Holy Ghost." The glorified Son had received of the Father the promise of the Holy Ghost and had sent Him unto His disciples, thus fulfilling His own promise to them (John 15:26). Every believer throughout the Church Age who has received this promise can testify that it has conformed to that of the one hundred and twenty at Pentecost in this regard; i.e., it has brought them into personal contact with the Lord Jesus.

2. THE PURPOSE OF THE BAPTISM

Jesus established the purpose of the baptism or filling with the Spirit in Luke 24:49—"But tarry ye in the city of Jerusalem, until ye be endued with power from on high." Again in Acts 1:8 He said, "But ye shall receive power after that the Holy Ghost is come upon you." It will not be possible for us to deal fully with this point in this volume. We only ask those who disagree with us to be patient until they are presented with a thorough treatment of the subject. We are not ignorant of opposing views, but, in conjunction with many Pentecostal and non-Pentecostal students of the Word, we affirm that the *primary* (we do not say the *only*) purpose of the baptism at and since Pentecost was and is the enduement of believers with "power from on high."

[197]

3. THE EVIDENCE OF THE BAPTISM

(a) It is a matter of record that the experience at Pentecost was a charismatic one; i.e., it was of a transcendent and miraculous character, producing extraordinary effects which were visible to onlookers. There its initial oncoming was signalized by utterances by the one hundred and twenty in languages never learned by them. It is our belief that the speaking in tongues on that occasion formed the pattern for every similar baptism or charismatic enduement. The apostle Peter evidently concurred in this view, for he described the reception of the Spirit by Cornelius and his household (Acts 10) in these words, "The Holy Ghost fell on them, *as on us at the beginning*" (Acts 11:15; 15:8).

(b) What about the wind and fire at Pentecost? Why should the speaking with other tongues be singled out of the three supernatural manifestations as the initial, physical evidence of the baptism with the Holy Ghost? This question is often asked of Pentecostal people today, and we believe that it deserves an answer.

The "sound as of a rushing mighty wind" and the "cloven tongues like as of fire" were accompaniments of the Holy Spirit in His official descent from heaven and in His outward and visible revelation of His presence. These demonstrations had occurred before Pentecost; whereas speaking in tongues (at Babel the new Tongues became the native languages of the speakers) was distinctly a Pentecostal and post-Pentecostal experience. The wind and the fire were outside the disciples themselves and in the realm of nature: but the Galileans themselves spoke with other tongues. The wind and fire preceded the filling of the believer; speaking in tongues, however, came as a result of the filling.

[198]

The wind and fire were never repeated after this occasion; on the other hand, speaking with tongues is the recorded accompaniment of several subsequent fillings with the Spirit in the Book of Acts.

We would also point out the superiority of tongues over these first two signs. As we have mentioned, the wind and the fire were natural forces, not of human volition. Now consider the speaking in tongues. Here the Lord must deal with the human will which He recognizes as sovereign, and which He will not set aside. To exert His will and power is not enough; He also needs the voluntary surrender of man to bring about the perfect manifestation. And in the case of the speaking in tongues, man must yield not only his will, but also his whole being—his physical, mental, vocal and spiritual faculties. Yet, we read that the disciples were "all with one accord" —in accord with one another (a miracle in itself!) and with God; i.e., in perfect yieldedness to the Holy Ghost. This speaking with other tongues, as the Spirit gave them utterance, was surely the transcendent miracle!

(c) It is true that the tongues spoken by the disciples were distinct; yet it is also true that they were basic. They were distinct in that they were understood by the audience, whereas there is no other Scriptural instance in which the tongues spoken at the reception of the Spirit were understood; they were basic in that they were tongues, given supernatural utterance by the Spirit, and thus providing the pattern for all baptisms or fillings of the Spirit.

The tongues spoken on Pentecost were no doubt used of the Lord to attract the interest of the "devout men, out of every nation under heaven," who were at Jerusalem at that time. We grant this because it is a matter of Scriptural history, but we do not agree with the expositors who regard this as the only reason for their appearance at Pentecost, for in later instances we find tongues exercised without a multitude being present. We do not desire to evade the fact that the *glossolalia* at Pentecost was of a special kind, but we do believe that it was only natural to expect an outstanding manifestation of tongues in their first appearance in the Christian era, ʌnd as a commemoration of the first filling of Christian believers; and, perhaps, as an indication of the plan of the Holy Spirit in this dispensation to carry the gospel to all nations. The tongues of Pentecost were distinct, and yet they set the pattern for future baptisms in the Holy Spirit.

(d) T. J. McCROSSAN has advanced an argument to the effect that all of the one hundred and twenty did not speak with tongues on the day of Pentecost. He writes:

"About four o'clock one morning we were suddenly awakened out of a sound sleep, when a voice said to us, 'Did you notice last night, when you read Acts 2, that one of the peoples which heard their very own (idios) languages (dialektos) spoken on the day of Pentecost, was the inhabitants of Judea?' We praised God for calling our attention to this fact, for we knew that the Galileans (the whole hundred and twenty were *Galileans*—Acts 2:7), and the Judeans spoke the very same language in Christ's day; viz., the Aramaic, called Hebrew in the New Testament.

"Schaff-Herzog's Encyclopedia (Vol. 1, p. 125): 'After the exile the Aramaic gradually became the popular language of Palestine; not only of Galilee and Samaria, but also of Judea. Christ and the apostles spoke it.' Here then we have positive proof that some of the hundred and twenty Galileans, after having been filled with the Holy Ghost, praised God in their very own language, but they did it only as the Holy Spirit gave them to utter forth. The Holy Spirit was running their tongues just as completely as He was running the tongues of those other Galileans speaking some foreign language. Now since the Holy Spirit made some of the one hundred and twenty Galileans praise the Lord in their very own tongues, we ought to expect that He will cause some of His saints to do the same today.'"[1]

In order for Mr. McCrossan to arrive at this conclusion it is necessary for him to overlook some important points in the narrative. The fourth verse distinctly states that all the disciples spoke with OTHER tongues; i.e., tongues other than their own. This statement is a flat contradiction to Mr. Mc-Crossan's claim that "the Holy Spirit made some of the one hundred and twenty Galileans praise the Lord in their very own tongue." Whatever else the words, "in Judea," may mean, they surely cannot be interpreted as contradictory to Acts 2:4.

There is a real basis for the belief that the language spoken by both Galileans and Judeans was the popular Aramaic, so an explanation must be offered for the astonishment which the Judeans manifested when they heard the Galileans speaking in the Judean tongue. This fact most certainly suggests a linguistic difference of some kind. It seems to us that Matthew Henry's comment helps to solve the

---

[1]*Speaking With Other Tongues, Sign or Gift—Which?* p. 35.

difficulty: "Thence we come in order to Judea, which ought to be mentioned because, though the language was the same with that which the disciples spoke, yet before, they spoke it with a north-country tone and dialect ('Thou art a Galilean, and thy speech betrayeth thee'), but now they spoke it as correctly as the inhabitants of Judea themselves did."

This speaking without an accent, and this forming of a number of strictly Judean words, was as impossible to the Galileans as it was for the Ephraimites to say, "Shibboleth" (Judges 12:6). It was as milaculous for their north-country tone and dialect no longer to betray them, as it was for their other *glossolalic* brethren to speak pure Latin, or Persian, or Arabic.

D. A. HAYES cites a modern manifestation of tongues which appears to be somewhat similar to this Pentecostal experience. During the Welsh revival of 1904, "young Welshmen and Welshwomen who could not speak a dozen words in Welsh in ordinary conversation were remarkably and, as it seemed to them, supernaturally empowered to pray fervently and fluently for five or ten minutes in idiomatic Welsh. This enabling to speak in what was supposedly an unknown tongue was to many people the most remarkable feature of that remarkable revival."

(e) One Sunday morning in Washington, D. C., we were somewhat startled to hear a non-Pentecostal pastor exhorting his people to seek the Lord for the infilling of the Spirit. Knowing that he belonged to an' organization which quite vigorously opposed tongues, we were rather curious to hear his views upon the results of that filling. And when he called their attention to Acts 2:4, we really did get curious!

"What happened when the disciples were filled with the Holy Ghost?" he asked. "They began to do something! And what was it they began to do? They began . . . to testify, and pray, and to lead souls to Christ!"

We sat in that lovely church wondering from what version of the Scriptures the good pastor was reading! All of the versions which we had ever consulted on Acts 2:4 gave rendering similar to that of the Authorized Version: "And they were all filled with the Holy Ghost, and began TO SPEAK WITH OTHER TONGUES, as the Spirit gave them utterance"! Nothing could be plainer than those words, and we found it exceedingly difficult to justify such a direct evasion of the speaking with tongues. We agreed thoroughly with the pastor that the other qualities would be part of the Spirit-filled life, but such an obvious attempt to detract the attention of his people from the immediate, outward result of that first outpouring of the Spirit was hardly defensible.

CHAPTER 11

The Spirit and the Samaritans

THE next case of receiving the Spirit is found in the eighth chapter of Acts.[1] Philip the evangelist preached Christ to the city of Samaria. "And the people with one accord gave heed unto those things which Philip spake, hearing and seeing the miracles which he did. . . . And there was great joy in the city. . . . When they believed Philip preaching the things concerning the kingdom of God, and the name of Jesus Christ, they were baptized, both men and women." This revival in Samaria was acknowledged by the church at Jerusalem by the sending of the apostles, and acknowledged by God by the sending of the Holy Ghost (Acts 8:14-17).

One striking feature of the Scriptural narrative of this reception of the Spirit is the absence of any mention of tongues. This would appear to be a fatal blow to the view expressed by Chrysostom and embraced by Pentecostalists today: "Whoever

---

[1] Acts 4:31 was a *re*filling of the disciples, and not a first filling or baptism with the Spirit.

was baptized in apostolic days, he straightway spake with tongues." Search as we will, we cannot find the words, "and began to speak with other tongues," added to verse seventeen. On the other hand, it seems that the critics of Pentecost are so happily proclaiming the absence of tongues that they do not take time to read what the record does say. As we examine the account, we are led to believe that the Pentecostal "evidence doctrine" can be sustained despite the absence of mention of tongues here. Since all courts will accept circumstantial evidence as support for a case, we propose to submit circumstantial facts here as proof that tongues were present, even though they were not included in the report.

We would notice first that the enduement of power given to the Samaritans was of the same charismatic character as that of the disciples at Pentecost. It was a definite, sudden, inspirational experience. This can be seen in the language used by Luke: "For as yet He [the Holy Ghost] was *fallen* upon none of them. . . . Then laid they their hands on them, and they *received* the Holy Ghost." These words describe the same kind of experience as that of Cornelius and his household: "While Peter yet spake these words, the Holy Ghost *fell* on all them that heard the word." Such language is not used to describe a quiet, gradual experience, nor is it used to depict a work of the Spirit which is only spiritual and invisible.

Verses 18 and 19 tell us, "And when Simon saw that through laying on of the apostles' hands the Holy Ghost was given, he offered them money, saying, Give me also this power, that on whomsoever I lay hands, he may receive the Holy Ghost." No one can doubt from these words that there was an outward evidence of the reception of· the Spirit. It does not seem plausible that a man of Simon's caliber would offer money for the ability to produce an invisible effect.

Now what did Simon see? What manifestation did he witness that made him eager to possess the power to impart this Gift?

It was not that those who received the Holy Ghost suddenly began to perform miracles of healing, or to cast out demons, for Simon had already witnessed these things in the ministry of Philip. Nor could it have been a sudden expression of great joy, since the revival under Philip had been the scene of many joyful shouts from the lips of those who had been delivered from physical infirmities and demonic bondage. Nor do we believe that Simon would have offered money for the ability to bring forth a spontaneous overflowing of love. Peter's denunciation of him leads us to believe that Simon had no real appreciation of spiritual qualities.

What, then, did Simon see? It is our conviction that Simon witnessed the *glossolalia*. This miracle of utterance was entirely new to him, and would arrest his attention as nothing else. How he would covet the power to impart this gift! "The voice they uttered was awful in its range, in its tones, in its modulation, in its startling, almost penetrating power; the words they spoke were exalted, intense, passionate, full of mystic significance." With this power he could again take his place before the people as at least the equal of Philip. The multitudes would wonder at him, and acclaim him again as "the great power of God!"

In Chapter 13 we shall see that the six Jewish brethren were convinced that "on the Gentiles also

was poured out the gift of the Holy Ghost" only
when they heard them speak with tongues. Why
should we believe that the brethren from Jerusalem,
especially Peter (Acts 10), would require any less
proof in this earlier instance at Samaria? "The Jew
looked upon the Samaritan as he looked upon the
Gentile. His hostility to the Samaritan was probably
greater, in proportion, as he was nearer."[1] See John
4:8. It is entirely within the realm of possibility that
back at the church in Jerusalem Peter allayed all
fears by saying of the Samaritans, as he did of
Cornelius' household, "God which knoweth the
hearts, bare them witness, giving them the Holy
Ghost, even as He did unto us." (Acts 15:8).

To prove that we are not alone in our belief
that the Samaritans spoke in tongues upon receiving
the Holy Spirit, we turn to the best-known commentators. Their testimonies in this regard, though
not infallible, do merit the respect of all, for they were
men sound in doctrine, orthodox in exposition and
exegesis, and scholars of the highest rank. And we
might add that their testimonies will be lacking in
prejudice, for they lived and wrote long before this
Twentieth Century Pentecostal Revival.[2]

1. MATTHEW HENRY (1662-1714): "How they
advanced and improved those of them that were
sincere; it is said (v. 16), that the Holy Spirit
was as yet fallen upon none of them, in those
extraordinary powers which were conveyed by the
descent upon the day of Pentecost; they were none of
them endued with the gift of tongues, which seems

---

[1]Conybeare and Howson, *Life and Epistles of St. Paul.*
[2]These quotations (with the exception of the last two) are
taken from *Life and Letters of St. Paul,* by P. C. Nelson.

then to have been the most usual, immediate effect
of the pouring out of the Spirit. See Acts 10:45, 46.
This was both an eminent sign to them that believed
not, and of excellent service to them that did. This
and other gifts they had not, only they were
baptized in the name of the Lord Jesus, and so
engaged in Him and interested in Him, which was
necessary to salvation, and in that they had joy
and satisfaction (v.8), though they could not speak
with tongues." (Matthew Henry finished his great
commentary on October 2, 1706, and the edition
from which we quote was printed in London in
1811.)

2. ADAM CLARKE (1762-1832), a Methodist:
"They prayed and laid their hands on the disciples,
and God sent down the gift; so, the blessing came
from God by the apostles, and not from the apostles
to the people. But for what purpose was the Holy
Spirit given? Certainly not for the sanctification of
the souls of the people: this they had on believing in
Christ Jesus; and this the apostles never dispensed.
It was the miraculous gifts of the Spirit which were
thus communicated—the speaking with different
tongues, and these extraordinary qualifications which
are necessary for the successful preaching of the gospel." (The volume from which this quotation is
taken was published in London in 1851. The
Commentary appeared between 1810 and 1826, a
volume at a time.)

3. THOMAS SCOTT (1747-1821), Episcopalian:
"Many teachers, and probably private Christians,
wrought miracles and spake with tongues, as the
Spirit gave them utterance, but the honor of communicating those gifts by the imposition of hands
and prayer, was, generally at least, restricted to the

apostles. When Simon, therefore, saw the effects which followed from the laying on of their hands, he concluded that they could, if they chose, impart to him a similar power, supposing that the whole power was at their disposal. (Note 2 Cor. 13:7-10.) This he supposed would admirably subserve his purpose of obtaining honor and wealth: for by enabling men at his own will to speak foreign languages, without the trouble of learning them, and to cure diseases by word, he would not only carry on a most lucrative trade, but be almost adored as a deity," etc. (This edition from which we quote was printed in Boston in 1830. Both Henry and Scott are quoted at greater length in the Comprehensive Commentary. Our edition was published in Philadelphia in 1857. First edition, 1796.)

4. JOSEPH BENSON (1748-1821), Methodist: "Then laid they their hands on them. . . . And they received the Holy Ghost—in answer to the prayers of these apostles; that is, these new converts spoke with tongues, and performed other extraordinary works," etc. (Edition of 1857.)

5. WILLIAM BURKITT (1650-1703), Episcopalian: "They prayed and laid their hands on them and they received the Holy Ghost. Whereby the Holy Ghost is not to be understood the sanctifying graces of the Holy Ghost, which the apostles never did nor could dispense, but the extraordinary gifts of the Holy Ghost, the gift of tongues and prophecy, and the power to work miracles." (*Expository Notes on the New Testament,* 1844.)

6. CHARLES JOHN ELLICOTT, Episcopalian: "When Simon saw that through laying on of the apostles' hands. . . . The words imply that the result was something visible and conspicuous. A

change was wrought: and men spoke with tongues and prophesied." (*The New Testament Commentary for English Readers*, London, third edition.)

7. HERMAN OLSHAUSEN (1796-1858), Lutheran: "Simon perceived the extraordinary effects of the laying on of the apostles' hands, in the gifts which were exhibited, particularly the speaking in tongues." (*Commentary on the New Testament*. Translated from the German by A. C. Kendrick, 1850.)

8. PHILIP SCHAFF (1819-1893), Reformed: "The gifts of the Holy Ghost were plainly visible. The laying on of the apostles' hands conferred something more than the inward spiritual grace; outward miraculous gifts of some kind or other were plainly bestowed." (*International Illustrated Commentary on the New Testament*. New York, 1888.)

9. *Lutheran Commentary* (New York, 1906): "When Simon saw"—lit., when Simon had seen the effects of the communication of the Holy Ghost, speaking with tongues, and like (comp. Acts 2:4; 10:46)."

10. BERNHARD WEISS, Lutheran, in his commentary on the New Testament, translated from the German by Schodde and Wilson: "We must not forget, in this connection, that the communication of the Holy Spirit in those days was manifested in the ability to work wonders, and was not purely subjective possession." (Edition 1906.)

11. ALBERT BARNES (1798-1870), Presbyterian: "The phrase, 'the gift of the Holy Ghost,' and the 'descent of the Holy Ghost,' signified not merely His ordinary influence in converting sinners, but those extraordinary influences that attended the first preaching of the gospel . . . the power of speaking

with new tongues (ch. 11), the power of working miracles, etc. Acts 19:6." (*Notes on the New Testament*, 1841.)

12. D. D. WHEDON (1808-1888), Methodist: "We have here, as at Caesarea (10:44-48), and at Ephesus (19:5-7), a miniature Pentecost, in which a new inauguration seems to take place by the repetition of the same charismatic effusion." (*Commentary on the New Testament*, 1890.)

13. ALEXANDER MACLAREN, Baptist: "The Samaritans had been baptized but still they lacked the gift of the Spirit. Now the context shows that that gift was attended with outward effects which Simon saw, and wishes to be able to impart. The Samaritans had not yet received the Holy Ghost, . . . that is, the special gifts, such as those of Pentecost. That fact proves that baptism is not necessarily and inseparably connected with the gift of the Spirit and chapter 10:44, 47, proves that the Spirit may be given before baptism." (*Expositions of Holy Scripture*, 25 vols.)

14. H. B. HACKETT (1808-1875), Baptist: "They received the Holy Spirit as the Author of the endowments conferred on them. Among these may have been the gift of tongues (see 2:4; 10:46), and also that of prophecy, as well as the power of working miracles." (*Commentary on the Original Text of the Acts of the Apostles*, 1858.)

15. WILLIAM ROBERTSON: "That prayer was answered by an outpouring of the Spirit, accompanied by some of the manifestations which marked His coming at Pentecost." (*Studies in the Acts of the Apostles*.)

16. J. S. EXCELL, Editor, *The Preacher's Homi-*

letical Commentary: "This shows that the recipients of the Holy Ghost must, in some external fashion, ... probably through speaking with tongues or working miracles, . . . have indicated their possession of the heavenly gift."

17. M. F. SADLER, *Commentary on the New Testament* (12 Vols.) : "It is clear from this that the manifestations of the presence of the Spirit were in outward gifts, such as healing, or speaking with tongues. If they had only been gifts of spiritual grace and holiness, Simon would not have discerned them, or would have held them in no account."

18. J. G. BUTLER, *Bible Word*: "They, like all the converts, had received the ordinary gifts bestowed in regeneration. Now they received the peculiar extraordinary gifts of Pentecost."

19. HENRY ALFORD, *Greek Testament—with English Notes*: "Idon (seeing). Its effects were therefore visible, and consequently, the effect of the laying on of the apostles' hands was not the inward, but the outward miraculous gifts of the Spirit."

20. W. R. NICOLL, *The Expositor's Greek Testament* (*with English Notes*) : "Dr. Hort, who holds that the reception of the Holy Spirit is here explained as in 10:44 by reference to the manifestation of the gift of tongues, etc., points out that the verb is not *elabon* (the aorist) but *elambanon*, and he therefore renders it, 'showed a succession of signs of the Spirit.' "

21. CONYBEARE AND HOWSON: "When the news came to Jerusalem, Peter and John were sent by the apostles, and the same miraculous testimony attended their presence which had been given on the day of Pentecost."

22. PULPIT COMMENTARY: "In this case, as at Pentecost, the extraordinary gift of the Holy Ghost was conferred."

Many more quotations could be added, but these should be sufficient. It should be observed: (1) that all the commentators quoted agree that there was some visible, outward, miraculous manifestation or evidence of the Holy Ghost; (2) that nearly all of them mention speaking with tongues as almost certainly the manifestation or as one of the manifestations.

We conclude this chapter by saying that we do not enter our conjectures as positive proof that the Samaritans spoke in tongues, but we submit these facts and testimonies as circumstantial evidence supporting what is definitely stated in other instances. The burden of proof would most certainly seem to lie upon those who assert that speaking with tongues was not present on this occasion.

CHAPTER 12

The Disciple at Damascus

THE principal character in the third recorded case of reception of the Spirit in Acts is Saul of Tarsus, later known as the apostle Paul. Again we Pentecostalists are confronted with the absence of tongues in the narrative. Again we are reduced to the task of securing circumstantial evidence. Our non-Pentecostal friends are particularly happy over this instance, for there are no implications whatsoever in the historical record that Paul's infilling with the Spirit was accompanied by tongues.

DR. WALTER L. WILSON makes a rather strange statement about Paul and tongues in his booklet *Facts or Fancies* (p. 22): "There is no evidence that Paul ever spoke with tongues. In 1 Corinthians 14:18 he tells us that he did, but no record is given about it."[1] This comment by Dr. Wilson puzzled us quite a bit. We knew that he did not intend to reflect upon Paul's honesty, or to doubt Paul's own testimony—"I thank my God, I speak with tongues more than ye all." We finally came to the conclusion

---

[1] Used by permission of Zondervan Publishing House, Grand Rapids, Mich.

that he was emphasizing the fact that the ninth chapter of Acts does not speak of the exercise of tongues by Paul.

Is it possible that Dr. Wilson has never made the discovery that the ninth chapter of Acts also fails to tell us that Paul was filled with the Spirit? It is true that Ananias put his hands on him, and said, "Brother Saul, the Lord, even Jesus, that appeared unto thee in the way as thou camest, has sent me, that thou mightest receive thy sight, and be filled with the Holy Ghost." But what saith the next verse? "And immediately there fell from his eyes as it had been scales: and he received sight forthwith, and arose, and was baptized." Not a single word about his reception of the Spirit! Not a single word about the fulfillment of the prophecy of Ananias, "That thou mightest . . . be filled with the Holy Ghost!" Of course, we all conclude that the will of the Lord was accomplished in this respect as well as in the restoration of his sight. However, if our non-Pentecostal friends insist on emphasizing the absence in the record of Paul's speaking in tongues, we can say, just as logically, that he was not filled with the Holy Ghost at that hour. How could there possibly be any mention of tongues in the narrative, when there is a complete absence of mention of the experience of which the speaking with tongues is but a part?

At the time that Paul was writing the First Epistle to the Corinthians it is certain that he possessed the gift of tongues (1 Corinthians 14:18). This being so, there must have been a first time when he was given this miracle of utterance. The logical place for this primary experience would have been, as in the case of all the other apostles, at the hour when he was filled with the Spirit. It is apparent, as we shall see in the next chapter, that speaking with tongues was the accepted evidence of the filling of the Spirit among the apostles and the other brethren at Jerusalem. It is unthinkable that the chiefest of apostles could have received an experience which did not measure up to the standard. And if Peter and his brethren found assurance in the glossolalic utterances of friendly Gentiles, how great was the assurance which Ananias received upon hearing the arch-persecutor of the church speak with tongues just like the very saints against whom he had been breathing out threatenings and slaughter!

CHAPTER 13

The Holy Ghost and Cornelius' Household

PETER and his six brethren journeyed to Caesarea with fear and misgiving in their hearts. To them it was "an unlawful thing for a man that is a Jew to keep company, or come unto one of another nation." What, then, was responsible for this unheard of journey to the Roman centurion's house? It was the vision given to Peter, the providential appearance of the three messengers in Joppa, and the voice of the Spirit to the apostle saying, "Arise therefore, and get thee down, and go with them, doubting nothing: for I have sent them" (Acts 10:20). But prejudice which extended back for centuries through generation after generation was not easily dismissed. (Peter himself, in spite of all that God showed him on this occasion, returned at a later date to the bigotry so common among his countrymen. Gal. 2:11.) Still, after hearing Cornelius' testimony at Caesarea, Peter did seem to grasp the fact that the Gentiles were to be included in the new kingdom.

Suddenly, something happened that convinced not only Peter but also his skeptical friends that God was "no respecter of persons." The Word declares, "While Peter yet spake these words, the Holy Ghost fell on all them which heard the word. And they of the circumcision were astonished, as many as came with Peter, because that on the Gentiles was poured out the gift of the Holy Ghost. For they heard them speak with tongues, and magnify God. Then answered Peter, Can any man forbid water, that these should not be baptized, which have received the Holy Ghost as well as we?"[1] The great wall of racial prejudice, more impregnable than the wall of Jericho, had come tumbling down, when God authenticated these Gentile recipients of the Spirit by giving them utterance in tongues.

We Pentecostalists, with our emphasis upon the evidential character of the speaking in tongues at that hour, are often accused of overlooking the distinctiveness of this first outpouring of the Spirit upon Gentiles. On the other hand, it seems to us that many non-Pentecostalists are so absorbed by the racial and dispensational aspects of this occasion that they overlook the evidential character of the tongues. But why must these two views be mutually exclusive? The *glossolalia* at Jerusalem had a significance beyond its relationship to the filling with the Spirit, and the same is true of its appearance here. At the same time, we believe that it is entirely possible for phenomenon, despite its special significance on both of these occasions, to signify also the reception of the Holy Spirit.[2]

---

[1] Acts 10:44-47.

[2] Often the Pentecostal view is opposed on the grounds that the three recorded instances of tongues in Acts occurred in *companies*, the supposition being that there was a special significance in the exercise of this phenomenon by a whole company. But even should there be some particular import connected with a company speaking with tongues, would that

It is a matter of fact that God used the speaking with tongues to break down the "middle wall of partition" between the Jews and Gentiles. But is it not also a matter of fact that Peter and his comrades looked upon tongues as positive evidence "that on the Gentiles was poured out the gift of the Holy Ghost"? Our dispensationally minded friend would have us to see only the phrase, "on the Gentiles"; whereas we would point out the importance of the latter part of the statement as well—"was poured out the gift of the Holy Ghost." Now what was it that made these astonished Jews so certain "that on the Gentiles was poured out the gift of the Holy Ghost"? "FOR (because, by reason of, on account of) *they heard them speak with tongues, and magnify God.*" This one supernatural sign was all the proof they needed. In their minds speaking with tongues must have been inseparably connected with the baptism with the Spirit, or else they never would have accepted it as the incontrovertible evidence of that experience. And it should be pointed out that if those who spoke with tongues at Caesarea had been Jews instead of Gentiles, their experience would have been acknowledged by them of the circumcision as a genuine baptism with the Spirit.

Why cannot our non-Pentecostal friends see a dispensational significance in the fact that both Jew and Gentile believers spoke with tongues upon receiving the Holy Spirit? Why cannot they see that the basically similar experiences at Jerusalem and Caesarea reveal God's plan for that experience throughout

---

invalidate the meaning of tongues to the individual within the company? The feeding of the five thousand established the Messianic claims of the Lord, but it also satisfied the hunger of everyone in that multitude.

this whole dispensation, in which there is "neither Jew nor Greek"? Surely this dispensational view is as tenable as that which attributes the presence of tongues on both of those occasions only to the initial outpourings of the Spirit upon Jew and Gentile, and which denies that this phenomenon was the common and accepted evidence of every individual experience of being filled with the Spirit in the early church.

A vigorous protest is lodged frequently against Pentecostal people for their insistence that all baptisms with the Spirit must conform to their own experience. This insistence, our critics say, is indicative of extreme spiritual pride. But Peter and his six brethren did not look thus upon their demand that the Gentiles conform to their experience. If Cornelius and his household had not spoken with tongues (i.e., had not received the Holy Ghost "as on us at the beginning"[1]) their experience would not have been recognized as up to the standard. And when we today judge the experience of others, it is not our purpose to make all conform to our personal experience, but to require that all measure up to the standard baptism with the Spirit which the believers of the early church experienced.

---

[1]The phrase, "as on us at the beginning," does not imply an exact duplication of Pentecost—wind, fire, recognized languages. God did not have to repeat the distinctive manifestations of Pentecost, since the basic manifestation of speaking with tongues was all that was needed.

CHAPTER 14

The Experience
of the Ephesians

THIS is the third case in which it is recorded that those receiving the Spirit spoke with tongues. It seems that our friends who offer a dispensational explanation for the other two cases (Acts 2:4; 10:46) are at a loss to explain the appearance of tongues at Ephesus. There was no racial significance here; indeed, no special purpose at all to which they can attribute the phenomenon. Hence, this is usually termed an "appendix." But it must be manifest even to these teachers that its very existence weakens their whole dispensational theory.

Happily for them, H. J. Stolee, Th.D., a teacher in the Lutheran Bible Institute, Seattle, Wash., has come to their rescue. Mr. Stole recognizes the problem that exists in this Ephesian episode., but he believes that he has the proper solution. The speaking in tongues was given here to accomplish the same purpose as its previous manifestations in Jerusalem and Caesarea, viz., the removing of doubts and prejudices and the establishing of facts and doctrines which were to be basic to the missionary program of the Church throughout the centuries. But what doubts and prejudices needed to be removed, and what facts and doctrines needed to be established here at Ephesus?

Mr. Stolee writes that the Lord was seeking to impress upon the Ephesian disciples the divine approval of the baptism which had just been administered unto them by the Apostle Paul. These twelve men had been taught that God had sent John to baptize, and had submitted to the baptism of John. Now, it was necessary for God to reveal to them— and all succeeding generations of Christian believers —that the baptism which was instituted and commanded by Christ was to be accepted as the true and permanent baptism. It was not enough for Paul to explain to them that John's baptism had been replaced by Christian baptism; the fact must be demonstrated by a supernatural sign.[1]

Thus, according to Mr. Stolee, we Pentecostalists are mistaken in citing the extraordinary experience of the Ephesians as the normal experience of early disciples. The chief purpose of the speaking with tongues here was not to make manifest that the Ephesians had received the Holy Spirit, he claims, but to confirm the fact that Christian baptism was the only baptism approved of God in the present dispensation.

---

[1]For his complete views, see his work, *Pentecostalism*, issued by the Augsburg Publishing House, Minneapolis, Minn.

It is difficult for us to see the need for a supernatural confirmation of Christian baptism. Mark tells us that "they went forth, and preached everywhere, the Lord working with them, and confirming the WORD with signs following," but we cannot find a single instance of a specific confirmation of an ORDINANCE by a miracle. For example, the Lord's Supper needed no miraculous confirmation to establish its precedence over the Passover Feast. The very fact that it was instituted by the Lord Jesus in place of the Passover meal, and that it was taught and practiced by the apostles whose ministry as a whole was approved by God with signs and wonders, assured its acceptance by the Church. Why, then, should water baptism merit what its companion ordinance did not merit? Had not this mode of baptism been instituted also by the Lord, and had it not been a constant practice in the Church for some twenty years?

The speaking with tongues at Ephesus had about as much vital connection with Christian baptism as the dove and the voice from heaven had with John's baptism. Those two signs were not given to establish the genuiness of John's baptism, a sign in itself, but to make manifest the deity of Jesus of Nazareth. Likewise at Ephesus, the *glossolalia* was not given to authenticate Christian baptism but to make manifest the presence of the Spirit of God, the Third Person of the Trinity. Where in the Scriptures has God sent a sign to confirm a sign? He employed tongues as a supernatural means to establish the supernatural fact of the infilling of the Ephesians with the Holy Ghost. Andrew Murray says: "Paul prayed for them and laid his hands on them, and they received the Holy Spirit; and then, in token of the fact that this whole transaction was a heavenly reality, they obtained a share in the Pentecostal miracle, and spake with tongues."[1]

Because the sixth verse says, "They spake with tongues, and prophesied," some would have us to believe that all twelve of the Ephesian disciples did not speak with tongues. It is said that in a description of any company statements are often made which would indicate that some action was indulged in by the whole company, when in reality only some took part. For instance, it might be said of an audience, "They laughed and cried, shouted and sang." It would not mean that every member of the audience performed every one of the acts, but that some did one thing, and some did another, but they together did all the things mentioned in the description. So at Ephesus some spoke with tongues, and some prophesied, but all together the twelve "spake with tongues, and prophesied."

Frankly, we do not believe it necessary to dwell at length on this desperate attempt to evade the plain statement of the record. If men are determined to sidestep truth, all manner of wresting the Scripture is possible to them, and no amount of reasoning from us could convince them of their error. "Because they receive not the love of the truth . . . God shall send them strong delusion, that they should believe a lie." 2 Thessalonians 2:10, 11. That delusion which to them is so plausible, so convincing, is the result of a substitution of a chain of human reasoning for the simple facts of inspired Church history.

In the first place, there were only twelve men in

---

[1] *The Full Blessing of Pentecost*, p. 18, Fleming H. Revell Co., New York, N. Y.

this company, and it does not seem reasonable that a principle applying to a huge audience would apply to just twelve men. Even so, at Jerusalem, where there were ten times as many disciples as at Ephesus, all spoke with tongues. And a larger company was assembled at Caesarea also when the Holy Ghost fell, but all spoke with tongues there. We could cite innumerable commentators to the effect that all twelve of the Ephesians spoke with tongues, but why should we do this when the Word of God itself is so clear? It is just as logical to argue that the "they" of verse 5 does not refer to all twelve, but who would dare to say that all of them were not baptized in the name of the Lord Jesus? Taking the record at its face value—"They spake with tongues and prophesied"—one must come to the conclusion that in addition to their speaking with tongues, the twelve men prophesied, but all spoke with tongues.

CHAPTER 15

Summary of the Five Cases

FOR the past five chapters we have been analyzing the relationship of tongues to the baptism with the Holy Spirit. Now we present a brief summary of our findings, with the hope that it will help to explain the meaning of the speaking with tongues in the Book of Acts.

1. *In three out of five cases* (i.e., at Jerusalem, Caesarea, and Ephesus) it is absolutely certain that speaking with tongues was the immediate, outward result of the baptism. Despite frantic efforts by some to prove otherwise, the plain and unmistakable statement of the Word is that every recipient in these instances was given utterance in tongues by the Holy Spirit.

2. *In four out of five cases* it is almost certain that all spoke with tongues. The record of the reception of the Spirit by the Samaritans so strongly implies the presence of tongues that every unbiased student of the Word is reasonably certain that it was manifested there too.

3. *In five out of five cases* (if we include Samaria) it is evident that all spoke with tongues at some time during their Spirit-filled life. Though it is not recorded that Paul spoke with tongues at his baptism, we know from his own testimony—"I thank my God, I

speak with tongues" (1 Corinthians 14:18)—that at a later time he was *glossolalic*. Surely, if our non-Pentecostal friends dare to base doctrine on the silence of the Word, we can safely base doctrine on the express statement of the Word!

May we pause here for a moment to give our opinion as to the absence of tongues in the record concerning the Samaritans and concerning Paul? This absence has caused many Christians to reject the Pentecostal position that speaking with tongues was the constant accompaniment of that experience in the early church. Perhaps a few remarks will help to remove this obstacle from the path of all honest-hearted believers who are earnestly seeking after truth.

We believe that Luke followed the same Spirit-inspired practice which John followed in his biography of the Lord Jesus. You will find John's practice laid down in three verses in the last two chapters of his Gospel. In John 20:30 we read, "And many other signs truly did Jesus in the presence of His disciples, which are not written in this Book." Why were not these other signs written in this Book? The reason is simple enough, "And there are also many other things which Jesus did, the which, if they should be written everyone, I suppose that even the world itself could not contain the books that should be written" (John 21:25). John was guided by the Holy Spirit to select those signs which were typical, and which were sufficient for his purpose. And what was his purpose? "But these are written that ye might believe that Jesus is the Christ, the Son of God; and that believing ye might have life through His name" (John 20:31). In other words, the beloved disciple did not write his Gospel to satisfy mockers and doubters, who

[230]

would demand that every miracle of Jesus be recounted in detail; but to strengthen the faith ("that ye might believe") of those who would see by the written examples of Jesus' words and works that He was indeed the Christ, the Son of the living God.

Likewise, Luke, in relating in Acts some of the miraculous happenings in the early church, describes them minutely, while of others he simply says, "And by the hand of the apostles were many signs and wonders wrought among the people" (Acts 5:12). He writes of the reaction of the once lame man to his miraculous healing, "And he leaping up stood, and walked, and entered with them into the temple, walking, and leaping and praising God" (Acts 3:8). On another similar occasion, however, Luke merely says, "And many . . . that were lame were healed" (Acts 8:7). No record of any "walking," "leaping," or "praising," but who would say that these same natural reactions to physical healing did not occur? No reporter is required to give all the details of an event, especially if he has mentioned them previously, or intends to mention them subsequently. His task is to report the most important facts, and to insert only enough sidelights to give proper color to the story. The most important thing about the lame Samaritans was that they were healed, and having said this Luke need not encumber his narrative with their reactions to their healing.

And it should be clearly understood that speaking with tongues was not, and is not, the most important element of the baptism with the Holy Ghost. Peter's rehearsal of the outpouring of the Spirit upon Cornelius and his household (Acts 11:4-17) did not contain a specific reference to tongues, even though that phenomenon had been the indubitable proof to him and his companions "that on the Gentiles also was poured out the gift of the Holy Ghost." While it is true that he said, "The Holy Ghost fell on them, as on us at the beginning," and thus satisfied the brethren that the Gentile experience was according to the pattern, still the actual words, "speaking with tongues," are not included in the Scriptural account of Peter's defense before the Jerusalem church.

And so it was with Luke's reporting on the *glossolalia* in the entire Book of Acts. It was not necessary for him to write of its presence in every instance of the baptism with the Spirit before we could accept it as the initial, physical evidence of that experience. Three out of five times are sufficient for all who read with an open heart, who do not demand an unnecessary recitation of details contrary to common practice in either secular or sacred reporting.

4. But some, in spite of this explanation, will continue to insist that, because specific mention of tongues is lacking in the cases of the Samaritans and Paul, it is not necessary for all to speak with tongues. But does their objection to our view relieve them of the necessity of conforming to at least the minimum number of *glossolalic* recipients of the Spirit, as found in the Word? Certainly, all will agree that the following proportion must prevail among those who receive the Spirit today, if they are to measure up to the Scriptural standard:

(a) Three out of five, or sixty per cent, *must* speak with tongues.

(b) Four out of five, or eighty per cent, *should* speak with tongues.

(c) Five out of five, or one hundred per cent.

should speak with tongues at some time during their Spirit-filled life.

But we ask you, is this proportion realized in non-Pentecostal ranks today? Do sixty per cent of those receiving the fullness of the Spirit speak with tongues? Do thirty per cent? Do ten per cent? Do one per cent? The answer to all these questions is, "NO!" In fact, it is difficult for us to see how there could be any speaking with tongues among them, since, in the great majority of non-Pentecostal groups, there is little or no definite praying for the enduement with power from on high.

It is our earnest hope that this investigation of the five cases in Acts will provoke among our non-Pentecostal friends a fresh searching of the Scriptures in regard to the infilling of the Holy Spirit. And should not we all be ever ready to conduct an examination of our doctrine and spiritual experiences to satisfy ourselves anew that they be in the faith?

CHAPTER 16

Seven Reasons Why God Chose Tongues

PENTECOSTALISTS are frequently called upon to answer the question, "Why should God choose tongues as the initial, physical evidence of the baptism with the Holy Ghost?" Perhaps the best way to introduce our answer is to ask a counter question, "Why should God choose blood as the atoning element?"[1]

To true Christians, the answer to our query is quite simple. God is sovereign. He may choose as He will without consulting anyone but Himself. But God is not only sovereign, He is also omniscient. He has known from the beginning that the life of the flesh is in the blood; that the blood is the most important element in the physical phase of the life of man and beast, and thus, when shed for another, it portrays perfectly the supreme sacrifice; that its value and symbolic nature are universally understood by the human race. Of course, other rea-

---

[1]See Leviticus 17:11.

sons could be given for God's choice of blood as the atoning element, but these are sufficient to reveal that though the choice lay ultimately in the sovereignty of God, it can be understood by the finite mind of man.

And likewise with the selection of tongues as the initial, physical evidence of the baptism with the Spirit. The High and Lofty One was not obligated to consult the opinion of man in making His sovereign choice of speaking with tongues, and yet there are a number of obvious reasons which all can easily grasp.

1. IT IS AN EXTERNAL EVIDENCE

This may seem to be a strange motive, in view of the fact that this is the most spiritual of all dispensations, the outward forms of Old Testament days having now become spiritual realities. Still there is a principle which can be observed in every dispensation; viz., as long as man is subject to earthly frailties, he is in need of at least a few outward symbols of spiritual truths. Even in this age, external signs have been given to the Church, and these signs are recognized by practically all of Christendom as a permanent part of divine worship; viz., the Lord's Supper and water baptism. That which is symbolized by these two ordinances is assuredly far more important than the ordinances themselves; but at the same time, if they had not been necessary, why did God so firmly establish them in the New Testament Church? Their very presence in the hour that now is, when the true worshipers of God worship in spirit and in truth, when the extreme ritualism of the Old Testament is done away, and when we walk by faith rather than by sight, is proof that we still need somewhat of the external.

CHRYSOSTOM tells us: "Whoever was baptized in apostolic day, he straightway spake with tongues; they at once received the Spirit; not that they saw the Spirit, for He is invisible, but God's grace bestowed some *sensible* proof of His energy. It thus made manifest to them that were without that it was the Spirit in the very person speaking." This quotation reveals clearly the reason for an outward evidence of the baptism with the Spirit. And we should remember that it was during this present dispensation that "God's grace bestowed some *sensible* proof of His energy." Therefore, to assume the attitude that speaking with tongues, because of its external nature, is no longer needed, is hardly according to New Testament truth.

And may we go a step farther, and point out that every aspect of God's work in the human heart is manifested outwardly in one form or another? While James stresses the outward, and Paul the inward, both are in perfect agreement on the fact that the inward, by its very nature, must express itself outwardly. Real love, according to Paul as well as James, will manifest itself in a practical manner (compare 1 Corinthians 13:4-8 and James 2:1-16); heart belief will produce confession of the Lord Jesus with the mouth (Romans 10:9, 10), just as it will produce the bridling of the tongue (James 1:26). Faith and works, the inner cause and the outer effect, are inseparable elements in the spiritual life.

Such a marvelous experience as the baptism with the Holy Spirit demands a marvelous manifestation. When we consider the mighty force of the onfall of the Holy Spirit upon the human spirit, what is man that he could restrain every physical and vocal reaction? How could man possibly remain silent, when He, whom the heaven of heavens cannot contain, suddenly fills His tabernacle? How could man hold his peace, when from out of his innermost being rivers of living water begin to flow with irresistible power? The rocks themselves would cry out! Let them who know not the power of the Holy Ghost remonstrate as they will, we can only look at the Scriptures, and say with Myer Pearlman: "The baptism with the Holy Ghost in apostolic days was an experience in which the Spirit of God made such a direct and powerful impact upon the spirit of man that a condition of ecstasy resulted, and in that ecstatic condition a person spoke ecstatically in a language he had never learned. When the Spirit of God makes the same impact upon us today that He made on those early disciples, we too will experience the same ecstatic condition and the same ecstatic utterance."[1]

2. IT IS A UNIFORM EVIDENCE

After quoting from Joel's prophecy the promise of the Father to pour out His Spirit on all flesh, Peter stressed the universality of the promise: "Repent and be baptized everyone of you in the name of Jesus Christ for the remission of sins, and ye shall receive the gift of the Holy Ghost. For the promise is unto you, and to your children, and to all that are afar off, even as many as the Lord our God shall call" (Acts 2:38, 39). These words disclose that the baptism with the Holy Ghost is available to all believers, regardless of their varying mental, emotion-

---

[1]*The Heavenly Gift.*

al, and spiritual capacities. It is a gift of grace, meeting the desperate need for all to "be endued with power from on high." This means that among those receiving the Spirit will be intellectual giants and ignorant heathen converts; staid, unemotional persons and passionate zealots; mature saints and babes in Christ.

It is only natural to expect the differences in temperament and capacity to cause different reactions to the gift of the Spirit. While all will greatly value the privilege of being filled with the Spirit, yet each one will react according to his own peculiar disposition. Thus, it would be impossible to establish the mental, emotional, or spiritual behavior of any single individual as a requisite in all. This reveals the need for a uniform evidence by which the experience of all, whether educated or uneducated, emotional or unemotional, mature or immature, could be authenticated.

How ideally this need is met by speaking with tongues! Think for a moment of the group of disciples assembled in the upper room. One hundred and twenty were in one accord, but each had a separate and distinct personality. Peter the leader and Andrew the follower, Thomas the materialist and John the mystic, Mary the maid with a demonic past and "Mary the mother of Jesus." Yet, when filled with the Spirit, every one of them began to speak with tongues, as the Spirit gave them utterance! No wonder Peter and his companions at Caesarea were so positive of the genuineness of the Gentiles' experience, when "they heard them speak with tongues and magnify God." We know of no other evidence which could be manifested anywhere by anyone,[1] at any time as conclusive proof of the in-filling with the Spirit.

3. IT REVEALS THE PERSONALITY OF THE SPIRIT

The philosophy of speech is given to us by Paul in 1 Corinthians 13:11, where, in describing his childhood, he says, "I spake as a child, I understand as a child, I thought as a child." By reversing the order of these verbs, we can see the manner in which speech works. First is the thought, second the understanding, and third speech. We think various thoughts on a subject; then, by a process of analysis and summary, we come to an understanding or comprehension; and then we speak. One thing is absolutely necessary in this process, however; our thinking, understanding, and speaking must be in a familiar tongue.

But at Pentecost, and in every similar experience, the disciples were speaking in unfamiliar tongues. The words which poured forth from their lips had not been previously in their thoughts and understanding. Since intelligent speech demands an intelligent speaker, we know that in back of their speech

---

[1]Pentecostal workers among the mutes inform us that these silent saints, when being filled with the Spirit, speak in tongues just like anybody else! Even if the divine economy had dictated an exceptional policy for these friends, should this have made void the necessity for tongues as an evidence of the infilling of normal believers? No more than their inability to confess with their mouth the Lord Jesus (Rom. 10:9, 10) makes such a confession less binding on us who have the powers of speech.

Let us not limit the Holy One of Israel. The God whom we serve "is able to do exceeding abundantly above all that we ask or think," yea, He is the One in whose praise the dumb their loosened tongues employ!

there must have been someone else who was thinking and understanding in those other tongues. That Someone was the Spirit of God! He it was who gave the disciples utterance in the languages of the multitude, declaring "the wonderful works of God." The wind and the fire were symbols of His presence; but this phenomenal speech manifested, as nothing else, the personality of the Spirit.

The Pulpit Commentary has a splendid thought in this connection: "Nor need it seem at all too far-fetched an inference, if anyone hesitated to count it *designed* arrangement, that through this *speaking* being so essentially the act of the Holy Spirit, a very strong suggestion of the *personality* of that Spirit should be borne in on the disciples then, and much more on disciples of succeeding ages. Absolute speech does not come from what is merely an influence, an energy, a power; it is the function of a person. And it is one of the highest prerogatives of the human being. The disciples had lost a personal presence, in the person of Jesus, which could never be replaced, and which never was to be replaced till He should 'so come' again, 'in like manner as they had seen Him go into heaven.' And yet, though the personal presence of Jesus was not to be replaced by another visible Presence, it *was* most surely to be replaced by the presence of a Person. Would it not be calculated to assist the disciples both to believe *correctly* and to feel grateful that the ever-invisible Spirit was none the less a personage, a Being—not a vague influence nor a phantom?"[1]

---

[1]Vol. 41, p. 75.

4. IT IS A SYMBOL OF THE SPIRIT'S COMPLETE CONTROL OF THE BELIEVER

The wild, untamable nature of the human tongue is vividly portrayed by James in the third chapter of his Epistle: "For every kind of beast, and of birds, and of serpents, and of things in the sea, is tamed, and hath been tamed of mankind: but the tongue can no man tame; it is an unruly evil, full of deadly poison" (James 3:7, 8). James also tells us that the tongue is a valuable indicator of the quality of a man's religion; for let a man seem ever so religious, yet if he bridleth not his tongue, his religion is vain (James 1:26). Whereas, the control of the tongue by means of true religion, manifests mastery over man's entire nature: "In many things we offend all. If any man offend not in word, the same is a perfect man, and able also to bridle the whole body" (James 3:2).

Not only is the tongue the last thing to yield to man's dominion, but it is also the last thing to yield to the Holy Spirit. Hence, it is an accurate recorder of the extent to which the believer has submitted to the control of the Spirit. How reasonable to expect the Spirit Himself to indicate His possession of the believer by making the stubborn tongue to speak forth whatsoever He bids it, even in unfamiliar languages. At the very entrance of the Spirit-filled life, then, the believer is given a remarkable illustration of the submission of his tongue, a submission which is to characterize that whole life.

5. IT MANIFESTS THE HOLY SPIRIT AS THE BELIEVER'S SOURCE OF TRUTH AND UTTERANCE

At the Feast of Pentecost two loaves of bread made

from the first fruits of the wheat harvest were waved before the Lord (Leviticus 23:16-21). When that ancient feast found its fulfillment on the New Testament day of Pentecost, the speaking with other tongues also became a kind of first fruits.

The Lord Jesus made it very clear that the truths which He spoke, and even the words with which He clothed them, and His mighty works—in fact, His entire life and ministry—were the result of utter dependence upon the Father. The Gospel of John especially abounds with references to His dependence upon the Father. See John 6:57; 14:10, 24; 17:18. And He sought constantly to impress upon the disciples their own need to rely, not upon their own understanding, but upon the Holy Spirit. "The Comforter, which is the Holy Ghost, whom the Father will send in My name, He shall teach you all things, and bring all things to your remembrance, whatsoever I have said unto you. . . . He shall testify of Me. . . . When He, the Spirit of Truth, is come, He will guide you into all truth. . . . He will show you things to come. He shall glorify Me: for He shall receive of Mine, and shall show it unto you" (John 14:26; 15:26; 16:13, 14).

How vividly this was sealed upon the hearts of the disciples, when on the day of Pentecost they began to speak with other tongues as the Spirit gave them utterance. This temporary suspension of their normal intellectual processes, undoubtedly, made them very conscious of the necessity of looking to the Holy Spirit as the Source and Revealer of truth. How impotent their own wisdom and speech must have seemed to them. Not that this phenomenal utterance caused them to believe that a Spirit-filled life would make them mere mental automata. On

[243]

the contrary, the Spirit would grant them full exercise of every faculty. Nevertheless, there were going to come times when eye would not be able to see, nor ear hear, nor heart receive; then they must turn to God for a revelation by His Spirit. "For the Spirit searcheth all things, yea, the deep things of God" (1 Corinthians 1:9, 10). There would come times when they were to take no thought how or what they should answer, or what they should say, for the Holy Ghost would teach them in the same hour when they ought to say (Luke 12:11, 12). Thus, this miraculous speech, this creation of the fruit of the lips (Isaiah 57:19), is symbolic of the entire life of the Spirit-filled believer, who trusts not in the excellency of man's wisdom or speech, but in the wisdom and words which the Holy Ghost teacheth.

6. IT SIGNIFIES THE HONOR WHICH GOD HAS PLACED UPON HUMAN SPEECH

The whole creation waited for an articulate expression of its praise to the Creator. The mineral, vegetable, and animal kingdoms yearned for a representative, one who in intelligent speech could give voice to their worship. To man, this distinctive privilege was given. Made in the image of God, man alone received the power to co-ordinate thought and tongue into intelligent speech. In a sense, as he audibly worshiped and communed with God, he became the high priest for every living thing.

And what tremendous power there is in speech! Its power as an evil influence, resulting fom man's fall, is shown very emphatically by James: "Behold, how great a matter a little fire kindleth! And the tongue is a fire, a world of iniquity: so is the tongue among our members, that it defileth the whole body, and setteth on fire the course of nature; and is set on fire of hell. . . . It is an unruly evil, full of deadly poison" (James 3:5, 6, 8). On the other hand, the tongue possesses great power for good. Especially is this true in the experience of the children of God. With the mouth confession is made unto salvation; angelic praise is not comparable with that which ascends from the lips of redeemed men; the salvation of a lost world is dependent upon the tongue, for God has decreed that by man shall the unsearchable riches of Christ be proclaimed. See also Matthew 12:37.

Surely, speech is representative of all the privileges and powers which are man's prerogative. How fitting it is, then, that the Holy Spirit should single out this most important faculty as the initial, physical evidence of the infilling with the Spirit. And did not the Lord Jesus indicate how closely related were the enduement of power and the speech? *"Ye shall receive power,* after that the Holy Ghost is come upon you: and *ye shall be witnesses* unto Me."* It is a marvelous tribute to man that God is mindful of him, and desires to converse with him; but how much more marvelous is it that at the filling with the Spirit He actually takes control of man's unworthy tongue and speaks *through* him! This significant act most certainly shows His esteem of this highest accomplishment of His highest creature.

7. IT IS AN EARNEST OF HEAVENLY SPEECH

Sin has brought more than a mere multiplication of languages; it has brought deformity to human speech itself. No longer does man possess the perfect articulation of Edenic days, or even of pre-Babel days. This gift, like all other gifts, has been corrupted from its original purity and power. Even we who have the firstfruits of the Spirit groan within ourselves, waiting for the completion of our redemption, when we shall receive not only glorified bodies but also glorified speech. Then, when that which is in part, that which is subject to earth's bondage, is done away, and that which is perfect is come, all of the saints of God, from north and south, east and west, shall understand one another, for all shall speak one pure and mighty human language. Together we shall proclaim the glory of the Lamb who hath redeemed us from every kindred, tribe, and tongue. Why should it be thought strange or unreasonable, then, that God should grant a token of that coming hour by substituting other tongues in the lips of those receiving the fullness of the Spirit, an experience which brings so near all the glories of heaven?

CHAPTER 17

Seven Objections Considered

1. THE GOD OF VARIETY IS NOT TIED DOWN TO ANY ONE EVIDENCE

IT has been pointed out that God in His wisdom has made everything and everyone different; i.e., no two grains of sand, no two flowers, no two snowflakes, and no two persons are exactly alike. And what is true in the natural is also true in the spiritual, for not two spiritual experiences are identical in one person, much less in two persons. Therefore, to insist that all speak with tongues at the baptism with the Holy Ghost is to defy this divinely ordained plan, and to limit the God of infinite variety.

We Pentecostalists are happy to acknowledge the distinctiveness of every created object and being, and we agree that this distinctiveness also exists in the spiritual realm. Nevertheless, we do not feel that this law can be invoked against our insistence upon tongues as the initial, physical evidence of every baptism with the Spirit.

The whole creation gives abundant testimony to the diversity of God's nature and His works. On the other hand, He has revealed to us in His Word that in some instances He has chosen to limit Himself. Especially is this true in His plan of salvation. Has He not chosen only ONE element to make an atonement for the soul—blood? Has He not decreed that there is only ONE name under heaven given among men whereby we must be saved—Jesus? Has He not set forth but ONE ordinance which typifies the identification of all believers with the death and resurrection of the Lord—water baptism? Has He not given but ONE ordinance whereby we show the Lord's death till He come—the Lord's Supper? These sovereign limitations reveal the fact that if God in His wisdom prefers to restrict His workings, He can do so without lessening His ability to work in a diversified manner.

ONE experience must be received by all who would enter the kingdom—the new birth. The reactions to this blessed experience vary according to the personality of the recipient, but this does not alter the fact that there is ONE evidence of the new birth shared by all—the witness of the Spirit (Rom. 8:16) ! In like manner, all believers are commanded to receive ONE experience—the baptism or filling with the Spirit. Again, physical, emotional and intellectual reactions are as varied as the recipients, but again ONE evidence uniformly accompanies the experience—*The witness of the Spirit through us in other tongues!*

But even though all speak with tongues, it is plain that the God of variety has not attempted to make every baptism identical in every respect. There were some differences in the receptions of the Spirit in the Book of Acts. At Jerusalem and Caesarea there was no laying on of hands as at Samaria, Damascus, and Ephesus. Certainly, the tongues which were spoken were diverse. And we should suppose, from our observations of present-day baptisms, that each individual believer had his own manner of speaking with tongues. But one thing is clear: while there was variety in some respects, there was also a uniformity in that every recipient spoke with tongues. It would be easier for us to believe that God had not established this phenomenon as the initial, physical evidence, if it were not for the fact that in the three outpourings in Acts 2:4; 10:46; and 19:6 every member of every company spoke with tongues.

2. ANY ONE OF THE NINE GIFTS OF THE SPIRIT CAN BE THE EVIDENCE.

DR. IRONSIDE writes: "The Holy Spirit is sovereign. No one has the right to demand that he be given any certain gift or gifts as an evidence of the Spirit's baptism."[1] T. J. MCCROSSAN also tells us: "When the Holy Ghost baptizes or fills us, each of us will be given at least one spiritual gift." He then quotes 1 Corinthians 12:7-11, 29-30, and asks, "Reader, will you believe Paul, or these many sincere and good men and women who, through ignorance of the original Greek text, which alone is inspired of God, are telling you that all must speak with tongues as the one and only infallible sign of being baptized or filled with the Holy Ghost?"[2]

In the next chapter we shall see that while there is no difference between the nature of tongues in Acts and the nature of tongues in Corinthians, there

---

[1] *Addresses on the First Epistle to the Corinthians.*

[2] *Speaking With Other Tongues, Sign or Gift—Which?* pp. 36, 40.

is a difference between the two in regard to purpose and operation. Here we would point out that even if the speaking with tongues in Acts is the gift of tongues of 1 Corinthians 12 to 14, it still deserves far more prominence than is accorded it in non-Pentecostal circles today. The mere fact that some groups profess to believe that speaking with tongues is only one of the evidences, does not excuse them for its utter absence in their midst, We have reasons to believe that some are sincere in this attitude toward tongues, but we also have reasons to believe that there are others who use this theory as a means to eliminate tongues altogether. How else can we explain their opposition to tongues in every shape and form, both as an evidence and as a gift? If they really believe that speaking with tongues is one of the evidences, why do they take every precaution against its manifestation in their services? Why do the leaders suppress all favorable comment about tongues in connection with the baptism? Can it be that they doubt their own theory? Surely they must know that their constant claim that all do not speak with tongues does not void the fact that at least some should experience this miracle of utterance. The Holy Spirit, who manifested His presence on three occasions by causing all to speak with tongues, surely wills to divide this gift at least to a few believers.

Briefly, our reasons for disagreeing with the view that any of the other gifts can be the evidence are these:

(a) If this theory were true, the Holy Spirit had an excellent opportunity to demonstrate it at Pentecost. Nine gifts divided among the one hundred and twenty would have meant one gift to about every thirteen disciples. Instead, the Spirit gave all one hundred and twenty disciples utterance in other tongues.

(b) Speaking with tongues was distinctly associated with the filling with the Holy Spirit at Jerusalem, Caesarea, and Ephesus.

(c) Tongues alone occurred in all three instances of which the full record is given. Prophecy was also manifested on one occasion, and perhaps two (Acts 19:6; 10:46), but it never was given as the only evidence.

(d) Peter and his six brethren knew that Cornelius and his household had received the Spirit, not because they witnessed manifestations of a number of gifts, but because "they heard them speak with tongues and magnify God."

Recently, a prominent radio evangelist stated that he, too, subscribes to the view that any one of the gifts of the Spirit can be the evidence. The gift which he received was "evangelical, expository teaching." Unquestionably, this highly esteemed brother does have a splendid ministry along that line, and we gratefully acknowledge it as a gift from God. But does "evangelical, expository teaching" fall in the category of the manifestation of the Spirit? If we mistake not, the gifts which Paul describes as the manifestation of the Spirit are those miraculous gifts listed in 1 Corinthians 12:8-10. Every true minister of the gospel has a particular ministry, in which, if he be diligent in study and prayer, he is pre-eminently blessed. But have not most Timothys found that it usually takes some time to make full proof of their ministries, that their profiting may appear to all? Whereas, the baptism or filling with the Spirit is an experience which, through a miraculous manifestation of the Spirit, speaking with tongues, is immediately recognized by all.

3. LOVE IS THE REAL EVIDENCE

Those who favor love as the only safe evidence lay great stress on the fact that all other evidences. whether visible or invisible, can be counterfeited, whereas love is inimitable. They must admit, however, that there are degrees of love. For example, there is a love which is in word but not deed and truth; there is an emotional love which is likewise very much on the surface; there is an intellectual love, which, though excellent in itself, is not complete; and then there is that perfect love so wondrously described in 1 Corinthians 13. Now the only possible way to determine the genuineness and the degree of love would be to observe it over a period of time, an observation that would necessarily be a gradual process. Does this correspond to the experience of the New Testament believers who could tell immediately whether or not one had been filled with the Spirit? Acts 10:46 does not read, "For they saw their *love* one for another," but, "For they heard them *speak with tongues* and magnify God." Of course, we believe that anyone who is filled with the "Spirit of power, and of *love*, and of a sound mind" (2 Timothy 1:7) will manifest love for God and man. But we see no need to substitute this fruit of the Spirit for the speaking with tongues which is the immediate, outward result of the filling with the Spirit.

4. FAITH REQUIRES NO VISIBLE PROOF

D. H. DOLMAN, in his book *Simple Talks on the Holy Spirit* (pp. 99, 100) asks us to consider Galatians 3:2 ("This only would I learn of you, Received ye the Spirit by the works of the law, or by the hearing of faith?") in the light of Colossians 2:6

("As ye have therefore received Christ Jesus, so walk ye in Him."). In other words, the manner of our reception of the Lord Jesus, i.e., by faith, should be the manner of our reception of the Spirit, or any other experience subsequent to conversion. Hence, Mr. Dolman is of the opinion that it is wrong to look for an external evidence of the reception of the Spirit.

In contending for tongues as the initial, physical evidence of the infilling with the Spirit, we Pentecostalists are not opposed to faith. It is the means by which the experience is received. There is no conflict between faith and speaking with tongues. Each has its particular part in the reception of the Spirit. Faith is the only principle by which the fullness of the Spirit, or any other divine blessing, is obtained (Ephesians 2:8, 9); speaking with tongues is the immediate, outward manifestation of that experience. Faith, then, is absolutely essential to the one who desires to be filled with the Spirit (Hebrews 11:6); speaking with tongues is also a prime necessity, if the experience is to be according to the Scriptural pattern. Therefore, since both faith and tongues fulfill their own particular purpose in the reception of the Spirit, why should they be considered as mutually exclusive?

In some circles today receiving the Spirit by faith is construed to mean the elimination of all outward manifestations, including tongues. Any expectation of visible results is considered to be dishonoring to the principle of taking the experience by faith. This conception of receiving the Spirit by faith can hardly be justified, however. Faith is not sufficient in itself; it is the means, not the end; it is the channel, not that which flows through the channel; it is the divinely decreed method of obtaining the blessings of God, not the blessings themselves. Now if no blessings are forthcoming, that faith, according to the Word (James 2:17), "is dead, being alone." And we are persuaded that much of the so-called "taking by faith" is nothing more than the giving of mental assent to a truth which never becomes alive in the individual's experience.

Receiving by faith does not in any way alter the character of a spiritual experience. For example, conversion, the receiving of the Lord Jesus by faith, is an experience of which we have every Scriptural right to expect certain accompanying evidences—the witness of the Spirit with our spirit that we are the children of God, and the joy and peace in believing. These things are not only the effects of conversion, but, in a definite sense, they are also an integral part of the same. Receiving the Lord Jesus by faith means taking this experience as a whole into the heart.

Likewise, receiving the Spirit by faith means taking the experience as a whole. By no means does it remove from the experience the supernatural element, which, according to abundant Scriptural precedent, is the constant accompaniment. In fact, the very context of Galatians 3:2, the verse which Mr. Dolman has cited, shows that the reception of the Spirit was made manifest by the presence of miracle and inspiration. The apostles themselves spoke with tongues as a result of being filled with the Spirit through faith, and required this phenomenon as a mark of genuineness in the experience of others. The doctrine of the early church regarding the reception of the Spirit accepted the principle of faith, as revealed in the receiving of the Lord Jesus by faith, and, at the same time, was complete enough to embrace speaking in tongues as the immediate, visible result of that experience, even as on the one hundred and twenty "at the beginning."

5. SOUL WINNING IS THE EVIDENCE.

JOHN R. RICE writes: "The issue I would raise everywhere is that soul-winning power is far more important than tongues and this is the evidence of the fullness of the Spirit. For Jesus said to His disciples, in Acts 1:8; 'But ye shall receive power, after that the Holy Ghost is come upon you: and ye shall be witnesses unto Me both in Jerusalem, and in all Judea, and in Samaria, and unto the uttermost part of the earth.' . . . The simple truth is that none of the well-known, world-wide interdenominational evangelists have spoken in tongues or believed in it. I do not mean that many of the Pentecostal group of people are not soul winners, but none of them have been interdenominational and world wide in their soul-winning influence.[1] I am not saying that speaking in tongues keeps people from winning souls. I am simply saying that not speaking with tongues does not prevent people from winning souls."[2]

First, let us say that in Chapter 19 we shall endeavor to explain the absence of tongues in the experience of many of the great soul winners, both past and present. Here we shall consider only the issue raised by Dr. Rice, that "soul-winning power is far more important than tongues and this is the evidence of the fullness of the Spirit."

---

[1]Dr. Rice did not anticipate that God would shortly raise up Oral Roberts, William Branham, Gayle Jackson, T. L. Osborn, Tommy Hicks and other Pentecostal evangelists who have become "world-wide in their soul-winning influence."
[2]*The Sword of the Lord*, p. 8, June 14, 1946.

This is an attempt, through the comparison of tongues with one of the vital elements of the Christian life, to eliminate tongues as a necessary part of the infilling with the Spirit. Soul winning, like love and faith, is not expendable; it is the chief business of the Church Militant. Considered abstractly, it is far more important than any other single thing in the life of the believer. But why should anyone try to emphasize the value of soul winning to the detriment of that which, according to the Book of Acts, is the immediate, outward result of the baptism with the Spirit? Without a doubt, a true baptism or filling with the Spirit will result in the winning of souls, provided, of course, the believer continues to walk in the Spirit, and to follow Christ who said, "Follow Me and I will make you fishers of men." (Matthew 4:19). Nevertheless, unlike tongues, soul winning is not a part of the baptism itself; it is not the initial, physical evidence of that experience. There can be little doubt that after Cornelius and those assembled with him received the Holy Ghost, they led souls to the Lord Jesus. But what made Peter and his Jewish brethren so positive of the genuineness of the Gentiles' experience was not soul winning, but speaking with tongues. There was no debating the comparative values of soul winning and tongues, or whether tongues would help or hinder believers in soul winning; the ambassadors from Joppa simply accepted tongues as the normal evidence of the reception of the Spirit, and that was that.

And as far as soul winning is concerned, we believe that statistics will indicate clearly that the average Pentecostal believer has witnessed to and won far more souls to the Lord than the average non-Pentecostal believer. The miraculous growth of the Pentecostal Movement during this Twentieth Century can be traced directly to the passion for souls and the power to witness derived from the charismatic enduement from on high. It is true that many Christians from other ranks have identified themselves with this Movement; and it is true that many unconverted members of other denominations have been converted in Pentecostal meetings; but it is also true that a vast number of present-day Pentecostalists have been brought in from among the unchurched multitudes.

In regard to the world-wide interdenominational stature of Pentecostal ministers, we have but a brief word. The Pentecostal Movement is conceded to be one of the strongest evangelical groups in the Church today. Some of its ministers have won thousands of souls to Christ, and, if accorded due recognition, would compare quite favorably with some of the leading soul winners among other groups. However, it is almost impossible for Pentecostal ministers to obtain wide recognition on an interdenominational basis, for, in most instances, they are scarcely acknowledged in an interdenominational gathering, much less given the opportunity to issue the evangelistic appeal. Be this as it may, we still feel that an experience should not be judged on the grounds of the exceptional minister or believer, but on the grounds of the average minister and the average believer. When the Pentecostal baptism is judged on this latter and truer basis, it will be revealed as the greatest impetus to soul winning in the world today.

6. LIMITING OF PHYSICAL EVIDENCE TO TONGUES PRODUCES FLESHLY EXTRAVAGANCES

Many have rejected the doctrine of tongues as the initial, physical evidence because they have been fearful of the fanaticism which, according to them, must follow such a doctrine. They insist that such a teaching is conducive to a seeking of tongues rather than a seeking of the fullness of the Spirit. One thing these objectors should bear in mind, however, is that the doctrine must be judged on its Scriptural merit, and not on its liability to abuse; for *what teaching is totally free from abuse at the hands of extremists?*

In one sense, we Pentecostalists do seek tongues and encourage others to seek tongues, but not in the sense in which our critics accuse us. Knowing that this miracle of utterance is an integral part of the baptism, and knowing that the experience is not up to the New Testament standard without the speaking with tongues, we naturally look for it. But we also know that the speaking with tongues is an effect, and not a cause; the Holy Spirit is the cause! He it is that gives the believer utterance in other languages. How foolish it would be, then, to concentrate on tongues, as if it were the sum and substance of the whole matter! The rivers of strange eloquence must flow out of the innermost being which is possessed by the Spirit of God. Unless the speaking with tongues at such a time is as the Spirit gives utterance, it is as "sounding brass or a tinkling cymbal."

Even so, we must admit to our shame that some Pentecostalists, in their zeal for all to conform to the Scriptural pattern, have seemingly forgotten that there is a spiritual as well as a physical side to the baptism. Psychic methods have been adopted which have had but one purpose—the causing of ecstatic speech. This practice has brought much reproach upon the Pentecostal Movement, driving many earnest inquirers away in disillusionment, and producing highly unsatisfactory experiences; for the seekers received no true baptism, and that which was supposed to be an utterance in tongues was nothing more than a fanatical gibberish. And yet, it is also true that some who have been dealt with in the same manner have actually been filled with the Spirit and have truly spoken with tongues. The only explanation of this is that God in His mercy saw the hungry heart of the seeker and the honest heart of the over-zealous worker, and answered the heart cry of both. It was not because of the unwise methods, but in spite of them!

Why have we spoken so candidly on this point, which we very easily could have excluded from this discussion? We want our fundamentalist friends to know that these things are not approved by the Pentecostal Movement as a whole. And we also want them to know that these fleshly practices are not widespread as some critics have suggested.

There is a proper attitude for prayer-helpers to take toward candidates for the fullness of the Spirit, and this attitude is endorsed and practiced by the vast majority of Pentecostal believers. It is always in order to surround these candidates with an atmosphere of prayer and praise, and to offer an encouraging word. When it is evident that they are being filled with the Holy Spirit, it is perfectly proper to exhort them to continue to yield to Him. The supernatural is a strange realm to these seekers, and when the praise on their lips begins to change from their own familiar tongue to a new and unknown tongue it is reassuring to have someone near who has already undergone that experience. All this can be done, however, without resorting to unwise and fleshly practices.

7. TONGUES ARE FOR A SIGN, NOT TO THEM THAT BELIEVE, BUT TO THEM THAT BELIEVE NOT

This statement by Paul is often cited as an objection to the Pentecostal evidence doctrine. But the apostle is not opposing the attitude of the believers in the Book of Acts, who regarded tongues as an evidential sign of the baptism with the Spirit—"For they heard them speak with tongues." In 1 Corinthians 14:22 Paul is referring to the effect of tongues upon unbelievers, an effect which we shall discuss fully in Chapters 22 and 23 of this volume. There is no more contradiction between these two views concerning tongues than there is between the views of Paul and James concerning faith and works. They represent merely the viewpoints of two different groups, believers and unbelievers, toward tongues. Much misunderstanding and controversy could be avoided if all of us would take time to determine the exact meaning of Scriptural terminology.

CHAPTER 18

The Evidence Distinguished From the Gift

FUNDAMENTALISTS, as a whole, look upon all speaking with tongues in the Scriptures as one and the same phenomenon. The attempt of Pentecostalists to distinguish between the exercise of tongues in Acts and the exercise of tongues in 1 Corinthians 12 to 14 is viewed as theological hair-splitting which has no Scriptural support. The miraculous utterance, wherever it occurs in the Word, is recognized as "divers kinds of tongues," one of the nine gifts of the Spirit (1 Corinthians 12:10). Since these gifts are divided severally as the Spirit wills, and since Paul's question in 1 Corinthians 12:30, "Do all speak with tongues?" plainly deserves a negative answer, the fundamentalists conclude that it is not Scriptural to demand that all speak with tongues as the evidence of the filling with the Spirit.

How vitally important it is to every believer to determine whether or not the Pentecostal claim can be sustained! If there is a clear distinction between the tongues phenomenon in Acts and that in 1 Corinthians, then the Pentecostal argument for tongues as the initial, physical evidence is well-nigh irrefutable. If not, then the Pentecostal theology on the evidence teaching suffers a severe blow. This is, perhaps, the decisive point of the entire controversy.

One of the first steps in this discussion should be the defining of our terminology. When referring to the speaking with tongues found in the Book of Acts, we shall use the word "evidence"; when referring to the speaking with tongues in 1 Corinthians 12 to 14, we shall use the phrase, "gift of tongues." In other sections of this volume, as a concession to popular terminology, we have employed these and synonymous terms interchangeably, but it is our belief that we are technically correct only when we employ these terms in the manner just specified.

And we would add a word here concerning the mistaken idea that the expressions, "new tongues," in Mark 16:17, "other tongues," in Acts 2:4, and "unknown tongues," in 1 Corinthians 14:2,[1] represent separate forms of the manifestation. These expressions are merely different ways of saying exactly the same thing. The believer is given supernatural utterance by the Holy Spirit in tongues that are "new" to his lips, "other" than his own native tongue, and "unknown" to him in the sense that he is entirely unacquainted with them, or "unknown" to him to the extent that he is unable at other times to give forth the expressions which fall from his lips when under the inspiration of the Spirit. In both Acts and Corinthians there are several references to tongues which are devoid of any qualifying terms whatsoever; it is simply said, "They spake with

---

[1]See Chapter 20 for a discussion of the "unknown" tongue.

tongues," or, "He that speaketh with a tongue."
Thus, in the absence of anything that would clearly
distinguish between "new," "other," and "unknown"
tongues, these three words can be accepted as synonymous expressions indicating the extraordinary character of the utterance, rather than separating one
form of the phenomenon from another.

A. SIMILARITIES IN NATURE

There are so many similarities between the evidence and the gift that it is small wonder that many
Bible students have concluded that they are identical.
That we do realize this basic sameness is revealed in
the earlier chapters of this volume, where, in refuting
various arguments, we have referred indiscriminately
to the statements about tongues in both Acts and
Corinthians. It has already been mentioned that both
are signs, and that expressions describing the language
spoken are equally applicable to both. There are
other features which also disclose their inherent
likenesses:

1. The same organs of speech are employed.
2. The mind is quiescent with respect to the actual
exercise of speaking with tongues.
3. In each form the tongues are the expression of
the human spirit under the inspiration of the Holy
Spirit.
4. The miraculous element is present in both.
5. Both phases are a form of prophecy. Peter
linked the speaking with other tongues at Pentecost with Joel's words, "And your sons and daughters
shall prophesy." Likewise, the gifts of tongues and
of interpretation are also equal to prophecy. 1 Corinthians 14:5. Of course, prophecy is an inspired
utterance in one's native tongue, while every form

of speaking with tongues is in other than one's own tongue.

6. Both are used to praise and magnify God.

B. THE DISTINCTION IN PURPOSE AND OPERATION

While we freely admit all these innate likenesses, we still insist that the evidence and the gift of tongues are not identical. They are alike in nature, but diverse in purpose and use; and herein lies the chief distinction between the two. Nor do we feel that this is an artificial distinction made merely for the sake of our Pentecostal theology. Multiplied illustrations from every realm could be cited as proof of the fact that a difference in purpose and operation ofttimes constitutes a difference in things which are fundamentally of the same nature.

For example, in the English translation of the Bible we often find different meanings given to the same Hebrew or Greek word. There is nothing unusual about this, for in every language there are words which are susceptible to various interpretations. The sacred writers, like all other writers, have, by their use of a word, determined its meaning. In one passage they have caused it to convey one idea, and in another passage still another idea, depending upon their purpose. Hence, though there may be but one root meaning for the word, that meaning cannot be given arbitrarily for its every appearance. The rule which the translators follow is that the word should be interpreted by its use, and not necessarily by its root.

With this illustration in mind, let us examine the setting in which the Author of the Scriptures has

placed the two basically similar but distinct manifestations of tongues.

1. PURPOSE

1 Corinthians 12 to 14 presents a picture of the
supernatural weapons of the Spirit-filled church,
the gifts of the Spirit. These gifts—their source,
distribution, spirit, and laws of operation—constitute virtually the entire discourse. Here we find the
gift of tongues with its twofold purpose of individual and collective edification, and the set of rules
governing its public operation.

Turning to the Book of Acts we find that the
predominant theme is the birth and growth of the
Church. We see bone being joined upon bone,
sinew upon sinew, flesh upon flesh, and the Spirit
of God breathing divine life into New Testament
Israel. Here are recorded the spiritual experiences of
the early Christians. This, then, is the setting in which
we find the speaking with tongues which we call
the evidence. And we would have the reader to note
particularly that the tongues phenomenon here had
one primary purpose, to make manifest to recipient
and onlooker that the Holy Ghost had been given.
It is part of a clearly defined experience, and not
a normal exercise of one of the nine regular gifts.

This is the clear import of Peter's sermon at
Pentecost. In his answer to the query, "What meaneth this?" he did not intimate that the utterance which
so confounded the multitude was something special,
having no relation or connection with Joel's prophecy. On the contrary, his words, "This is that
which was spoken by the prophet Joel," would lead
anyone to believe that the speaking with other
tongues was the normal fulfillment of the "promise

of the Father" to pour out His Spirit on all flesh.

In the account of Cornelius' household it is certain that Peter did not consider the phenomenon as the gift of tongues—defined by religious thought today as something additional, having no direct relation to the baptism itself. In the minds of Peter and his friends the speaking with tongues was associated with, and was a primary result of, the outpouring of the Spirit. When the Gentiles broke forth in rapturous, ecstatic worship in other tongues, Peter never thought of gifts, but of the baptism in the Spirit. "Can any man forbid water that these should not be baptized, *which have received the Holy Ghost* as well as we?"

Nor at Ephesus was the speaking with tongues an occasion for ministering to one another as a means of mutual edification. The Holy Ghost so filled the scene, and the disciples were so occupied with His personality, that there was no thought of edifying one another (Compare 2 Chronicles 7:1, 2). Again the mighty impact of the Spirit had produced the characteristic effect of ecstatic speech.

If the evidence and the gift are the same, why are their purposes apparently distinct? In 1 Corinthians 12 to 14 there is not the slightest hint that the gift of tongues is associated, in any direct sense, with the filling with the Holy Spirit, certainly not in any greater degree than the other gifts. Its sole purpose is the personal edification of the speaker, and, when coupled with interpretation, the edification of the hearers. Whereas, in Acts the speaking with tongues is always the direct result of the filling with the Spirit. The only reasonable solution to this lack of similarity in purpose is that the evidence is one phase of the phenomenon, and the gift is another.

2. OPERATION

We shall now see whether or not the distinction in purpose is substantiated by a distinction in operation.

(a) It is clear from 1 Corinthians 12:10, 11, 30 that all do not have the gift of tongues; as one of the nine gifts of the Spirit, it is "divided severally as He will." But in every case in Acts, where the immediate results of the giving of the Spirit are recorded, *all* spoke with tongues. How shall we account for this difference in distribution, unless we differentiate between the tongues in Corinthians and Acts?

And what about Paul's words, "Do all speak with tongues?" (1 Corinthians 12:30). This oft-quoted question raised no issue in the early church with respect to the accepted evidence of the reception of the Spirit. By the time Peter and his friends went to Caesarea, at the very latest, speaking with tongues was recognized as the initial, physical evidence of the experience. Whether or not all spoke with tongues as having the gift did not change in the slightest the relation of tongues to the infilling with the Holy Ghost.

Mark 16:17—"They shall speak with new tongues"—is perhaps not a specific reference to the utterance associated with the filling with the Spirit and that alone, for it would seem to be a general promise including the tongues phenomenon as a whole. Nevertheless, this verse definitely conveys the impression that all may speak with tongues, if they will only believe. And what more likely place is there for all to speak with tongues than at the baptism with the Spirit? Then it was that the promise was fulfilled in the experience of the disciples, and so it will be fullfilled in all them that believe today. Unlike Zacharias, who was stricken dumb for his unbelief (Luke 1:20), they will begin to speak with other tongues because of their belief.

We would also call your attention to the healing of the sick which is promised in this passage—"They shall lay hands on the sick and they shall recover." v. 18. This form of divine healing is basically the same as the gift of healing (1 Corinthians 12:9), but, like tongues, it differs from its counterpart among the gifts of the Spirit in that it is available to all, whereas the gift is not available to all (1 Cor. 12:11, 30). Another promise to the sick is found in James 5:14-16: "Is there any sick among you? Let him call for the elders of the church, and let them pray over him, anointing him with oil in the name of the Lord: and the prayer of faith shall save the sick, and the Lord shall raise him up." Surely all they that believe and obey Mark 16:18, laying hands on the sick and seeing them recover, and all elders who anoint with oil and pray the prayer of faith, cannot be said to have the gift of healing. It is evident, therefore, that a miraculous exercise can be the same in essence, and even can fulfill the same purpose, and still not be identical with the gift which it so closely resembles.

(b) In 1 Corinthians 14 there are certain apostolic instructions governing the operation of the gift of tongues in public gatherings. That the speaking with tongues in Acts is not the gift, in the limited and prescribed sense of 1 Corinthians 12 to 14, must be accepted, or else we find the practice of the apostles in Acts in conflict with these instructions.

The matter of interpretation furnishes us with

a clear example of this. All who speak with tongues are admonished to pray that they may interpret those tongues for the edification of the church. In fact, since the main purpose of their gathering together was mutual edification, uninterpreted tongues not only are disparaged but are actually forbidden (1 Corinthians 14:28). But look at the failure of the apostles to enforce this injunction in Acts. At Jerusalem it was not necessary that tongues be interpreted, because they were understood by the audience; but how about the other cases? We find there was no demand for interpretation at Caesarea by Peter, or at Ephesus by Paul. Why not? The tongues on these occasions were not given primarily to provide edification, but to announce the arrival of the Spirit.

(c) Another restriction which Paul through the Holy Spirit set upon the public exercise of tongues is the maximum number of utterances in a single meeting—"If any man speak in an unknown tongue, let it be by two, or at the most three, and that by course" (1 Corinthians 14:27). Yet at Pentecost there were one hundred and twenty speaking in tongues, all at one time! How many spoke at Caesarea we know not, but surely their number exceeded three. And at Ephesus Paul himself allowed twelve to speak with tongues in one meeting, and that not by course! Now if all speaking with tongues is the gift, then all these believers, the apostles included, were out of order. How are we to explain this contradiction between apostolic instruction and practice, unless we distinguish between the two phases of tongues? Certainly, the Holy Spirit would not inspire and give utterance in Acts to that which He afterwards condemns in Corinthians!

(d) The chief reason for the restriction of tongues

as a regular gift in constant operation in the church is the preservation of a balanced form of worship. "Divers kinds of tongues" is but one of the nine gifts, and deserves no more prominence than any other gift. But in Acts tongues is exalted out of all proportion as *the* evidence of the *reception* of the Spirit. Again we affirm our belief that the only way to reconcile this apparent disagreement is to recognize the tongues in Acts as the initial, physical evidence of every baptism with the Spirit, and in this capacity it fulfills a definite and specific purpose without interfering in the slightest with the balanced distribution of the gifts of the Spirit.

(e) T. J. McCROSSAN has endeavored to prove from the Greek text that the utterances at Pentecost were identical with the utterances at Corinth. Since he has devoted fourteen pages to this one argument, we shall quote only his conclusion in which he sums up his main points:

"These hard and fast grammatical rules hold good throughout the whole range of Greek literature, and so when we find in Acts 2:4; 10:44-46; and 19:6, that the words denoting 'the baptism' or 'the infilling of the Holy Spirit' are always expressed by the aorist tense, while 'the speaking with tongues' is always expressed, as we have clearly shown, by the imperfect tense, this is positive and absolute proof (1) that they did not speak with tongues until the filling with the Holy Ghost had become a completed or past action, and (2) that when they did speak with tongues they continued so to do. It was from that time a continual, customary, and habitual thing. This is the exact meaning of the imperfect tense, as we have clearly shown. In each case, therefore, 'the speaking with tongues' was 'the gift of tongues'—

something continued, repeated, habitual—and not God's sign or seal to them of their baptism. To any Greek scholar this is so evident that there can be no possible room for doubt. Praise God for the Greek language.

"Friend, let us remind you again that if you spoke with tongues at the time of your baptism or infilling, and have not done so since, you were not baptized according to Acts 2:4."[1]

Mr. McCrossan has again explored the Greek to substantiate a theory which is contrary to the text itself and to the context. It seems so illogical to insist that the technicalities of a language can be employed in such a way that the evident meaning of the language is defeated. We do not take issue with Mr. McCrossan on the fact that the word "filled" signifies a definite, complete experience, and that the verbal phrase, "began to speak," signifies a continuing action. But how can we possibly construe Acts 2:4 to mean that the speaking with tongues had no vital connection with the infilling with the Holy Spirit? Acts 10:46 would be totally inexplicable if we were to take such a position. And how can we believe that Luke by his use of the imperfect tense ("began to speak") meant to convey the thought that the disciples continued to speak with other tongues all through their lives? Doubtless many of them, if not all, did speak with tongues after the day of Pentecost, but that it is not what Luke meant in Acts 2:4! It would be as logical to conclude from this sentence, "And they were all baptized (aorist tense) in water, and their clothes began to drip (imperfect tense)," that the wet garments had nothing what-

---

[1]*Speaking With Tongues, Sign or Gift—Which?* p. 19.

ever to do with the baptism in water, and that those garments kept right on dripping forever and aye!

The temporary nature of evidential tongues, as opposed to the permanency of the gift, should also be emphasized. Peter and his brethren concluded immediately that Cornelius and his household had received the Spirit, "For they heard them speak with tongues" —then and there. They did not require a continual manifestation of tongues over a period of years, or months, or weeks, or days, or even hours. It is not mandatory for one who has been baptized according to Acts 2:4 to speak with tongues as a "continual, customary, and habitual thing," though, in many cases, evidential tongues are succeeded by the permanent gift.

Thus, our study of the tongues phenomenon in Acts and 1 Corinthians brings us to the conclusion that there is a definite distinction between the evidence and the gift. While it is obvious that there are many similar features betwen the two, it is impossible not to see that there is also a sharp contrast in their purpose and operation.

CHAPTER 19

The Dispensational Aspect

A. PRE-PENTECOST SAINTS WHO DID NOT SPEAK WITH TONGUES

If tongues were proof of the infilling with the Holy Spirit in New Testament times, why is it that some who are described as Spirit-filled did not speak with tongues? We refer to Zacharias (Luke 1:67), Elisabeth (Luke 1:41), John the Baptist (Luke 1:15), and the Lord Jesus (Luke 3:22; 4:1).

In answering this oft-repeated question, we would point out first of all that there is a clearly marked distinction between the filling with the Spirit prior to Pentecost and the filling with the Spirit on and after that eventful day. John the Baptist indicated this truth by declaring, "He shall baptize you with the Holy Ghost and fire" (Matthew 3:11); i.e., the Lord at some future time would give to His followers an experience which was not then available. The disciples themselves received an enduement of power before Pentecost (Matthew 10:1), but they were commanded to tarry for another and distinct enduement of power from on high (Luke 24:49), And the Lord spoke of a future event when He cried, "He that believeth on Me as the Scripture hath said, out of his belly shall flow rivers of living water. (But this spake He of the Spirit, which they that believe on Him should receive; for the Holy Ghost was not yet given: because that Jesus was not yet glorified" (John 7:38, 39).

The fact that the anointing of Jesus with the Holy Ghost at Jordan was not attended by speaking with tongues, does not prove that this supernatural manifestation is not the initial, physical evidence of the baptism with the Spirit in this dispensation. His experience there was unique, and never repeated; "for God gave not the Spirit by measure unto Him" (John 3:34). What need had the Son for the Spirit to testify, when the Father Himself spoke from heaven? Just because the Spirit gave Him no utterance in tongues, does not make void His provision to them that believe. "In My name . . . they shall speak with new tongues," said He (Mark 16:17). Nor does it invalidate the record of speaking with tongues in the Book of Acts. One might as well tell Peter to demand that the Spirit should descend upon him like a dove, rather than in the form of a fiery tongue, as to tell him that the *glossolalia* should not be considered as an inseparable part of the infilling with the Spirit, simply because this miracle of utterance had not been imparted to the Lord Jesus at Jordan.

It seems logical to conclude that it was God's will that the new experience, so distinctly a part of the new dispensation, should be made manifest by a new sign. Hence, at Pentecost the disciples spoke with other tongues, an unprecedented manifestation, which became the immediate, outward result of every complete baptism or filling with the Holy Spirit from that time forth, notwithstanding its absence in pre-Pentecostal experiences.

B. POST-APOSTOLIC SAINTS WHO HAVE NOT SPOKEN WITH TONGUES

It would appear from the available records that most of the great saints of this dispensation, who lived previous to this Twentieth Century, did not receive an infilling with the Spirit which included speaking with other tongues. This is cited frequently as proof of the error of the "tongues-evidence" teaching.

One thing immediately apparent about this argument, which carries so much weight among non-Pentecostalists, is that it is based upon men rather than upon the Scriptures. That these men had marvelous spiritual experiences and were mightily used of God is unquestioned, but we believe that we do have a perfect right to question the advisability of turning to them as the final court of appeal. The infallible Word of God is the only sure rock upon which we can build our doctrines. What we find there should be accepted as the touchstone for all teachings and experiences, regardless of its corroboration or contradiction in the lives of the most eminent of Church leaders. And we are persuaded that these men of God would be the first to insist that the Word, and not their own teachings or experiences, be the criterion for the Church with respect to the baptism or filling with the Holy Ghost. One thing is sure: if these persons are to be our final authority on one doctrine, then they must be our final authority on all doctrines. But what Calvinist refers to the Arminians among these men as his authority? Or what immersionist builds his case upon the views and practices of the "sprinklers" or "pourers"?

Nevertheless, we Pentecostalists cannot afford to

dismiss lightly this argument which has caused so many believers to reject our evidence teaching. Some satisfactory explanation must be given for this apparent refutation of our belief that speaking with tongues accompanies every true baptism with the Spirit. But as we endeavor to meet this argument, we would emphasize again this point: whether or not our reasoning in regard to the absence of tongues in the experiences of these men of God is absolutely correct, it does not alter the fact that the charismatic baptisms in the Book of Acts must remain the pattern for all Christian believers. The doctrine stands or falls on its Scripturalness, or lack of it. The experiences of men must be judged by the Scriptures, and not the Scriptures by the experiences of men.

1. THE DISPENSATIONAL PRINCIPLE

One definition of dispensation might well be that it is a period of time in which certain truths are revealed by God as a standard by which all men during that period are to be judged. It has been necessary at times, however, for God to suspend judgment according to the standard, because His people, through their sin and failure, have rendered themselves incapable of conformity to it. Rather than to cast them out altogether, He in His grace has condescended to meet them on a lower plane. Still though the initial plan has not been enforced in every particular, God has taken steps to restore it. Thus each generation is measured by the truth given in the beginning, but it is judged according to its position along the line of the recovery of that truth. This applies even to those whose hearts were perfect toward Him, but who, because of an imperfect knowledge of some portion of the original standard, failed to measure up in every regard.

As an illustration, we call your attention to God's attitude toward polygamists in Old Testament days. The original pattern was one wife for one man (Genesis 2), but this proved to be too high a standard for hard-hearted men, and so they introduced their own plan which allowed for a plurality of wives. God's plan remained exactly the same, but He was forced to meet them according to this lower, man-made plan. Now His permission of polygamy made it, in a sense, a substitute for monogamy: consequently, succeeding generations adopted it as a legitimate practice. Many godly men were allowed a number of wives, even though that was not according to the highest revelation of marriage, as shown by God in the beginning, and as ultimately restated by the Lord Jesus in Matthew 19:4-9.

2. LOSS AND RECOVERY OF NEW TESTAMENT TRUTHS

This principle is also revealed in the loss and recovery of New Testament truths and experiences by the Church. The failure of the post-apostolic Church plunged many New Testament truths and experiences into an almost total eclipse. For one thousand years Christendom was under the darkness of the perverted teachings and pagan practices of Papal Rome, and very few rays of light were able to penetrate that gross darkness. Then came the Reformation with its burning and shining lights—Luther, Zwingli, Calvin, and countless others—reviving and proclaiming long-lost Scriptural truths. The Church was awakened out of her millennium of sleep, and arose to walk again in the pathway of truth and the highway of holiness.

But even in that glorious hour the recovery of the apostles' doctrine was not complete. It was too much to expect that the reformers would leave all the error of their predecessors, or that they would restore all New Testament truth to its former radiance. It seems that they, and their successors as well, had blind spots in their spiritual vision. Some portions of truth were hidden from them, awaiting another hour for their full revelation. But each new generation brought its own theologians and revivalists who added more and more to the knowledge of the truth, and the gospel was preached in ever-increasing fullness. Precept was upon precept, line upon line, here a little and there a little, as God patiently led His Church back to the New Testament standard of doctrine and religious experience.

3. RESTORATION OF THE PENTECOSTAL BAPTISM

The baptism with the Holy Spirit was among the truths which were not fully revealed to those great men of God. With the exception of a few isolated instances, this experience had ceased to be a reality in the lives of believers, and as yet had not been restored to the Church. Many of these men realized a partial restoration of the New Testament pattern; they saw the filling with the Spirit as a definite experience subsequent to conversion, and desperately needed by every child of God; but they did not grasp its supernatural character. The fact that they could have such a baptism, opening to them the entire miraculous realm of the gifts of the Spirit, signs and wonders, had not yet been revealed to them. Now there is a vital connection between seeing a truth in the Word and possessing it as an actual experience. The law is, "According to your faith, so be it unto you." And what is the source of faith? "Faith cometh by hearing . . . the Word of God." It is only in the exceptional case that God brings a soul into an experience which has not first been perceived by that soul in the Word.

At the dawn of the Twentieth Century a deep spirit of prayer gripped many of the people of God in behalf of a great world-wide revival. This fervent intercession was accompanied by an intense study of the Scriptures. Long, prayerful hours spent in searching the Book of Acts and the Epistles convinced these believers that the early Christians enjoyed a much richer and fuller experience than they themselves had yet received. By pursuing much the same analysis as that which we have pursued in this book, they came to the conclusion that the early Christians received an enduement of power characterized by a phenomenal utterance in tongues; and further, that this should be the experience of all Christian believers. They began to concentrate their prayers on another mighty outpouring of the Holy Spirit in which the experience of the First Century disciples would become the normal experience of Twentieth Century disciples. God heard and answered that prayer, and today multiplied thousands of believers in all the world can testify to the baptism with the Holy Spirit according to the Scriptural pattern.

Just why the Lord has chosen to wait until this present century to restore this particular truth, we cannot say positively. It would be difficult to believe that it was God's desire that the miraculous aspect of the infilling with the Spirit should be sealed up until these last days. There are indications that He has tried to restore this full baptism to the Church before the Twentieth Century. At various times it seems that certain ones caught a glimpse of the truth and pressed through to a Pentecostal experience, but this was rare indeed. God's ability to give was limited by man's capacity to receive.[1] The Church was not ready for the miraculous element, and therefore He was forced to suspend the charismatic phase of the experience until now.

Another reason for the delay may be that in accomplishing His overall plan for this dispensation God has designed the full revelation of the baptism to coincide with the peculiar hour in which we live. There seems to be no escaping the fact that we have entered into the last days predicted by Paul (2 Timothy 3:1) when "perilous times shall come." The intensification of the sinful nature and deeds of man; the world situation so closely approximating the prophetical picture for both Jew and Gentile; the constant reiteration of outstanding statesmen that our whole civilization is in imminent danger: all these things make Bible students supremely conscious that we are approaching the climax of the age. How reasonable, then, to expect a fuller revelation of divine truth to meet the need of this hour!

As a general rule, when God moves in a distinctive manner, He precedes that action with the revelation of a closely related truth. Thus, to meet some partic-

---

[1] The two tables of the Law, which represented the divine standard for Israel, were broken by Moses, not because they had been set aside by God, but because the people through their sin had rendered themselves incapable of receiving them. And as a result of the failure of Israel, even the godly Levites within the nation were denied for a time the revelation of the commandments. Nevertheless, the people repented, and enabled the Lord to restore the standard which He had originally designed for them.

ular need, truths which have been but dimly discerned by the wisest of His servants are suddenly unveiled, and become common knowledge to all; while other truths, long apparent to the Church, assume a special importance. This is the underlying cause for the vastly increased light which has been shed in recent years upon the second coming of the Lord Jesus. He is coming soon! And likewise with the unfolding of the New Testament experience of the baptism with the Spirit. The revelation and preaching of this experience have enabled the Lord to send forth a marvelous Latter Rain outpouring of the Spirit, which an increasing number of believers are recognizing as God's answer to these awful days of apostasy and anti-Christian activity.

4. LIMITATION OF THEIR EXPERIENCE

The saints referred to earlier in the chapter were exceptional men, having a conception of truth and consecration deep enough to walk in the power of the experience which they did receive. It was through no fault of their own that their experience was not up to the Scriptural standard, not a full baptism with the Holy Ghost, not of a miraculous character, and not accompanied by tongues. They walked in the light which they had, and received an experience which was according to their particular period in the recovery of the truth. We reaffirm our belief in their greatness of character, and we acknowledge the marvelous results of their ministry, but we must also say that these men were limited by the time in which they lived. From the standpoint of character and ministry as forerunner of the Lord Jesus, John the Baptist was as great as any man; but from the standpoint of privilege, John was not equal to the least in the kingdom. And from the standpoint of privilege, the saints of other years of Church history are not as the least of Pentecosal saints who live in these last days when once again the fullness of the Spirit is being received as in New Testament days.

If these men were here today, they would be the first to admit that their truth and experience would not be sufficient for this hour. Their views concerning the filling with the Spirit, and many other truths which they failed to grasp fully, would need revision. Nor do we believe that these men would be adverse to necessary changes in their views and practices. Like the prophets of old, they were continually searching after and diligently inquiring about Scriptural truths upon which they had little light in their day. CHARLES G. FINNEY, in the preface to his *Systematic Theology,* expresses undoubtedly the attitude of all these men of God toward the ever-increasing knowledge of New Testament truths:

"I have not yet been able to stereotype my theological views, and have ceased to expect ever to do so. The idea is preposterous. None but an omniscient mind can continue to maintain a precise identity of views and opinions. Finite minds, unless they are asleep or stultified by prejudice, must advance in knowledge. The discovery of new truth will modify old views and opinions, and there is perhaps no end to this process with finite minds in any world. True Christian consistency does not consist in stereotyping our opinions and views, and in refusing to make any improvement lest we should be guilty of change, but it consists in holding our minds open to receive the rays of truth from every quarter and in changing our views and language and practice as often, and as fast, as we can obtain further information. I call this Christian consistency, because this course alone accords with a Christian profession. A Christian profession implies the profession of candor and of disposition to know and obey all truth. It must follow, that Christian consistency implies continued investigation and change of views and practice corresponding with increasing knowledge. No Christian, therefore, and no theologian should be afraid to change his views, his language, or his practices in conformity with increasing light. The prevalence of such a fear would keep the world, at best, at a perpetual standstill on all subjects of science, and consequently all improvements would be precluded."

5. COMPARISON OF RESULTS

The following question is sometimes raised: "If you Pentecostalists have received a greater experience, why is it that your results are not proportionately greater? When have you ever had revivals even to equal those of Wesley, Whitefield, etc.?"

The Pentecostal revival has swept around the world in an amazingly short time, bringing many thousands to a saving knowledge of the Lord Jesus, and leading many other thousands into a deeper life in God. In some respects, this revival movement compares quite favorably with the revival movements of other eras. Nevertheless, it should be pointed out that results are not always the yardstick of a spiritual experience; and we mean genuine, not spurious, results. The times, circumstances, and sovereign dealings of God must be considered in making a proper estimate of results. What apostle ever had a city-wide campaign to equal that of Jonah at Nineveh, in which the entire population of the metropolis, from the king to the lowest beggar, turned to God? But, because of the greater results of Jonah's revival.

do we prefer his spiritual revelation and experience to that of the apostles?

Then, too, on the basis of comparative results, some radio preachers today should be rated as vastly superior to the revivalists of bygone days, for they reach more people in one broadcast than the most powerful evangelists of the past reached in a lifetime; and, for that very reason, their record of conversions may be greater. Yet does this mean that these broadcasters are, necessarily, of a greater stature than those men of God who did not have the privilege of a radio ministry?

The outstanding men of the past were remarkable and unusual men, and thus, not men who should be used as a criterion. Not only were they endowed with extraordinary talents, but the very nature of their tasks made them outstanding. Consequently, they tower not only over Pentecostal believers today, but also over their own contemporaries. Not all who received the Spirit at Pentecost became apostles by virtue of that experience, though this does not mean that they did not receive the Spirit even as did those sovereignly chosen leaders of the Church. It is evident that the baptism accomplished every bit as much, proportionately, in and through them, as the experience did for those whom God had designed a larger sphere of ministry.

6. COMPARISON OF PRESENT DAY LEADERS AND PENTECOSTAL BELIEVERS

Another objection to our explanation concerning the absence of tongues in the experience of men of God in the past is advanced on the basis of the great work being done today by non-Pentecostalists. The wonderful ministry which has been given to these men is cited as positive proof that it is not necessary to receive a charismatic baptism in order to minister effectually even in these days.

However, we would remind the reader that the great non-Pentecostalists of today are like their counterparts in Church history; they are remarkable and unusual men who should not be regarded as the standard. The only satisfactory way to determine the true value of the full baptism with the Spirit is to compare the average non-Pentecostalist with the average Pentecostalist.

What difference has this baptism made between the two? Individually, the Pentecostal believer is distinguished on the whole by a greater joy in his salvation, more power in prayer, and more zeal for souls. Collectively (i.e., as a congregation) there is more of the old-fashioned revival atmosphere and freedom in worship. As an entire Movement, Pentecostalists are experiencing a growth that exceeds that of any other group of Christians. And the direct cause of all this is the mighty Pentecostal baptism! Not that we Pentecostalists feel that we have, by any means, apprehended all that we have been apprehended for. We are deeply conscious of our failure to live constantly the Spirit-filled life, of which the baptism is but the door. Still, what God has been able to do in and through these earthen vessels should be an indication of what He wants to do in and through the Church as a whole. We have no corner upon this experience; it is for all—"even as many as the Lord our God shall call"!

In regard to non-Pentecostal leaders and groups, our attitude is much like that of Aquila and Priscilla toward Apollos. To them, the eloquent disciple of John the Baptist was a great man with a wonderful ministry. Nonetheless, his conception of the truth and his spiritual experience were not complete. He needed what they had. Consequently, they sought an opportunity to "expound the way of God more perfectly unto him." Now Apollos might well have disdained them as lowly tent makers, and said, "Dost thou teach me? The truth that was good enough for my teacher is good enough for me!" But how happily for him that God had given him a broken and contrite spirit, a humility which allowed him to be taught by two lay members. He recognized in their exposition the fulfillment of his own heart cry and that of his teacher. He saw that their message was the complement, not cancelation, of what he had believed and preached up until that time. And because of his humble acceptance of the truth, his own revelation of truth and ministry increased to such an extent that one assembly held him as an equal to the two foremost apostles of the Church!

The Pentecostal message can also be despised by the great non-Pentecostal men of today; but if these present-day Apolloses can realize that this is the spiritual awakening for which they have been praying, that this is what the Church needs, and that in accepting this truth, they need not repudiate their former ministry in the slightest degree, only God knows what could be done in these closing hours! We are not thinking of what these men are now, in comparison to what the average Pentecostalist is, any more than Aquila and Priscilla compared Apollos in his former state with themselves. We are thinking, rather, of what these men are now in comparison to what they could be with this mighty Pentecostal baptism! They are great now; they would be almost apostolic then!

Would to God that some of them might have the courage to lead the way into the reception of the New Testament fullness of the Spirit. We have no desire merely to convert outstanding men to our doctrine, so that they and their followers might come into the Pentecostal Movement. Our sole hope and prayer is that the whole Church of the Living God shall be filled with the Holy Ghost! This is the only plan which God has to meet the apostasy in the Church and the anti-Christian spirit in the world. *The Church of Jesus Christ must not be content with what was good enough in the past. God's truth marches on, and the Church must keep pace!*

Part B

The Gift of Tongues

CHAPTER 20

Devotional Tongues

THE gift of tongues is twofold in its operation: devotional and congregational. The devotional or private phase of the gift attracts less attention than the more spectacular congregational or public phase, but it is none the less important. There are few spiritual exercises more edifying to the individual believer than this miraculous form of communion with God, and it is our earnest hope as we examine its nature and distribution that every *glossolalic* believer will re-echo Paul's exultant words, "I thank my God, I speak with tongues . . . ," and that all others will covet this gift for themselves.

1. MY SPIRIT PRAYETH

All speaking with tongues belongs to the realm of the human spirit. This is evident from 1 Corinthians 14: "Howbeit in the spirit he speaketh mysteries" (v. 2) ; "If I pray in an unknown tongue, my spirit prayeth" (v. 14) ; "I will pray with the spirit . . . I will sing with the spirit" (v. 15) ; "when thou shalt bless with the spirit" (v. 16). We know from the second chapter of this same Epistle that the things of man are known only by the spirit of man which is in him, even as the things of God are known only by the Spirit of God (1 Corinthians

[291]

2:11) ; i.e., our own nature is hidden to us, except through the agency of our spirit which transcends the perceiving qualities of even our intellect. Thus, in a sense, the spirit is the high priest of our whole being, knowing the needs of every part and translating them in prayer unto God, who is able to supply all our need, according to His riches in glory by Christ Jesus.

Now the spirit makes its requests known at the throne of grace by praying in a tongue unknown to our intellectual comprehension. "For if I pray in an unknown tongue, my spirit prayeth, but my understanding is unfruitful." 1 Corinthians 14:14. The theory most generally accepted by commentators is that praying with the spirit is praying with the understanding with an access of spiritual power, but this theory is refuted by these words of Paul. Prayer in an unknown tongue and prayer with the understanding are both excellent forms of prayer, but they are not one and the same. No other saint has ever prayed with a more intelligent concept of his spirittual needs than Paul, yet even he had to acknowledge that, "We know not what we should pray for as we ought." And when we, too, realize our insufficiency, then it is that the Holy Spirit "helpeth our infirmities by making intercession through us with groanings which cannot be uttered," and by giving our spirit utterance in other tongues.

2. THOU VERILY GIVEST THANKS WELL

In the giving of thanks and blessing of the Lord with our spirit (i.e., in a tongue) we can share somewhat the inspired utterance of the psalmist, though he, like all other sacred writers, was inspired in a degree unattainable by us. HAROLD HORTON has written eloquently of the privilege of such miraculous worship:

"Every consecrated believer must have felt at times a consuming desire to open his heart to God in unspeakable communication and inexpressible adoration. There is a deep in the spirit of the redeemed that is never plumbed by the mind or thought. That deep finds expression at last in the baptism of the Spirit, as unaccustomed words of heavenly coherence sweep up to the Beloved from the newly opened well of the human spirit, . . . flooded as it is with the torrential stream of the divine Spirit. Only deep can call unto deep at the noise of God's full-flowing cataracts. 'He that speaketh in a tongue speaketh not unto men but unto God: for no man understandeth him; howbeit in the spirit he speaketh divine secrets.' 1 Corinthians 14:2. The gift of tongues sinks a well into the dumb profundities of the rejoicing spirit, liberating a jet of long-pent ecstasy that gladdens the heart of God and man. Blessed fountain of ineffable coherence, of inexpressible eloquence! Have you never in the presence of Jesus felt inarticulate on the very verge of eloquence? This heavenly gift will loose the spirit's tongue and burst upon the speechless heart with utterance transcending sages' imaginings or angel rhapsodies. Have you ever wept to think how helpless your words are to express emotion in the presence of Him whom your soul loveth? Other tongues alone can give you utterance equal to the holy task. . . . Other tongues will capture the escaping thought, the elusive expression, the inarticulate longing, lending worthy and soul-satisfying utterance to profoundest gratitude and worship. . . .

"And what a rest to weary mind and nerve, to relax from mental concentration in praying and praising, and break forth in effortless utterance in the Spirit! Notice the blessed connections in Isaiah 28:11, 12: 'With stammering lips and another tongue will He speak to this people. . . . This is the rest wherewith ye may cause the weary to rest; and this is the refreshing!' What heavenly rest in spiritual exercise has the Lord designed in these heavenly tongues! Hallelujah!"[1]

3. I WILL SING WITH THE SPIRIT

How wistfully many sing, "Oh, for a thousand tongues to sing my great Redeemer's praise!" Yet when God attempts to answer that prayer in part by giving them utterance in tongues, they draw back in horror. If they only knew with Paul the joy of singing spiritual songs with the spirit, they would gladly accept the gift of tongues. Why should it be thought strange that the spirit of man desires to break forth in an ecstasy of adoring song to the Lord Jesus to the glory of God, the Father of spirits?

We have heard this singing in tongues often by a whole congregation, occasionally by a smaller group and even by a single believer; and at times it is in a voice vastly superior to the natural voice of the singer. Such singing makes us think of the ancient aeolian harps rippling out strange but beautiful harmonies as the winds blew softly over their strings. It transports us like John to that distant heavenly scene, where:

"The four beasts and four and twenty elders fell down before the Lamb, having every one of them

---

[1] *Gifts of the Spirit*, p. 138, 139, and 142.

harps, and golden vials full of odors, which are the prayers of saints. And they sung a new song saying, Thou art worthy to take the book, and to open the seals thereof: for Thou wast slain, and hast redeemed us to God by Thy blood out of every kindred, and tongue, and people, and nation; and hast made us unto our God kings and priests: and we shall reign on the earth. And I beheld, and I heard the voice of many angels round about the throne and the beasts and elders: and the number of them was ten thousand times ten thousand, and thousands of thousands; saying with a loud voice, Worthy is the Lamb that was slain to receive power, and riches, and wisdom, and strength, and honor, and glory, and blessing. And every creature which is in heaven, and on the earth, and under the earth, and such as are in the sea, and all that are in them, heard I saying, Blessing, and honor, and glory and power, be unto Him that sitteth upon the throne, and unto the Lamb for ever and ever. And the four beasts said, Amen. And the four and twenty elders fell down and worshipped Him that liveth for ever and ever" (Rev. 5:8-14).

4. AN UNKNOWN TONGUE

And speaking of heavenly scenes, what about the "unknown" tongue? Some have thought that the word "unknown," appearing in 1 Corinthians 14:2, 4, 13, 19, 27, indicates a heavenly language unknown to man. In support of this view, they cite Paul's statement concerning "tongues of angels" (13:1), and "no man understandeth him" (that speaketh in an unknown tongue—14:2). It should be observed, however, that the word "unknown" is in italics, having been supplied by the translators. This does not mean that the Greek scholars who gave us the Authorized Version have violated the Greek text in adding "unknown" to the English translation, for it is plain that the *glossolalic* utterances were rarely understood by the hearer, and never by the speaker.

But it is wrong to infer from the phrase, "unknown tongue," that one special tongue was being spoken by the Corinthians, since the gift had already been designated as "divers kinds of tongues." And it is wrong to interpret the clause, "no man understandeth him," in anything more than a general sense, for to do so would be contradictory to Acts 2:5-12. As to the reference by Paul to angelic tongues, it seems to us, though we may be mistaken, that the apostle spoke in a hyperbolical sense, describing the highest possible exercise of tongues, even as he spoke of understanding "*all* mysteries, and *all* knowledge," and having "*all* faith so that I could remove mountains." Not that we doubt that the God who can cause the dumb beast to speak in the tongue of man (Numbers 22:28-30) can also cause him who is "a little lower than angels" to speak in angelic tongues; but while such an extraordinary utterance is possible, it seems improbable.

5. HE THAT SPEAKETH . . . EDIFIETH HIMSELF

In commenting on the belief that tongues tend to the edification of the individual believer, D. A. HAYES says, "We cannot dispute this, since the statement rests upon individual conviction alone." Though it is true that the blessing and richness of this gift can be known only by personal experience, it is not true that it "rests upon individual conviction alone." It rests upon "thus saith the Lord," for Paul declared that "the things I write unto you are the commandments of the Lord." And he wrote, "He that speaketh in an unknown tongue edifieth himself." Paul should have known, for according to his own testimony he excelled in exercise of devotional tongues, and only eternity will reveal the tremendous benefit which the apostle received from this supernatural communion with God.

And we who speak with tongues today can also testify to its edifying power. We have found this gift to be a real tonic for the building up of our spiritual health in general. Especially is this true in the matter of prayer. Like all other believers, we have experienced times when the heavens seem as brass, when the spiritual atmosphere is oppressive and heavy, when the presence of God seems far away, and when sleep appeals to us far more than effectual, fervent prayer. But God, seeing beyond our outward lethargy into the awakened heart, provides a means whereby we are quickened to call on His name; viz., the *glossolalia*. It is almost incredible how quickly this praying with the spirit dispels every bit of drowsiness and dullness, and enables us to discern spiritual realities. The whole man, made alive unto God, finds it easy to pray, to lay hold of the promises, and to consecrate his all to the Lord. This exercise of devotional tongues may be difficult for some to comprehend, but to us who by the grace of God have been privileged to have this blessed experience, it is a wonderous source of edification.

6. I WOULD THAT YE ALL SPAKE WITH TONGUES

Speaking with tongues as a means of sacred and supernatural communion with God is a gift of the Spirit to be cherished and cultivated by its fortunate possessors, and a gift to be coveted and sought by them who have it not. It is true that all who covet and seek this gift do not receive. All do not speak with tongues. We must be content with the gift or gifts which the Spirit divides to us. If He, in His sovereignty and wisdom, withholds the *glossolalia* from you, there is no cause for you to feel that your spiritual attainment is necessarily inferior to that of one thus gifted. Nevertheless, until you have prayed definitely and persistently for this supernatural form of communion with the Lord, you must not conclude that it is not for you. The very fact that the gift of tongues was quite commonly distributed among the believers in the church at Corinth is proof that the Spirit wills a wider distribution of the gift today. The Holy Spirit, like the Lord Jesus on the Emmaus Road, may appear "as though He would go further," but a yearning and burning heart can ofttimes constrain Him to abide and bestow upon it more than the usual quota of His gifts.

Hear again the words of the apostle: "He that speaketh in an unknown tongue edifieth himself. . . . I thank my God I speak with tongues. . . . I would that ye all spake with tongues."

CHAPTER 21

Congregational Tongues

THE New Testment, unlike the Old Testament, lays down no set form of worship to which we as children of God must adhere. It gives us freedom to conduct our worship together according to our individual inclinations or desires, the only stipulation being that the worship must be "in spirit and in truth." This freedom has produced innumerable forms of worship, ranging from extreme ritualism to the almost complete absence of form. But though the New Testament gives us no prescribed rules whereby we are to mold our services, it does reveal a few elements of early church worship which should serve as basic principles for the entire Church.

Perhaps the most prominent feature of the worship prevalent in those days was the recognition of the presence and power of the Holy Spirit. He who was greater than Joshua had come to take the place of Him who was greater than Moses, and to Him the disciples deferred even as they had to the Lord Jesus during His earthly ministry. That the Spirit's authority was acknowledged as supreme by the apostles and the whole church is evident from His sovereign choice of Barnabas and Saul (Acts 13:2), His selection of the fields of labor for the apostles (Acts 10:19, 20; 16:6, 7), and His direction of church government (Acts 15:28). Furthermore, in the twelfth, thirteenth, and fourteenth chapters of 1 Corinthians, which take us right within the doors of the early church and give us a glimpse of its worship, we find that the Spirit was regarded as the Divine Leader of the service. When the saints assembled themselves together, they sought diligently the mind of the Spirit, for only in following His leading would it be possible for them to worship in the highest manner.

If there is one point in which the average church today fails to measure up to the New Testament standard of worship, it is in the failure to give the Holy Ghost His rightful place. Even some born-again ministers are falling short in this respect; for while they recognize their utter dependence upon the Spirit to convict and regenerate the sinner, they seem to forget His equally important ministry of enabling the believer to worship "in spirit and in truth." This accounts for their apparent inability to visualize a service which is under the direct control of the Spirit, in which human leadership is present but not predominant, in which there is a spontaneous lifting up of all voices in one accord of prayer and praise, in which supernatural gifts are in operation, and in which every believer is free to contribute openly to the profit of all. If these elements of New Testament worship are to be restored to the church at large, there must be, first of all, a restoration of the New Testament attitude toward the Holy Ghost.

But we must leave this fundamental principle,

and go on to a consideration of the relationship between divers kinds of tongues and interpretation
of tongues, two gifts which were a distinctive part
of the Spirit-inspired worship of the First Century
Church. Having discovered in previous chapters the
nature of tongues, let us now turn to an examination of its companion gift, the interpretation of
tongues.

A. WHAT IS THE GIFT OF INTERPRETA-
TION OF TONGUES?

This gift is commonly viewed as an extraordinary perception of spiritual truth, or the ability
to clarify the more difficult portions of the Scriptures. Yet in order to accept this idea of the gift, it
is necessary to ignore or deny its identification with
the *glossolalia*, which the Word of God plainly
reveals to be miraculous. Nor is it merely a natural
interpretation by one who hears his native tongue
supernaturally uttered by a believer. The men who
recognized their own tongues at Pentecost had
not received the gift of interpretation of tongues,
for they were not then members of the Church to
which the Holy Spirit bestows this gift. And Paul's
exhortation to him that speaketh in a tongue to pray
that he may interpret, should put an end to all
attempts to reduce the gift to a purely natural level.

Interpretation of tongues is the supernatural power
to understand and utter the significance of the mysteries spoken in divers kinds of tongues. It is the gift
which transforms an utterance in an unknown
tongue, edifying only to the speaker, into a "manifestation of the Spirit . . . to profit withal." It
enables him who speaks in an unknown tongue to
speak not only to God, but also to men, for, as

a rule, without this gift "no man understandeth him." Unlike tongues, the gift of interpretation involves the understanding, for the words are in a known tongue and thus clearly understood by the interpreter and congregation. Like tongues, however, interpretation does not originate in the mind of the believer but in the mind of the Spirit of God. Even the words themselves are the result of an immediate inspiration of the Spirit, rather than of a calm selection by the interpreter. In this respect, interpretation of tongues bears a resemblance to the manner in which the infallible Word came into being. "No prophecy of the Scripture is of any private interpretation. For the prophecy came not in old time by the will of man: but holy men of God spake as they were moved by the Holy Ghost" (2 Peter 1:20, 21).

We saw in the previous chapter that the utterances in tongues are chiefly devotional in character. Since the primary purpose of interpretation is to reveal the meaning of these utterances, we can expect the interpretation, in many instances, also to be devotional. Hence, a prayer in a tongue will, through interpretation, become a prayer in the language of the congregation; an utterance of praise will still be praise when interpreted; and a giving of thanks will be thanksgiving to which all may say, "Amen." How can the interpretation be genuine if it fails to express accurately the thought content and the mode of worship of the *glossolalic* utterance?

Some friends are of the opinion that the devotional aspect constitutes the entire sphere of operation of these gifts, and therefore they object to any utterance or interpretation which is in the form of a declaration, exposition, or exhortation. They argue that any utterance in a tongue, or its interpretation, which is directed toward man rather than toward God, is not Scriptural, for "he that speaketh in an unknown tongue, speaketh not unto men, but unto God" (14:2). But these friends are taking an extreme view which is not justified by a full study of the Scriptures. We do not believe that these two gifts are confined to the utterance and interpretation of inspired worship, and that alone.

It is true that the chief purpose of tongues is to provide the human spirit with an opportunity to worship God in ecstatic prayer, praise, thanksgiving, and song; and in so doing, the believer is speaking not unto men, but unto God. This does not mean, however, that the Holy Spirit does not employ tongues and interpretation as a means to communicate truth directly to men. Paul explains his statement, "He that speaketh in an unknown tongue, speaketh not unto men, but unto God," by adding the words, "for no man understandeth him" (1 Corinthians 14:2). One can hardly be said to be speaking to men, if men cannot understand him. "For if the trumpet give an uncertain sound, who shall prepare himself to the battle? So likewise ye, except ye utter by the tongue words easy to be understood, how shall it be known what is spoken? For ye shall speak into the air." (1 Corinthians 14:8, 9). The apostles does not have in mind so much the direction toward which the utterance is aimed, as he does the audience who can understand.

The purpose of prophecy is to "speak unto men unto edification, exhortation and comfort." Yet we find ofttimes in the Scriptural examples of prophecy that, mingled with the declarations and exhortations, there are praises and giving of thanks. See Luke

1:46-55, 67-79. In other words, he that prophesieth can and does occasionally speak unto God, as well as unto men. Why, then, cannot tongues at times contain truths which, when interpreted, will be a message that edifies, exhorts, and comforts the church? Paul tells us expressly in 1 Corinthians 14:5 that tongues and interpretation are equal to prophecy, and this can only mean that these two gifts must fulfill the purpose of prophecy. For that matter, there would seem to be an intermingling of various gifts of the Spirit, the word of wisdom and the word of knowledge often being included in the tongues, interpretation, and prophecy.[1]

B. WHO MAY POSSESS THE GIFT OF INTERPRETATION?

Like the other gifts of the Spirit, interpretation of of tongues is divided "to every man severally as He will." While the gift is not distributed to all, 1 Corinthians 14 seems to indicate that those who speak with tongues are usually recipients also of the interpretation of tongues. Verse 5 reveals that it is possible for him who speaks in a tongue to interpret also, and verse 13 specifically commands him to pray that he may interpret.

There are several reasons for the lack of a wider distribution of the gift. One is the doubt as to the will of the Spirit in the matter. Many are hesitant about praying definitely and importunately for the

---

[1]T. C. Edwards' Commentary is quoted by Weymouth in his notes to his translation of 1 Corinthians 14:6: "A man's spirit may, even in a state of ecstasy, receive a revelation which, interpreted, becomes a prophecy; or the ecstasy may quicken the action of thought and lead to knowledge, which may be taught as doctrine."

ability to interpret, because they fear that the gift is not for them. But since there are few who are zealous enough for the edification of the church to seek the gift, and since the Lord earnestly desires to impart it on a more abundant scale, we are confident that, in most instances, this much needed supernatural exercise will be given in answer to believing prayer; or else the discovery will be made that God in His sovereignty desires to withhold it. Of one thing we can be sure: no believer who speaks with tongues has obeyed God's command in 1 Corinthians 14:13 until he has prayed that he may interpret.

Then too, a strong and courageous faith is necessary for the exercise of this gift. Sometimes the Spirit suggests only a word, or a phrase, or a sentence to the mind of the interpreter, and the rest of the interpretation is revealed after he has begun to speak. This arouses a fear in the interpreter that he may inject his own thoughts, thus making it a private interpretation rather than the result of being borne along by the Holy Ghost. We should thank God for a wholesome fear to presume upon the exercise of a supernatural gift. May we ever shrink from any kind of an attempt to simulate the manifestation of the Spirit! But we must not allow our fear of an imperfect exercise of the gift, and the resultant criticism from others, to keep us from desiring and receiving interpretation of tongues.

It would be foolish for us not to recognize the possibility of human imperfection in this, as well as in every other realm. An interpreter, like a prophet (but unlike the sacred writers), is liable to error, and thus may express not only the thoughts of God, but also his own thoughts. On the other hand, God in His wisdom has designed that this

miraculous gift should operate through the understanding, and is able to keep the interpreter from
injecting his own thoughts. We are confident that, as
we yield ourselves wholly to Him, He will enable
us to distinguish between that which is merely human
and that which is divine.

C. JUDGING AN INTERPRETATION

If a prophecy is subject to judgment (1 Corinthians 14:29), the interpreter can expect his utterance also to be judged. This calls for humility
and courage on his part, and for charity and ability
on the part of those who would judge righteous
judgment. Now the question is, How shall we know
what constitutes a genuine interpretation?

1. It will be helpful to consider the Scriptural
title of this gift. It is "interpretation—not translation
—of tongues." The term "translation" suggests a
literal rendering of the original into another language,
a searching for exactly corresponding words; whereas
interpretation is more of a free translation, a striving
to catch the spirit of the original, rather than the
exact wording. Hence, when judging an interpretation we must not question its genuineness solely
because it is shorter or longer than the utterance in
tongues. Even a natural interpretation is not always
the same length as the utterance whose significance it
endeavors to express. The purpose of the spiritual gift
is to interpret the meaning of the mysteries in divers
kinds of tongues; it is not necessary to translate literally the unknown tongue.

2. It is our personal conviction that the supernatural character of tongues and interpretation is
strong evidence for a revelation of truth superior

to that found in the usual prayer or testimony.[1] There should be a depth of spiritual insight, a penetration of the mind of God, and vigor or forcefulness of expression which is not otherwise present. We cannot conceive that, in the economy of God, such an extraordinary utterance would be imparted, if it were to contain only ordinary thoughts. Of course, the utterance which contains present truth, truth needed at that particular time, can certainly be considered profitable, whether the truth is old or new, common or exceptional. But we believe that even familiar truth will be spoken with an unaccustomed forcefulness and anointing which the entire congregation will feel.

3. Another feature that we must bear in mind is that the personality of the interpreter has a direct influence upon the interpretation itself. "The temperament, natural gifts and training, as well of course as the nationality of the possessor of the gift, will influence the statement, but the gift is not for that reason the less supernatural. Two youths, for instance, might be sent by their employer with the same message to the same person. One might say, 'My governor cannot let you have the things you ordered.' The other, sent as a safety measure in case the first somehow miscarried, might say, 'Mr. Smith regrets that owing to a careless oversight in the hardware department he finds himself unable to supply the goods he promised.' Both messengers convey the principal message; the difference in disposition, training, and experience accounts for the difference in

---

[1]It stands to reason that the Holy Spirit will never inspire an utterance whose substance is contrary to the Word of God. If the interpretation does not agree with the Word, it is not to be accepted by anyone as genuine.

expression. The Lord equally entrusts His revelations to sanctified farm hands and God-fearing, anointed philosophers. The farm hand will deliver his message with the blunt forthrightness of an Amos; the philosopher with the refinement of an Isaiah. But remember that much correspondence with the heavenly sanctities will transform the crudities of a Galilean bumpkin into the miraculous and exalted subtleties of the Epistles of John."[1]

D. RESTRICTIONS ON PUBLIC TONGUES AND INTERPRETATION

It is only fair that we Pentecostalists who cite Paul as the foremost exponent of tongues should also be willing to bow to the restrictions which he, through the Holy Ghost, was constrained to place upon the congregational use of the gift. And we are persuaded that the great majority of Pentecostal churches do abide by these rules. Any failure to do so, we believe, stems more from an incorrect interpretation of the apostle's words than from a direct revolt against the indisputable authority of the Scriptures.

1. BY TWO OR AT THE MOST BY THREE

One error which exists among some Pentecostal believers is the failure to take literally Paul's command in 1 Corinthians 14:27: "If any man speak in an unknown tongue, let it be by two, or at the most by three, and that by course." There are a number of theories which serve to make elastic this rule which the Holy Spirit intends to be rigid.

---

[1]Harold Horton, *The Gifts of the Spirit*, p. 155.

(a) The first of these is the belief that there can be an unrestricted number of utterances in tongues, so long as not more than three persons take part. This belief is based upon the fact that "Two or at the most three" refers not to utterances but to persons. The context would seem to indicate that Paul does have references to persons, for we read, "Let one interpret" (v. 27), and "let the prophets speak two or three." v. 29. Nevertheless, we cannot agree with this theory, for in practice it would destroy the balance in congregational worship, about which Paul is so manifestly concerned; it would allow two or three persons to dominate the entire service. Speaking with tongues is not to be given so much prominence that it excludes the other gifts of the Spirit which are equally supernatural and equally edifying. The words, "two or at the most three," undoubtedly refer to persons and not specifically to utterances, but the plain implication is that three utterances are the most to be permitted in any single service, regardless of the number of persons—one, two, or three—exercising the gift. This is borne out by the instructions given to the prophets. Limited to three prophecies in a service, they are to prophesy one by one, i.e., each is to give a prophetic utterance, and then to yield to the next prophet.

(b) Another attempt to liberalize the restriction is made by designating an utterance as a fragment of a message, and allowing the gifted one to speak as many times as he feels necessary for the completion of the message. This policy, however, would produce any number of utterances, for who could decide arbitrarily whether the utterance was complete or fragmentary? Verse 27 says "speak," no mention being made of full or incomplete messages, and the simplest explanation is that whether the speaking in tongues is brief or lengthy, it is to be considered as a complete message.

(c) Some would infer from the words, "and that by course" (v. 27), that there can be an unlimited number of public utterances, just so they are in series of three each—three addresses in tongues with their interpretations in one part of the service, three more in another part, etc. To this we reply that the plain meaning of, "and that by course," is that each utterance is to be separate from the other, and is to be followed by an interpretation. To infer anything else is to distort and needlessly complicate a simple passage of Scripture. And we would also point out that prophecy, which is, at least, the equal of tongues and interpretation, is restricted to "two or three," with nothing at all being said about it which could be construed as permitting more than three.

Much unnecessary confusion and reproach will be avoided, if we Pentecostal people will be careful to limit public utterance in tongues to "two, or at the most by three" in any one service. For every instance in which an address in tongues exceeding the Scriptural maximum has brought edification, there have been scores of instances in which it has been proved most conclusively that it pays to conform to the wise counsel, yea, the command, of the apostle. There must be a limit even to supernatural gifts, and speaking with tongues is no exception.

2. LET ONE INTERPRET

"Let one interpret" means that only one believer should attempt to interpret at a time. These words do not indicate a certain individual who has been designated as "the interpreter" for the church. The gift is not imparted to all, but 1 Corinthians 14:13 reveals that every one who speaks with tongues is a potential interpreter. Anyone to whom the Spirit distributes the gift may interpret, "that the church may be edified."

3. IF THERE BE NO INTERPRETER

No one should find any difficulty in understanding Paul's insistence upon the silence of *glossolalic* believers when no interpreter is present. Ten thousand words in uninterpreted tongues are not as profitable as five words in a familiar tongue. But some may ask, "How are we to know whether or not there is an interpreter in the congregation?" In the first place, one usually worships in his own church, and thus is acquainted with the distribution of the gifts among the believers. But if he should find himself in a strange church, he must trust the Spirit to check him when no interpreter is present. As a rule, one can expect this gift to be operative in the average Pentecostal assembly, though this is not always true. In the exceptional case, the believer should hold his peace, and that church should renew its efforts in prayer for the impartation of that gift by the Holy Spirit, for it is unquestionably the will of the Lord that every local gathering of saints should experience this means of edification.

4. LET YOUR WOMEN KEEP SILENCE

Book after book and pamphlet after pamphlet, written in opposition to the Pentecostal Movement, lay great stress upon 1 Corinthians 14:34, 35: "Let your women keep silence in the churches: for it is not

permitted unto them to speak; but they are commanded to be under obedience, as also saith the law. And if
they will learn anything, let them ask their husbands
at home: for it is a shame for women to speak in the
church." Since these verses are a part of the fourteenth
chapter, which discusses so fully tongues, interpretation, and prophecy, they deserve due consideration in
this volume. Especially so, since we are told by our
critics that the permitting of women to preach and to
exercise vocal gifts in our midst is in direct contradiction to the Word, and reveals the false nature
of the entire movement.

One observation should be made, however, before we endeavor to define our position in this matter.
If we Pentecostalists are to be disqualified on this
account, then all other revival movements which have
accorded women this privilege must also be disqualified. But such a disqualification could scarcely
apply to all the outstanding men and movements
which have been signally blessed of God, even
though they have held views similar to ours on the
conduct of women in the church. Consequently, while
we do not ask that all agree with our interpretation of
verses 34 and 35, we do ask that our critics shall
not condemn us *in toto* on this account, unless they
are prepared also to condemn these other groups.

Perhaps it is the better part of discretion to introduce this rather delicate discussion with a word of
appreciation for all Christian women. We are indeed
grateful for the emancipation and ennoblement which
the gospel has brought to womanhood, and for the
fact that the members of the fairer sex have proved
themselves doubly worthy of the graciousness of
their Lord. Though the ministry of women has not
been as prominent as that of men, no one who knows

the facts of Church history would dare to say that women, by their faithful, loving, holy, and prayerful lives, have not established themselves as at least the equal of men in advancing the cause of Christ.

Nevertheless, it is apparent that in Corinth there was a need for the position of women in this present dispensation to be defined. The women in the local church were overestimating the freedom which the gospel had brought to them. Their conduct in public worship was not according to natural custom or divine sanction, and Paul was forced to speak quite sharply concerning it. They were not to assume that natural custom could be defied without bringing reproach upon both themselves and their fellow-Christians (1 Cor. 11:3-16). Neither were they to cause confusion in the service by asking their husbands questions.[1] But the issue went much deeper than "head-covering" and "husband-calling": these Corinthian women were attempting to claim full equality with men.

To correct the situation, Paul called their attention to the vital principle which was being violated; viz., the subjection of women to men. He took pains to remind them that this was no new principle; it dated back to the law (14:34), and even back to Eden itself (11:8, 9; see also 1 Timothy 2:11-15). And, by virtue of apostolic authority, he revealed that it was to be enforced during the Church Age,

---

[1]We are told that the women of that day were seated separately from the men, and this helps us to understand the reason for this particular admonition. It is difficult to believe that it applies with as much force to the women of today who may whisper a question to their husband sitting beside them, as it did to the women of that day who were forced to call aloud to their husbands sitting on the other side of the congregation.

it being as necessary now as it was in Old Testament days. Any attitude or action which would defy this God-ordained principle was to be viewed as disobedience to the commandments of the Lord.

It is our opinion that the words of the apostle in 1 Corinthians 14:34, 35 and 1 Timothy 2:11, 12 are to be considered as a general rule, rather than an absolute rule which will admit no exceptions. Women must not attempt to usurp authority over men. They are to maintain silence in the church in regard to doctrinal and governmental issues, and they are not to claim equality with men in the public proclamation of the gospel. Nevertheless, we find that in Old Testament times, when the subjection of women was very strictly enforced, Deborah judged Israel (Judges 4:4), and Huldah prophesied unto men. 2 Chronicles 34:22-28. In the New Testament we read of Priscilla teaching doctrine to Apollos (Acts 18:26), and if her ability to expound the Word was at least the equal of that of Aquila, as the record seems to imply, then it is reasonable to conclude that the church which was in their house (Romans 16:5) must have enjoyed her expositions as well as those of her good husband. But these and similar instances are exceptional and not the rule.

Perhaps the present day Pentecostal Movement has been somewhat lenient in its enforcement of 1 Corinthians 14:34, 35. This leniency may be due to a reaction against the extremely legal attitude of other groups; or it may be that we have been influenced by the Twentieth Century idea about women's rights; or it may be that we have emphasized the Scriptural exception rather than the rule. Nevertheless, we do feel that the spirit of the rule is in effect in our midst. On the whole, women are not given undue prominence in the movement; they represent a very small percentage of the ministry; and they are virtually silent with respect to doctrinal and governmental questions. We have endeavored conscientiously to abide by the Word in this matter, following the general rule, and at the same time recognizing that, in some instances, women may speak in the church without violating their subjection to men.

Of one thing we can be sure: If these passages under discussion are to be interpreted in an absolute sense, then we Pentecostalists are not the only ones who are failing to measure up to the standard. We know of no group which requires women to remain in *absolute* silence. Even those who interpret these verses most literally permit the women to lift up their voices in special and congregational singing, responsive readings, and occasionally in testimonies. But if "silence" and "speak" are to be taken literally, women must maintain utter silence "when the church be come together in one place."

But, as we have already mentioned, the Word itself qualifies the command. On the very first day of the Church's history, the mother of Jesus and other women spoke with other tongues as the Spirit gave them utterance. This was certainly a coming together of the church in one place, and women were not only permitted to speak, but actually inspired by the Holy Ghost to do so! And that despite the presence of many men in that audience! Peter's explanation was that, according to the promise of the Father, the Spirit had been poured out upon the handmaidens, and consequently the daughters were prophesying.

In 1 Corinthians 11 Paul himself recognizes the

privilege of women to pray and prophesy. Now it must be conceded that whether prophecy is exercised by the four daughters of Philip (Acts 21:9) or by Agabus (Acts 21:10), it is the same in essence, purpose, and operation. The prophetic words are given by immediate, divine inspiration; they are spoken "unto men to edification, and exhortation, and comfort"; and they are for public (not private) use. Some may object that the tacit permission of the apostle in 1 Corinthians 11 for women to prophesy refers to gatherings of women only, but the passage itself does not justify this view. If anything, it strongly indicates the presence of men. And it is inconceivable that the Holy Spirit would allow Paul in chapter 11 to write, without condemnation, of prophesying by women, only to forbid it in chapter 14.

There is no evading the fact that women, as well as men, are members of the Body of Christ,[1] and thus are entitled to receive and exercise the miraculous gifts of the Spirit. We may not be able to reconcile this with the apparently absolute command that women are to keep silence in the church, but the fact remains that the Spirit has imparted such gifts to women in New Testament days and through the centuries of Church history. The most reasonable position, then, would seem to be the insistence upon the underlying principle of the whole matter, the

---

[1]"For by one Spirit are we all baptized into one body, whether we be Jews or Gentiles, whether we be bond or free; and have all been made to drink into one Spirit." 1 Corinthians 12:13. "For ye are all the children of God by faith in Christ Jesus. There is neither Jew nor Greek, there is neither bond nor free, there is neither male nor female: for ye are all one in Christ Jesus." Galatians 3:26-28.

subjection of women to men, the enforcement of the general rule concerning their conduct in the church, and the allowance of the exception to the rule.

5. LET ALL THINGS BE DONE DECENTLY AND IN ORDER

The Holy Spirit never renders anyone incapable of self-control. "The spirits of the prophets are subject to the prophets" (1 Corinthians 14:32). He does not cause a believer to act in any way contrary to the Word which He has inspired. This means that all those who possess the gifts of the Spirit should acquaint themselves thoroughly with the Scriptural regulations for their manifestation, and seek to conform every manifestation of the gifts to them. There is no real bondage in obedience to these regulations, and no real liberty in casting them aside.

It is possible for the gifts of the Spirit to "be exercised in such maturity, order, and love that there shall be, as far as possible, nothing repellant in their nature, or likely to cause an unnecessary stumbling-block to anyone. When thus exercised these gifts are singularly beautiful, and we trust that familiarity will never weaken our personal sense of awe and wonderment when the Spirit of God is truly manifesting His presence in the assembly in this way."[1] "Even so ye, forasmuch as ye are zealous of spiritual gifts, seek that ye may excel to the edifying of the church" (1 Corinthians 14:12).

---

[1]Donald Gee, *Concerning Spiritual Gifts.*

Part C

Tongues---A Sign

CHAPTER 22

A Sign of Confirmation

THE great problem of the Church today is world evangelization. All other problems assume importance only as they relate to this all-important business. And with the time for witnessing growing so short, the Church must awaken to the fact that what will be done must be done quickly.

"O Zion haste, thy mission high fulfilling,
To tell to all the world that God is light;
That He who made all nations is not willing
One soul should perish, lost in shades of night.
Publish glad tidings, tidings of peace,
Tidings of Jesus, redemption and release."

If ever there was a time when outward conditions were favorable to world evangelization, it is now. Radio has indeed given "the winds a mighty voice," with broadcasts of the gospel winging their happy way to the uttermost part of the earth. Huge printing presses make possible the distribution of millions of Bibles, Testaments, Gospels, tracts and other forms of Christian literature to the increasingly literate multitudes. Airplanes, launches, motorcycles, and other modern vehicles provide means whereby the missionary can visit more swiftly his own territory, and also evangelize the regions beyond.

Yet the evangelization of the world lags. Why? Is it because of the intense activity of wicked spirits in high places? The deeply entrenched systems and philosophies of heathen nations? The fierce enmity manifested toward the gospel by a sinful and adulterous generation? Doubtless, all of these combine to impede the progress of the "good news." But is this the real cause? When has opposition by demons or men ever been sufficient of itself to frustrate the plan of God? Sacred and secular history alike attest the fact that God's purposes are never broken off solely on the ground of demonic or human resistance.

The real cause for failure is the Church. Upon her refusal to be and to do what her Lord desires her to be and to do, lies the blame. Thus it has been in the past, and thus it is today. When we speak of failure in the Church, we do not refer to a deficiency in money, machinery, or messengers, for these are but secondary matters which will be added when the Church seeks first the kingdom of God and His righteousness. We refer, rather, to a deficiency in spiritual health and in following God's perfect plan for evangelism.

How the Church needs a revival in these last days! How impotent she is to meet her God-given responsibility! Weakened from within by corruption and compromise, she has little heart, and even less power, for the tremendous task of reaching this generation with the gospel. We agree wholeheartedly with Dr. Vance Havner that "the Church will not get on its feet until first its gets on its knees in repentance."[1] If the Church would fulfill her high mission, she must purge herself from all sin and

---

[1] *Jesus Only*, Fleming H. Revell Co., New York, N. Y.

ungodliness. Then, and only then, will she become "a vessel unto honor, sanctified, and meet for the Master's use, and prepared unto every good work." 2 Timothy 2:21.

But even this is not enough. The Church, penitent and purged, is merely prepared for the good work of evangelism; she is ready to know and to follow the divine plan for the publishing of the gospel to every creature. Now the question is, where can she find God's best program for awakening nominal Christian lands out of their calloused indifference to the cause of Christ, and reaching the uttermost part of the earth with the message of salvation?

The answer is so obvious that it seems strange that the question need ever be asked. The place where we find the message is the very same place where we find the method of propagating it—the Holy Scriptures! Why do we emphasize such an elementary truth? For the simple reason that the Church, in its scrutiny of early church methods of evangelization, has overlooked a most vital part, viz., divine confirmation of the message with miraculous signs. The failure of the Church since apostolic days to seek and receive such confirmation is a major factor in her slowness in carrying out the Great Commission.

It is not necessary to repeat our arguments of Chapter 5 concerning the reasonableness of expecting God to bear us witness today "both with signs and wonders, and with divers miracles, and gifts of the Holy Ghost." Hebrews 2:4. But it should be stressed that since this expectation is legitimately ours, we should seize every opportunity to lift up our voices to God, and pray with the fervency and faith of the early church: "And now, Lord, behold their threatenings: and grant unto Thy servants, that

[323]

with all boldness they may speak thy word, by
stretching forth Thy hand to heal; and that signs
and wonders may be done by the name of thy holy
child Jesus" (Acts 4:29, 30).

And what can we expect when the God of all grace
answers this prayer?

First, *these signs will bring glory to the Lord
Jesus Christ*. Peter appealed to the phenomena at
Pentecost as a positive token of His exaltation: "This
Jesus hath God raised up, whereof we all are witnesses. Therefore being by the right hand of God
exalted, and having received of the Father the promise
of the Holy Ghost, He hath shed forth this, which
ye now see and hear. . . . Therefore let all the
house of Israel know assuredly, that God hath made
that same Jesus, whom ye have crucified, both Lord
and Christ" (Acts 2:32, 33, 36). All they who
love the Lord Jesus in sincerity ought to rejoice
over any thing which will bring Him praise and
glory.

Second, *these signs will enable the Church to become what the Lord has designed her to be*; viz.,
"fair as the moon, clear as the sun, and terrible as an
army with banners" (Songs of Solomon 6:10). Too
long the Church has waged half-hearted warfare
against the gates of hell, cringing before the on-
slaughts of unbelieving men, compromising in order
to gain the favor of the world that crucified her
Lord, conceding the anti-Scriptural hypotheses of
"science falsely so called," and contradicting her message of the resurrection by her apparent lack of contact with a supernatural Leader.

How different the triumphant early church! Confronted on every hand with much the same opposi-

tion, those first soldiers of the Cross did not content themselves with passive resistance, but carried the battle to the enemy. And even a cursory reading of the Book of Acts shows that miraculous signs were the spearhead of the entire attack. To those who daily witnessed manifestations of divine power, the ascension of Jesus to the right hand of the Father was more than a Mount Olivet memory; it was a constant reality. And who could live in the midst of such miracles, and doubt that Jesus of Nazareth was the Lord of life and death? His lordship over every earthly realm was revealed by the signs mentioned in Mark 16:17, 18. How conscious of the presence of God must have been those early disciples as He "worked with them, confirming the word with signs following." What dignity, solemnity, and authority this visible approval of God imparted to them, to say nothing of the boldness to declare the message of salvation.

The objection against what is commonly termed "sign-seeking" would not have carried much weight in the First Century church. These disciples had heard their Master rebuke the Pharisees who sought a sign from Him, and yet they themselves prayed a Spirit-inspired prayer for "signs and wonders to be done by the name of Thy holy child Jesus." It was the difference in motive which evoked a denial for signs to a sinful and adulterous generation, but which granted them to Holy Ghost-filled believers. A carnal desire for miracles as a means of attracting popular attention to oneself, or for financial gain, or for satisfying an occult curiosity, must ever bring a stinging rebuke from heaven. But an unselfish desire to see Christ glorified and sinners converted must ever bring a favorable response from the heart of God.

Third, *the effect upon the world.* Apathy toward the gospel is impossible where God is "confirming the word with signs following." Persecution there may be, but never indifference. The day of Pentecost is indicative of the power of supernatural manifestations to arrest the attention of men to eternity's values. DR. HAVNER writes: "Two questions were asked by the people that day: 'What meaneth this?' and 'What shall we do?' Today we are trying to reverse the order. We are trying to make men ask, 'What must I do to be saved?' before they have seen enough in our churches to make them inquire, 'What meaneth this?' We are emphasizing evangelism without revival, which is not God's order. When men have been amazed by a church drunk with the wine of Pentecost, we may expect them to inquire further as to the way of salvation."[1]

Although Dr. Havner does not mention the phenomena which occurred on that day, we believe that his conclusion has a special application to the sound like as of a rushing, mighty wind, the tongues like as of fire, and the *glossolalia,* for the amazement of the multitude was primarily due to these manifestations. And since human nature is the same today, we can expect the miraculous to bring forth amazement and wonder among all kinds of men. The miraculous is no respecter of persons, and no matter what a man's station in life, he is only natural, and thus is startled by the supernatural.

Of course, every reader is familiar with the fact that the first question at Pentecost, "What meaneth this?" referred specifically to tongues. This miracle of utterance was a sign which opened the hearts

---

[1] *Jesus Only,* Fleming H. Revell Co., New York, N. Y.

of the multitude to Peter's message. Long before the Lord Jesus had prophesied that they that believe should speak with new tongues (Mark 16:17), Isaiah had uttered words which Paul identified with the *glossolalia*: "In the law it is written, With men of other tongues and other lips will I speak to this people; and yet for all that will they not hear Me. saith the Lord. Wherefore tongues are for a sign, not to them that believe, but to them that believe not" (1 Corinthians 14:21, 22). It must be conceded that the Old Testament prophecy was speaking of the unknown tongues of foreign invaders, but Paul, led by the Holy Spirit, identified it with the New Testament speaking with tongues.

Many well-authenticated testimonies from all over the world could be given to support the fact that tongues are a sign. MR. HAYES may say, "In the average church community of America I think there is no doubt that they (tongues) will do more harm than good among the unbelievers."[1] But in America, where so many diverse tongues are spoken, a manifestation similar to that at Pentecost could have a marked effect upon those who heard their own tongue. And it has actually occurred. But even when there is no one present who understands the utterance, it serves as a sign of the presence of God in the midst of the congregation.

We regret that in some Pentecostal circles there has been an excessive restriction of the public aspect of the gift of tongues. It has been taught that this gift is to be exercised only in worship services or believers' meetings, and that the preacher should never be interrupted by an utterance in tongues. This

----

[1] *The Gift of Tongues.*

attitude, a reaction to an unwise use of the gift, would exclude tongues entirely from evangelistic services, and is a long step toward eliminating tongues altogether.

As for the first teaching, there is nothing in 1 Corinthians 14 to warrant the belief that the gift is to be manifested only among believers. If anything, the chapter teaches that the value of tongues as a sign is according to its exercise among unbelievers. Also, when tongues and interpretation fulfill the purpose of prophecy, they may reveal the secrets of the heart and cause the sinner to confess and repent of his sins. As for the second teaching, while we would not encourage a constant interruption of the speaker, we certainly do not feel that this is a restriction which must be observed at all times. When we look away from the traditional form of service to the apostolic form, as revealed in Acts and Corinthians, we see that it was not a "one-man show," but that quite a number of believers took part. And the closer we get to the pattern, the more content we shall be to submerge our individuality, and allow the possessors of the gifts to contribute to the profit of all, and the less we shall attempt to say to the Spirit of God, "Thus shalt Thou work, or not at all!"

DONALD GEE has some splendid thoughts which are worthy of consideration in this connection:

"Difficulties in combining an exercise of spiritual gifts with evangelism reveal something wrong with our understanding either of the gifts of the Spirit, or of true evangelism, or both.

"This supposition that the two cannot be combined has become more than an idea; it has become a policy. There are Pentecostal leaders and assemblies who are rightly keen upon aggressive evangelism, and yet feel that the only way they can successfully pursue their object is to frown upon all exercise of spiritual gifts, at least in public meetings. Under such a policy distinctive Pentecostal testimony and experience usually come to a full stop with converts receiving the baptism with the Holy Spirit. Frequently there gradually creeps in a marked tendency to resort to purely natural methods of attraction to, and conduct of, the services rather than a dependence upon the supernatural power of the Spirit. It is difficult to believe that some of these methods do not actually grieve the Holy Spirit. The vision of a truly New Testament church becomes blurred and lost.

"It is only fair to add that there are other leaders and assemblies that make much of at least some of the gifts of the Spirit, but are plain failures when it comes to evangelism. Yet they sometimes boast of being 'real Pentecost,' and regard these others as miserable backsliders. 'Real Pentecost' for these folk evidently does not extend beyond the verse 4 of Acts 2; it has no interest in verse 41! Barrenness on the line of soul-winning seems to give them no concern; they are content to stay in their little meetings having 'good times,' and (presumably) 'letting the Lord have His way'; as though the Christ of Calvary had ceased to care any longer for the rolling tide of human woe and suffering. Sometimes these little companies take a commendable interest in foreign missions, but evangelical interest that is centered abroad and not equally as much at home is in danger of becoming merely sentimental, and is certainly not 'Pentecostal' in the true, Scriptural sense.

"*Can the two be combined?* Such a question ought

never to be seriously asked before an open Bible. They were combined in the early church, with conspicuously successful results. They must be combined today, if we are to attain to all that which 'Pentecost' really stands for.

"The pre-eminent place of the Holy Spirit in all true evangelism will be conceded by all. It is His particular work to convict of sin (John 16:8); it is He who lifts up Christ (John 15:26; 16:14); through His gracious energy we are born again. John 3:5. Gifts that come from Him and are His 'working' (1 Corinthians 12:7-11) cannot, therefore, be antagonistic to the evangelism but must have a valuable and well-defined place in all that has to do with soul-winning. . . .

"This gift (tongues) is one of God's 'signs' to the unbeliever (1 Corinthians 14:22), and must therefore have a legitimate place on occasions when the unbeliever is present. On the day of Pentecost it produced a double result of amazement and derision (Acts 2:13, 14), but it plainly had a big part in attracting the attention of the people to the gospel message preached by Peter. The only Scriptural ground (and therefore the only right ground) to take is that this gift is not antagonistic but is positively helpful to evangelism when rightly used. If it has proved a hindrance to evangelistic work it can only be because it has been wrongly used, probably by earnest but misguided people.

"Perhaps we might add that as a 'sign' to unbelievers in connection with evangelistic services we think this gift will be used by the Holy Spirit very seldom. 'Familiarity breeds contempt,' and a 'sign' used two or three times in every meeting soon becomes nauseating rather than convicting. Occasionally used, however, it can have startling results, and this would seem to be the divine purpose. We are not referring to private uses of the gift for devotional purposes (1 Corinthians 14:2), but to its place in the public meeting.

"The gift of *interpretation of tongues* has unique value in connection with the 'unlearned' (which may apparently include the 'unbeliever' also—see 1 Corinthians 14:23—with whom we are particularly interested in evangelism), in that it brings utterances in 'tongues' by the saints in the assembly within the grasp of his understanding. Verses 13-16. This involves the possibility of the utterance having the same effect upon him as prophesying. v. 24. 'Interpretation' is not always necessary when the Spirit is using the gift of tongues for a direct sign to unbelievers. Judging from Acts 2, there are occasions when the tongue spoken will be well enough understood by the one for whom the sign is intended. The gift of interpretation is primarily for the church. v 5."[1]

And now, to conclude the chapter, we would repeat our assertion that the confirmation of our message "with signs following" is a vital part of God's plan for world evangelization. The early church is a shining example of the effectiveness of the miraculous to quicken the spread of the gospel. A miracle is understood by all people in all lands, and while some would not believe though one were to rise from the dead, there are many who, by reason of witnessing the outstretched hand of the Lord, would believe. This fact has been abundantly proved since the beginning of this Twentieth Century, in which one of the major factors has been the super-

---

Pentecost, pages 82, 83, 84, 88, 89.

natural workings of the Holy Spirit. Even so, we believe that as the Church draws nearer to the coming of the Lord, we shall witness an era of miracles of which this Pentecostal revival is but the forerunner. May God stir His people to come boldly to the throne of grace with the earnest prayer:

> "Lord, send the old-time power, the Pentecostal power,
> Thy flood-gates of blessing on us throw open wide;
> Lord, send the old-time power, the Pentecostal power,
> That sinners be converted and Thy name glorified!"

CHAPTER 23

A Sign of Judgment

"MENE, MENE, TEKEL UPHARSIN"—strange words in an unknown tongue, written upon the wall of the palace by the fingers of a man's hand, bringing terror to a Babylonian king and his guests. The wisest of Babylon's court could not read or interpret them; only Daniel, the Hebrew, "in whom was the spirit of the holy gods," knew their awful significance. Astonished and troubled by the supernatural writing, the banqueting throng listened in horrified silence to the interpretation which fell from the prophet's lips. Each word was like the tolling of the bell of doom for Belshazzar and his fellows—"God hath numbered thy kingdom and finished it. . . . Thou art weighed in the balances, and art found wanting. . . . Thy kingdom is divided, and given to the Medes and Persians."

Why was the handwriting on the wall in an unknown tongue? Would not the warning have been as impressive in the language of the Chaldeans? Evidently not, otherwise God would have designed it that way. As it was, the miracle was heightened by the mystery which surrounded the words themselves,

[333]

making necessary a revelation of divine wisdom which was hidden to wise men after the flesh. Hence, the sign, though spectacular in itself, was even more startling through the employment of an unknown tongue.

Does not this fact suggest an answer to those who complain that they see no reason for a message from God to man in a language unfamiliar to its hearers? An unknown tongue is not the usual manner by which God speaks to man, but this instance at Babylon is proof that He occasionally has employed such means to convey a message.

In Chapter 22 we considered the *glossolalia* as a sign of confirmation. Here we shall consider its relationship to unbelievers who will not repent. The gospel, as a whole, is either a savor of life unto life or a savor of death unto death, depending upon whether it is accepted or rejected by those who hear. And what is true of the whole is also true of the part. Speaking with tongues is both a confirmatory and a condemnatory sign. It causes some to acknowledge the power and presence of God in the midst of His people, and to believe, whereas it produces upon others no transforming effect whatsoever. To the latter group it is what the handwriting on the wall was to blasphemous Belshazzar and his friends, a sign of impending judgment.

Most students of the Scriptures are familiar with the term, "law of first mention." This law may be defined on this wise: The first mention in the Word of a subject establishes the primary character and purpose of that particular subject, though secondary characteristics and purposes may appear later in the Word. Let us see how this law applies to tongues.

The initial reference to tongues is found in Isaiah 28:11, 12: "For with stammering lips and another tongue will He speak to this people. To whom He said, This is the rest wherewith ye may cause the weary to rest; and this is the refreshing; yet they would not hear." If the reader will study the context, he will discover that God had sought repeatedly to bring His people to a heart knowledge of truth, sending unto them prophets and teachers. But this was all in vain, for they rejected His warnings and set themselves against the Lord. Consequently, His justice required that His long-suffering be replaced by His strange work of judgment. Foreign armies would soon sweep down upon the rebellious nation, and then the people, hearing the strange tongues in their midst, would know that God was speaking in His wrath.

Following the gracious restoration of Israel to the land, the Lord sought once again to draw them unto Himself, but, as before, the stiffnecked and uncircumcised in heart resisted the Holy Ghost, persecuting and slaying the prophets. In the fullness of time God sent forth His Son, approving Him in their midst with signs and wonders and miracles, only to have Him rejected and crucified. Surely Israel's place as the chosen of God had been forfeited; her cup of iniquity was full. And when the Lord Jesus, the brightness of the Father's glory, "was taken up; and a cloud received Him out of their sight," the word "Ichabod" was truly inscribed over the nation.

How clearly this fact was revealed to Israel on the day of Pentecost. Sign after sign had been given to this disobedient and gainsaying people in the hope that they might return to the Lord, but on that day God spoke to them through the miraculous utterances of the Galileans, as He had spoken to their fathers by the tongues of invading armies. "What meaneth this?" they cried. Well might Peter have replied: "This meaneth that the wrath of Jehovah abideth over Israel; that because of your wicked rejection of the Lamb of God, the angel of death will not pass over you; that the salvation of God is sent unto the Gentiles, and they will hear it."

Judgment upon Israel was inevitable after this sign of condemnation, even though it did not follow immediately, as in Belshazzar's case. It was not until approximately forty years later that the blow fell. The legions of Titus were the scourge by which the Lord executed His wrath upon the apostate nation. Jerusalem was destroyed, and not one stone of the magnificent temple, of which Israel had been so proud, was left upon another. Behold the severity of God.

We wish that it were possible to trace the aftermath of the manifestations of the tongues phenomenon through the long years of Church history, for we are quite certain that these manifestations were also followed by judgments. At least, we have Scriptural grounds for believing that a major reason for the public exercise of tongues by persecuted peoples was as a sign of condemnation to their persecutors. Spiritual and moral judgments have always followed the sporadic outburst of the *glossolalia*, and there are a few instances in which even physical judgment seems to have fallen upon the enemies of the gospel.

And now, what meaneth this present-day speaking in tongues? It must have a special significance in this the most important and most revolutionary century since the time of Christ. Never has man advanced so far in material and scientific knowledge.

And yet, for all his vaunted wisdom, which has enabled him to penetrate the very secret of the physical universe, atomic energy, he has not made corresponding progress in spiritual knowledge. On the contrary, he is at the lowest moral and spiritual ebb of all his tragic history. Iniquity abounds on every hand. Total destruction through atomic and rocket warfare is a constant threat to the entire civilization. A world government, whose reins eventually will be taken over by the Antichrist, is becoming more than a prophecy; it is even now materializing.

What meaneth, then, this speaking with other tongues in the Twentieth Century? It means that the times of the Gentiles are being swiftly fulfilled! It means that a last and final sign is being given to an adulterous and sinful generation! It means that the nations tremble on the brink of destruction! It means that, *as local judgments have followed local manifestations of the glossolalia, even so universal judgment will follow its universal manifestation today!* It means that soon the seals will be opened, the trumpets sounded, and the vials of wrath poured out on this present evil world!

But we have not been "appointed unto wrath, but to obtain salvation by our Lord Jesus Christ," and to us this speaking with tongues means that our "redemption draweth nigh." It means that the midnight cry, "Behold, the Bridegroom cometh; go ye out to meet Him," will soon be heard. Then in that happy hour, notwithstanding the gross darkness of this world, we shall arise and shine, for He who is our Light shall come. Even so, come quickly, Lord Jesus!

SECTION IV

CONCLUSION

"Men and brethren, what shall we do?"
Acts 2:37

CHAPTER 24

"Wherefore, Brethren"

THE multitude listened intently as Simon Peter, the Galilean fisherman, gave the divine answer to the question "What meaneth this?" Slowly and deliberately, and yet with great fervency, Peter forged link after link in a chain of logic from which there was no possible escape. He explained, he expounded, he denounced, until, unable to restrain themselves any longer, his conscience-stricken hearers cried out, "Men and brethren, what shall we do?"

"Then said Peter unto them, Repent, and be baptized every one of you in the name of Jesus Christ for the remission of sins, and ye shall receive the gift of the Holy Ghost. For the promise is unto you, and to your children, and to all that are afar off, even as many as the Lord our God shall call. And with many other words did he testify and exhort, saying, Save yourselves from this untoward generation. Then they that gladly received his word were baptized: and the same day there ware added unto them about three thousand souls" (Acts 2:38-41).

Oh, what power and blessing are in words taken from the Scriptures, the very fountains of truth;

words inspired by the Holy Ghost, the Spirit of Truth; words set on fire of heaven; words like a hammer that breaketh the rock in pieces; words like a two-edged sword piercing even to the dividing asunder of soul and spirit! Would to God that our humble attempts to answer the question, "What meaneth this?" had an abundance of such words! But we must content ourselves with the consciousness that we have done our best to "speak the things which we have seen and heard." And so, with a few final words, we would testify and exhort our various readers.

First, *a word to the unsaved*. Although we anticipate largely a Christian reading of this volume, there may be some readers who have never been brought into personal contact with our wonderful Christ. If you are among that number, we would urge you to delay no longer in becoming acquainted with Him. The Scriptural, historical, and experimental facts which we have presented within these pages are abundant proof that Jesus of Nazareth is not among the dead, but is indeed the risen Saviour. These facts testify to the glorious possibility of God's being actually present in the life of them that love and obey Him, working spiritual, moral, intellectual, and physical miracles. Will you not this moment fly to the bosom of Him who loved you enough to die for you, that you might be forgiven? Will you not enter now into the presence of Him who can save you from the guilt and power of sin, and who can bring a deep, settled peace into your soul? Will you not this day surrender your all to Him who surrendered His all for you? Do it NOW! You will never regret it.

Second, *a word to non-Pentecostal Christians*.

Those of you who are included in this particular group have an opportunity now to examine minutely the Pentecostal view of speaking with other tongues. You can see whether or not this view agrees with the Word of God, and whether or not your objections to it have been met satisfactorily. However, we would remind each of you that the reading of this volume means that you must ultimately make a decision, either to accept or to reject the Pentecostal answer to the question "What meaneth this?" But though you must decide, we would not encourage you to make a hasty decision, for, no matter which way you choose, the price is great. If you accept our belief concerning tongues, you face the possible loss of religious reputation, ecclesiastical position, life-long friendships, and even temporal comforts. On the other hand, if you reject it, you will be rejecting that which an overwhelming amount of evidence proclaims as truth. Wherefore, brethren, we beseech you to count the cost carefully and prayerfully, and to ask God for grace to suffer the loss of all things rather than to sacrifice the priceless pearl of truth.

Pentecostal truth has, at times, fallen among thieves, who have stripped it of its dignity, beauty, and power, and have wounded it, and departed, leaving it half dead. And by chance there have come certain priests and Levites that way, who, fearing the reproach and ostracism of their fellows, have passed by on the other side. But certain Samaritans, as they have journeyed, have come where the truth has lain fallen in the street, and seeing what that truth might be if restored to its original health and vitality, have identified themselves with it, regardless of the cost. (Some would like to play the good Samaritan, but would withhold the oil and wine and two pence.) "Which now of these three, thinkest thou, was neighbor unto him that fell among the thieves? And he said, He that shewed mercy on him. Then said Jesus, Go, and do thou likewise."

Third, *a word to Pentecostal Christians*. It is our sincere hope, brethren, that this volume has strengthened your belief in the Scripturalness of our Pentecostal teaching with regard to speaking with other tongues. We trust that this Pentecostal answer to the Pentecostal question, "What meaneth this?" is reasonable enough to satisfy your mind, as well as your heart. How we should thank God for bringing us into the light of Pentecostal truth! We do well, however, to remember that this blessed privilege also brings a solemn responsibility. We must walk in the light which God has graciously shed upon our pathway, and this can be accomplished "not by might, nor by power, but by my Spirit, saith the Lord of hosts." Wherefore, brethren, let us pray for a constant, personal strengthening of might by His Spirit in the inner man, and for a new outpouring of His Spirit upon the Movement and the entire Church in these last days.

And now before we write "finis" to this study of the *glossolalia*, we would turn the eyes of all to that fast-approaching hour when that which is perfect shall come. Gone then will be "this poor, lisping, stamm'ring tongue"; yea gone even the Spirit-inspired utterance in divers kinds of tongues—for tongues will have ceased. Then in a nobler, sweeter song we shall join with that great multitude, which no man can number, of all nations, and kindreds, and tongues, and sing His power to save. Then "at the name of Jesus every knee shall bow, of things in heaven, and things in earth, and things under the earth; and every tongue shall confess that Jesus Christ is Lord to the glory of God the Father."

> "O Lord Jesus, how long, how long—
> Ere we shout the glad song,
> 'Christ returneth, Hallelujah!
> Hallelujah! Amen!' Hallelujah! Amen!"

THE END

Bibliography

The following works have been helpful in gathering material for this volume. With the exception of the standard reference works and those published by the authors themselves, the publisher is listed in each instance.

Anderson, Sir Robert, *Spirit Manifestations and the Gift of Tongues,* Loizeau Bros., New York, N. Y.

Barratt, Thomas B., *In the Days of the Latter Rain,* Elim Publishing Co., London, England.

   The Baptism With the Holy Ghost and Fire, Gospel Publishing House, Springfield, Mo.

Bushnell, Horace, *Nature and the Supernatural,* Chas Scribner and Sons, New York, N. Y.

Church of God Evangel, Church of God Publishing House, Cleveland, Tenn.

Clarke, Adam, *Commentary on the Whole Bible.*

Conybeare and Howson, *Life and Epistles of St. Paul.*

Crockett, Horace L., *Conversations on "The Tongues,"* Pentecostal Publishing Co., Louisville, Ky.

Cummings, Robert, *Unto You Is the Promise,* Gospel Publishing House, Springfield, Mo.

Cutten, George Barton, *Speaking With Tongues,* Yale University Press, New Haven, Conn.

Dalton, Robert Chandler, *Tongues Like as of Fire,* Gospel Publishing House, Springfield, Mo.

Dolman, D. H., *Simple Talks on the Holy Spirit,* Fleming H. Revell, New York, N. Y.

Drummond, Andrew L., *Edward Irving and His Circle,* J. Clarke and Co., London, England.

Encyclopedia *Brittanica.*

Erickson, E. C., *The Bible on Speaking in Tongues.*

Fisher, J. Franklin, *Speaking With Tongues.*

Foursquare Magazine, Echo Park Evangelistic Assoc., Los Angeles, Calif.

Frodsham, Stanley H., *With Signs Following*, Gospel Publishing House, Springfield, Mo.

Gee, Donald, *Concerning Spiritual Gifts, God's Great Gift, and Pentecost*, Gospel Publishing House, Springfield, Mo.

Hastings, James, *Dictionary of the Bible.*

Havner, Vance, *Jesus Only*, Fleming H. Revell, New York, N. Y.

Hayes, Doremus Almy, *The Gift of Tongues*, Jennings & Graham, Cincinnati, Ohio.

Henry, Matthew, *Commentary on the Bible.*

Horton, Harold, *The Gifts of the Spirit*, Northcote Printing Works, Clapham Junction, London, England.

Hoy, Albert, *The Gift of Tongues.*

Huegel, F. J., *Bone of His Bone*, Zondervan Publishing House, Grand Rapids, Mich.

Ironside, Harry A., *Addresses on the First Epistle to the Corinthians*, Loizeau Bros., New York, N. Y.

Irving, Edward, *Complete Works of Edward Irving.*

Jeffrey, George, *Pentecostal Rays*, Elim Publishing House, London, England.

Kinne, Seeley D., *Spirituals.*

Kuyper, Abraham, *The Work of the Holy Spirit*, Funk & Wagnalls Co., New York, N. Y.

Mackie, Alexander, *The Gift of Tongues*, Doubleday and Company, New York, N. Y.

Maclaren, Alexander, *Expositions of the Holy Scriptures.*

McCrossan, T. J., *Speaking With Other Tongues, Sign or Gift —Which?* Christian Publications Inc., Harrisburg, Pa.

McPherson, A. S., *This Is That*, Echo Park Evangelistic Assoc., Los Angeles, Calif.

Miller, Elmer C., *Pentecost Examined*, Gospel Publishing House, Springfield, Mo.

Myland, Wesley T., *The Latter Rain.*

Nelson, P. C., *Life and Letters of St. Paul*, Southwestern Press, Enid, Okla.

Ness, Henry, *Manifestations of the Spirit.*

Oliphant, Mrs. Margaret, *Life of Edward Irving*, Harper Bros., New York, N. Y.

Pearlman, Myer, *Knowing the Doctrines of the Bible*, and *The Heavenly Gift*, Gospel Publishing House, Springfield, Mo.

Panton, D. M., *Irvingism, Tongues, and the Gifts of the Holy Ghost*, Chas. J. Thynne & Jarvis, Ltd., London, England.

Pentecostal Evangel, Gospel Publishing House, Springfield, Mo.

Pentecostal Holiness Advocate, Pentecostal Holiness Publishing House, Franklin Springs, Ga.

Pethrus, Lewi, *The Wind Bloweth Where It Listeth*, Philadelphia Book Concern, Chicago, Ill.

Pollock, A. J., *Modern Pentecostalism, Foursquare Gospel, Healings and Tongues*, The Central Bible Truth Depot, London, England.

Price, Charles S., *Golden Grain*, Charles S. Price Publishing Co., Pasadena, Calif.

Pulpit Commentary, Funk and Wagnalls Co., New York. N. Y.

Rice, John R., *The Sword of the Lord*.

Schaff, Philip, *The History of the Christian Church*.

Simpson, A. B., *The Holy Spirit, or, Power from on High*, Christian Publications Inc., Harrisburg, Pa.

Smith, Aaron A., *The Holy Spirit and His Workings*.

Smith, F. G., *What the Bible Teaches*, Gospel Trumpet Co., Anderson, Ind.

Spence, Hubert T., *The Person, Work and Witness of the Holy Spirit*, Pentecostal Holiness Publishing House, Franklin Springs, Ga.,

Stemme, Harry, *Pentecost Today*, and *Faith of a Pentecostal Christian*.

Stolee, H. J., *Pentecostalism, the Problem of the Modern Tongues Movement*, Augsburg Publishing House, Minneapolis, Minn.

Stover, Gene, *He shall Baptize You With the Holy Ghost*.

Swift, Allan A., *The Spirit Within and Upon*.

Torrey, R. A., *What the Bible Teaches*, Fleming H. Revell, New York, N. Y.

Turner, W H., *Pentecost and Tongues*.

White, Alma, *Demons and Tongues*.

Wilson, Walter L., *Facts or Fancies*, Zondervan Publishing House, Grand Rapids, Mich.

INDEX